The Search for Major Plagge

The Search for

THE NAZI WHO SAVED JEWS

MICHAEL GOOD

Major Plagge

FORDHAM UNIVERSITY PRESS   NEW YORK 2005

Library of Congress Cataloging-in-Publication Data

Good, Michael.
   The search for Major Plagge : the Nazi who saved Jews / Michael
Good.—1st ed.
      p.   cm.
   Includes index.
      ISBN 0-8232-2440-6 (hardcover)
      1. Jews—Persecutions—Lithuania.   2. Holocaust, Jewish
(1939–1945)—Personal narratives.   3. Good, William Z.   4. Good,
Pearl.   5. Plagge, Karl, 1897–1957.   6. Righteous Gentiles in the
Holocaust—Germany—Biography.   7. Good, Michael—
Correspondence.   8. Lithuania—Ethnic relations.   I. Title.
   DS135.L5G66   2005
   940.53'1835'092—dc22   2004028106

Printed in the United States of America
07 06 05 5 4 3 2 1
First edition

For my parents, William and Pearl Good, whose ability to remember without bitterness and whose appreciation of their own good fortune opened a world of discovery for their American son.

I believe that the time has come for all right-minded, well-disposed people to extend their hands to each other across national boundaries to form a community of "the solitary among the nations." For whoever seeks truth and justice nowadays remains solitary in the midst of a blind multitude crying for power and violence.

—Karl Plagge

CONTENTS

An American Awakening

INTRODUCTION

On a warm spring day in June of 1999, I stood in the courtyard of the Heeres Kraftfahr Park (HKP[1]) labor camp in Vilnius, Lithuania. Flanking the courtyard were tall buildings that had once housed over 1000 Jewish workers and their families, all slave laborers for the German war effort. I listened as my mother told the story of how she and her parents had survived the Holocaust, unlike so many other members of our family. She explained that her survival was largely due to the efforts of the German Army officer in charge of the HKP camp, a certain "Major Plagge." "He was better than Schindler!" she exclaimed as she told how Major Plagge had protected his prisoners from the murderous intent of the SS.

I had traveled to Lithuania with my parents, wife and teenage children to see our city of origin, to hear of all those who were lost during the war and to retrace my parents' tales of survival during the Holocaust. As I pondered the miracle of my family's existence, I asked my mother what had become of this German major. "No one knows," she replied. Plagge had left Vilna[2] with the retreating Germans in July 1944 and vanished into the chaos of the final months of the war. No one had heard of him since.

Squinting in the bright sun as I listened to my mother that morning, I had no idea what was beginning. I thought I had reached the pinnacle of our family journey, overcoming my fears of facing history, and then organizing my family to fly across the globe in search of a distant time and place. I could never have guessed that hearing my mother's story would mark a beginning, not an ending.

1. "Military vehicle repair park" in English.
2. The toponymy of Vilna is very complex given the number of times the city has been controlled by different nations. Thus, it is called Vilnius by the Lithuanians who live there today, for the Poles it is Wilno, and the Germans call it Wilna. The Russians and Jews call it Vilna. Different ethnic groups within the city thus refer to it by different names. Following the usage of my parents, I will call it Vilna when referring to the city they grew up in before and during the war, but will refer to it as Vilnius when describing it today.

It had taken a long time to get to that courtyard in Vilnius. Growing up in Southern California during the 1960s, the last thing I was interested in was exploring my European roots. What I wanted more than anything else was to be a regular American. My parents were from another realm, another planet really. In their thick European accents, they told stories of their youth, filled with dark tales of war and genocide. As a child, it seemed to me that my parents had come from a vicious, ancient place filled with Nazis, concentration camps and dead Jews. These were all things that I wanted desperately to escape from. Like many children of immigrants, I was determined to leave the world of my parents behind as I strode into my American future. I was actually quite successful in this endeavor. Backyard swimming parties and little league baseball led to high school plays and senior proms. College led to medical school, which carried me to marriage, children, and work as a family physician. I was the immigrants' son who had fulfilled his parents' dreams of what a better life in a new land should be.

Yet over the years, flickering images of the past would intrude on my American paradise. These episodes began soon after I started to build my new family in Connecticut. One day in 1994 I was talking to my friend Vera Schwarcz, a professor of history at Wesleyan University and a daughter of Holocaust survivors herself. We were discussing my reluctance to involve my young family in the local conservative Jewish congregation. I was worried they might reject my children and me because my wife Susan was not Jewish. Looking at me, Vera said softly, "You are wrong, Michael, your avoidance has nothing to do with Susan. It is because of the Holocaust. Your soul understands what dangers the world presents to Jewish children." This statement left me dumbstruck. I had lived all my life in the United States, suffered virtually no anti-Semitism, and could not imagine that I was unconsciously paralyzed by my parents' history. Yet as I talked with Vera, tears streamed down my face. Given the force with which her words struck me, I knew that there must be a large measure of truth to what she said.

Then there was the family tree. After medical school, I had married Susan Possidente, an Italian-American woman of great beauty, talent, and insight. We had met at the University of Rochester where I was a medical student and she was writing her master's thesis in psychiatric nursing. Susan is the granddaughter of Italian immigrants, with a vast family of aunts, uncles, and cousins. As we dated, I was introduced to her relatives at the annual Posside-nte 4th of July picnic, a large event steeped in family history. Every year since

1946, when all four of her uncles had returned home safely from World War II, Susan's family has gathered for a giant annual Independence Day picnic. There are usually over 130 relatives from four generations present. As a new-comer to these clamorous gatherings, I had considerable trouble figuring out which relative belonged to which branch of the family. To help me sort all of them out, I decided to catalogue the Possidente family tree using a computer genealogy program. This process proved to be quite helpful, both to me and to the other young men who had married into the family.

Having completed my wife's genealogical tree, I decided to move on to my own family. Interviewing my parents, I gathered names, birth dates, places of birth, and stories of never seen relatives who had populated Russia, Poland, and Lithuania. There was my paternal great-grandfather Chone Gdud, a man of legendary strength who single-handedly picked up an entire tree that had fallen in the road after a group of Polish peasants had been unable to move it. There was my father's Uncle Zelig, who had murdered his beautiful wife in a fit of jealousy when he caught her in an affair with another man. There was my mother's saintly Aunt Emma, who ran an orphanage and who tragically cared for her only son as he slowly died from an incurable heart infection. Then there were the pictures, faces from long ago: a picture of Uncle Kasriel (Zelig's brother) showed a man who was the spitting image of my own father; a photo of my mother's Aunt Rachel confirmed her reputa-tion as being a vivacious beauty. A whole cast of vibrant and boisterous characters came alive as I collected names and stories for our family tree.

When I assembled the information collected from both the Italian and Jewish sides of our family to show to my children, I was forcibly struck by the contrasting pictures. My wife has 56 first cousins. I, on the other hand, have no cousins. The color portraits on the Possidente side of the family are filled with people who are alive today. My side of the family tree is filled with old, faded, black-and-white pictures of people whom none of us have ever met. The Good side comes to a sudden halt in 1941, with lives and families cut short, branch after branch showing lines that do not continue. Alongside my parents, one can see that there were once numerous relatives, almost 80 strong. But a close look at the dates of death reveals the same story: almost everyone died between June 22, 1941, and July 13, 1944, in Nazi-occupied Poland.

It was this memory of lives cut short, families murdered in the world's greatest crime, that I had been trying to escape from for the first 40 years of my life. As a child my nightmares had always been the same: gray men in Nazi uniforms with SS insignia coming to catch me, chasing me, trying to kill me. I did not want my children to suffer from such dreams. As a father I could easily imagine the desperation my relatives must have experienced in those final days as they tried to find ways to save their children. Thoughts and dreams such as these had caused me to avoid looking squarely at the Holocaust and my own family history; it was too painful. Reading books, watching films, or hearing stories about the war always caused me over-whelming pain and anxiety as I realized that mankind could not have changed fundamentally in 40 years; it could happen again, it could happen to my family, my children. When this topic came up, I always turned away; better to concentrate on life here in the United States, where such thoughts and terrible images rarely intruded.

Yet, I could not ignore my heritage and history. Staring at my family tree I could see that, even with so many lost, there were some that survived. What could we learn from the small tendrils of growth reaching down toward my children's generation? There were my two parents, William and Pearl Good, who had survived. They had three children: my older brother Leonard, my twin sister Anne, and myself. There is a small group of second cousins in Mexico from my mother's side of the family and a similar group of distant cousins from my father's family who set roots in Argentina. Thus, in addition to the myriad of Possidentes, Marcons, Lambertis, and Sebbens from the Italian side of the family, there are small groups of Jews: Gduds, Gersteins, and Goods all traveling toward the 21st century. I began to look more carefully at Holocaust survivors both from my family and from various friends' families. My father had survived the war after escaping execution by the Germans and hiding in the forests surrounding Vilna with the help of local peasant families. My mother, her parents, and her cousins from Mexico were all survivors of the HKP labor camp; they credit Major Plagge with saving their lives. My step-grandmother, Gita Gdud, whose husband and two children died in the Vilna Ghetto, had been hidden by Catholic nuns after escaping from the Germans. When I thought about our Holocaust survivor friends and their tales of survival, I found similar themes. In addition to their stories of terror, each also had survival stories that inevitably involved three elements: luck, tenacity, and an act of kindness during a crucial hour of need. As a result of these acts, they did not perish and went on to rebuild lives after the war. After examining many survivors' stories, I came to a new realization: that each Holocaust survivor represents a miracle of life and that almost all survivors owe their lives in small or large part to someone else's kindness, bravery, or courage. Thus, for many survivors of the Holocaust and their descendants, an examination of the war does not necessarily lead only to the bloody horrors that mankind is capable of; it can also point to the ultimate triumph of good over evil.

With this newfound perspective, I found myself gradually able to look at the past without averting my eyes. This exploration led me to plan a trip to Vilnius with my parents and family. It was on this journey that I came to stand in the HKP camp courtyard, listening to my mother retell her story. As I listened, a host of questions began to form in my mind. Who was this Major Plagge? How exactly had he saved his workers' lives? What had become of him after the war? Did his family know of his heroic acts during the war? Why did he, a staff officer of the Wehrmacht (German Army), work to save Jewish lives when his nation was committed to exterminating them? In trying to answer these questions, a new journey of exploration began, one that would lead from my home in Connecticut, through the Internet, traveling from New York, Montreal, and California to Hamburg, Frankfurt, and Darmstadt, Germany. This journey would eventually lead to answers about an amazing man who not only saved my mother's life, but the lives of more than 250 Jews during the Holocaust. On this journey I would discover a man whose story exemplifies the choice that humans have to select good over evil.

FAMILY JOURNEY

Why would you want to take our children there?
Look at your parents, look at you, look at all the scars you bear.
Aren't two damaged generations enough?
—Susan Good, 1998

The summer of 1999 approached. In my medical practice, one partner a year can take a one-month summer "sabbatical" vacation, and the summer of 1999 was my first opportunity to take such a vacation. As it neared, I gradually decided that it was time to ask my parents and family to go to Vilnius and explore our roots. My father was immediately eager to go; my wife and my mother, however, had reservations.

After 17 years of observing me and my family, Susan had ample opportunity to discover some of the peculiar scars that we carry from the war. Once in 1982, shortly after we met, I was showing her around my parent's home in Southern California, where I grew up. As we were preparing her bed, I opened a trap door on the desktop, which led to a hidden closet, and took out the pillows she was to use that night. When she commented that this storage area was an interesting design feature, I replied that it was a good hiding place for us kids should we ever need to conceal ourselves from dangerous intruders. It was only then that it occurred to me that not all families prepare hiding places for themselves in their homes. Similarly, when having breakfast one day with my parents, my mother commented on one of our neighbors, saying that when she first met them, she was unsure whether she could trust them to hide us in case the Nazis ever came looking for Jews. She went on to explain that upon meeting someone in the neighborhood, the first thing she tried to judge was whether they would be friends or foes in case of a dangerous turn of events. Being an insightful woman trained in psychiatric nursing, I'm sure Sue has seen many other examples of how the war left its mark on my parents, siblings and me. For instance, she has seen how, when things start to go a little bit wrong, we have a tendency to feel that events can suddenly spin out of control and lead to disaster. I know that, compared to others, I have more of a tendency to feel that people who oppose me or who are attacking me are actually trying to destroy me. This is a fearful feeling and causes me to overreact to the usual conflicts encountered in normal life. Having made such observations of my family and me, Susan was understandably worried that a trip to Lithuania and Poland would immerse our two children (Jonathan, age 15, and Rebecca, age 12) in a suffocating flood of graphic Holocaust images that would harm them psychologically.

While my parents are both from Vilna, and both are Holocaust survivors, their reactions to the prospect of going back to Vilna (now Vilnius, Lithuania) could not have been more different. My father immediately seized on the idea. "Yes, let's go!" he exclaimed. My mother on the other hand said, "I have no desire to go there and see all those murderers." To understand my father's eagerness to take the trip and my mother's reluctance, it is important to understand their prewar lives and their relationships with their non-Jewish neighbors.

My father (William Z. Good, born Wowka Zev Gdud) was from a small village called Niemenczyn, about 20 kilometers outside of Vilna. His father, Dov Gdud, owned and ran a turpentine factory, which was attached to the family home in the middle of the thick forest that surrounded Niemenczyn. Growing up in a rural community outside of Vilna, my father played with mostly Gentile peasant children from farms surrounding his home. Together they rode horses, kayaked in the river, and rode their bicycles down the dirt country roads.

My grandmother, Hannah Kopelowicz, was a strong-minded woman who my father describes as having been both artistic and charitable. She had broken the traditions set out by her Hassidic parents and, rather than staying home to learn to cook, clean, and sew like other girls, had insisted on going to school to earn her high school diploma. She met Dov Gdud soon after he was ordained as a rabbi, and he was quickly won over by this powerful and talented woman. After they were married, they moved to Niemenczyn. Hannah, whose father had been in the turpentine business, showed her husband the ropes in starting an enterprise and running a turpentine factory. My father recalls that she wrote poetry and tended to the ill throughout the community as a lay nurse. Because she was frequently at home alone with the children, Hannah insisted that my grandfather provide her with a handgun, which she learned to use. The locals all knew that Hannah Gdud was caring and charitable, but was also an armed woman not to be messed with!

My father also had a younger brother, Mot'l, who was three years his junior. Mot'l had some physical handicaps, being blind in one eye and quite clumsy. He was a poor student and was kept back three grades in school. In the natural competition between siblings he always lagged behind my father, who was both athletic and academically adept. However, in one area he was unsurpassed—playing the violin. Mot'l from an early age showed intense interest and talent in the violin. Before long he cared for nothing else and spent hours every day practicing the instrument. He auditioned with one of Vilna's most sought after violin instructors and was accepted as a student. By age 13 he was playing with the Vilna philharmonic.

My paternal grandfather, Dov Gdud, came from a family of fishermen and timbermen from the village of Greisdorf in Russia. After becoming orphaned at the age of 13, he was fed and educated as a charity case in several Jewish religious schools (called yeshivas) and eventually became a rabbi. Even though he was an ordained orthodox rabbi, he chose to make his living working the land. Grandpa Gdud employed many locals in his turpentine-making factory and was well liked by the area's populace, both Jews and Gentiles, because of his honesty and generosity. He was always on the look-out for local families who were in financial difficulty and would try to employ them at the turpentine factory or give them loans to help them through hard times. Everyone knew that he was scrupulously honest and would come to him to discuss confidential matters, looking for his advice. The Gdud home was a favorite stop for the local beggars, who knew they would never be turned away without a meal. While there was some underlying anti-Semitism in the attitudes of the locals, this was transcended by their good feelings toward the Gduds. Regardless of their attitudes to Jews in general, to their neighbors the Gduds were different, they were "Good Jews."

When he was 12, my father, his younger brother Mot'l, and their parents moved to Vilna so that he could attend the esteemed Tarbut Hebrew High School. Vilna was a great center of Jewish culture and learning, known as the "Jerusalem of Lithuania" before the war. During the 1930s there were over 80,000 Jews living in Vilna (out of a total population of 200,000), and they played a large role in life throughout the city. In Vilna one could find the whole spectrum of European Jewish society. There were the Jewish socialists, different sects of religious Jews such as the Hassids or the followers of the

"Gaon of Vilna" a famous Jewish scholar. There was the group my father belonged to, the Zionists, who were dedicated to the rebirth of Palestine as a Jewish state. Finally, there were the more secular, assimilated Jews to whom my mother's family belonged; they followed a modern path of education and enlightenment. Vilna thus contained an amazing mix of Jewish politics, religion, and art; it was a vibrant center of Jewish life.

When my father moved to Vilna, he immersed himself in the study of Hebrew as well as in secular studies. He and his classmates were passionate Zionists, speaking only Hebrew at school, eschewing Yiddish, which in their eyes was the language of oppression spoken by the Jews of the Diaspora[1]. He graduated from high school in June 1941 at the age of 17. Still, even after five years of living in Vilna, and having been immersed in its exciting Jewish culture, his family retained its warm ties to their Gentile neighbors in Niemenczyn. My grandfather Dov still traveled out of town every day to run the turpentine factory. These ties would prove crucial in enabling both my father and grandfather to survive the approaching Holocaust.

My mother (Pearl Good, born Perela Esterowicz) came from an entirely different segment of the Vilna Jewish community. Her father, Samuel Esterowicz, was a Jewish intellectual who had studied law in St. Petersburg during the Russian Revolution and had graduated from the University of Berlin with a degree in political economy. Grandfather Samuel had left religion behind as a teenager and, like many of Vilna's assimilated secular Jews, was an avid student of Western history, art, and culture. He came from a family of businessmen who had worked as estimators and business agents in the timber industry, which was a large part of the local economy. He too went into the business world, where he worked as a very successful sales representative of Elektryt, the largest radio tube and light bulb manufacturer in Vilna. In her memoirs, my mother gives the following description of her father:

> Father was very brilliant, with great knowledge of art, literature, and history. He had a photographic memory. He was a very good, honest and straightforward man, but was also stubborn, self-centered and did not posses even a modicum of the necessary hypocrisy for getting along with people; he was truthful to the point of impracticality. For example:

1. The word "Diaspora" comes from the Greek word meaning dispersion, and is used to refer to the dispersion of the Jewish people outside of Israel, especially after the destruction of the second temple in 70 AD by the Romans.

> Mother: "You shouldn't have called him a thief to his face."
>
> Father: "Why not? He knows it himself."

Fortunately for Samuel Esterowicz, he married a sensitive and insightful woman, Ida Gerstein, who helped guide him through the worldly realities of the secular Jewish community. My mother and grandmother worried about my grandfather's bluntness and social missteps, but, like my grandfather Dov, his honesty in prewar life later played a role in his family's survival during the war[2]. While Grandfather Samuel was the sales representative for Elektryt, he had a customer named Boleslaw Poddany, the owner of a large car dealership and repair shop. In his memoirs, my grandfather explains what occurred between himself and his customer Poddany:

> Boleslaw Poddany was a car dealer, the exclusive representative of "Ford," "Opel," and "Buick" cars. Poddany was purchasing from me replacement car batteries and light bulbs as well as some other products.
>
> When my relatives . . . learned that in me they had the primary wholesale source of car batteries, they demanded that I should sell to them directly. This put me in a difficult situation, since if I should sell batteries from the factory storehouse directly to the consumers, who would buy from my clients, the retail merchants? I finally found a solution to this difficulty—I sold them batteries at prices somewhat higher than wholesale and then every month I sent the difference (amounting to less than a hundred zloty) to Poddany, my largest customer.
>
> To Poddany, (a Pole from Poznan, a town famed for its exceptional hatred of the Jews), who had a completely different concept of the honesty of Jewish business people, my action made a memorable, almost stupefying impression—he became a faithful client of mine. It was Boleslaw Poddany who contributed greatly to my survival during the Hitlerian cataclysm, which had swallowed almost all the Jewish population of Vilna, including all my relatives.

2. I would like to make clear that while I feel that the honesty of both my grandfathers and their congenial relationships with Gentiles before the war were central factors in their unusual ability to save themselves and some of their family members, it should by no means imply that those who perished were in any way less exemplary in their conduct or morals. My parents have often emphasized that in their minds one of the most important factors in surviving the war was pure and simple luck, as we will see amply demonstrated in my father's story told in chapter 3.

Later, during the war, when the Germans commandeered his car repair business, Mr. Poddany made sure that his Jewish friend Samuel Esterowicz had a job in the workshop that he continued to run under the supervision of German overseers. This placed my grandfather under the auspices of Major Plagge and his HKP unit, which would ultimately prove to be so vital to his family's surviving the Holocaust.

My mother recalls a happy childhood as an only child, pampered and sent to a very modern Montessori school where she learned to read and started a lifelong love of books. Grandfather Samuel, having followed the rise of Hitler and Nazism in Germany over the previous six years, predicted war with Germany. However, probably as a result of having spent happy years during his youth in Berlin earning his university diploma, he had a generally high opinion of Germans. He did not have an acute a sense of foreboding about what was to come. Even if he could have understood Hitler's true intentions, he, like most of Europe's Jews, did not have the opportunity to flee suddenly from Vilna. The world had long since closed the tightly controlled routes of escape for those European Jews who wanted to leave their homelands. The Gdud and Esterowicz families were trapped in Poland along with 3.5 million of their fellow Jews as the German blitzkrieg rolled across Europe. They were soon to be caught in the mouth of a killing machine that neither they nor the world could ever have imagined possible.

As we will see later in my parent's stories, their wartime experiences were very different. After narrowly escaping executions, my father and grandfather Dov spent most of the war hiding in the forests, supported by their friends from the Niemenczyn area. While my father encountered some locals who collaborated with the Germans, his family's friends who risked their lives in opposing the Nazi genocide countered these experiences. My mother, on the other hand, spent the war in Vilna, first in the ghetto and later in the HKP labor camp. Other than Boleslaw Poddany and Major Plagge, there were almost no Gentiles whom she and her parents could identify as non-hostile. In Vilna, there were many Poles and Lithuanians who supported the Germans in their efforts to find and annihilate the Jewish population. Lithuanian Nazis and paramilitary police carried out many of the executions of Jews in the Vilna Ghetto.

Fifty-five years later, my parents brought their separate war time perspectives to bear when contemplating a trip back to their city of origin. My father thought of the people who had helped him during the war and was eager to see them again and show them his family. My mother remembered the many hostile forces that confronted her family in their struggle to survive, a major threat being the local city dwellers who were all too quick to denounce a Jew hidden in their midst. She feared that as she walked the streets of Vilnius she would once again see the hostile stares and wonder who among them had relatives who helped in the destruction of her family.

Thus, in late 1998, it came down to a father and son trying to convince a mother and daughter-in-law to travel halfway around the world to encounter the place, unseen for more than fifty years, where so much family history had taken place. Eventually, my father and I prevailed. To Sue, we promised to try to be sensitive to the well-being of the children, emphasizing the exploration of our prewar family roots and avoiding Holocaust museums and graphic images of genocide. We also decided to go to Italy after Vilnius, giving us the opportunity to explore Sue's family roots and meet her relatives. With regard to my mother, Dad and I convinced her that this would be her best opportunity to tell her story not only to her son, but also to her grandchildren. She realized that the Holocaust generation was aging and that such opportunities might not appear again. Thus, even with some trepidation, my wife and mother agreed to take the journey to Vilnius.

So it came to be that on June 21, 1999, two segments of the Good family met at Newark Airport to begin our long-awaited journey together. Susan, Jonathan, Rebecca, and I drove to Newark Airport to meet my parents, who flew cross-country from Los Angeles. After a long overnight flight, we arrived at Vilnius International Airport. Peering out of the aircraft window, it was clear that we were entering a different world. All the buildings surrounding the airport were grim squatting structures, products of Stalinist architecture and visual reminders of fifty years of Soviet control of Lithuania. However, as we approached the end of the taxiway we suddenly turned toward a new building, the recently built Vilnius Terminal, a tall, gleaming, glass-filled edifice, a symbol of newly independent Lithuania's budding capitalism. It was an emotional arrival for all of us. My parents had fled illegally in 1945, leaving their childhood names and homeland behind. Now Wowka Zev Gdud and Perela Esterowicz were proudly returning as Americans named William and Pearl Good, with their children and grandchildren in tow.

We were met at the airport by my parents' friend Irena Veisaite. Irena was a Jewish orphan who was adopted after the war by friends of my parents, the Brauns, and had remained in Vilna, one of the few remaining Jews there today. After a warm round of hugs and handshakes, Irena gave us a tour of the city and then took us to her apartment for some lunch. Sue, Jonathan, Rebecca, and I got our first taste of real Russian black bread eaten with local cheese, honey, and tea. I watched in delight as Irena drank her tea the same way my mother and grandparents had when I was growing up: sugar cube held in the front teeth with scalding hot tea drawn through the sweet cube.

Next, we went to the our hotel. Amazingly, it was situated in the very apartment building that my father had lived in during the prewar years of 1936 to 1941! My father excitedly showed us around his old home and neighborhood. Stepping out of the hotel, we passed down a winding path to the Vilya River. Standing on its banks I saw a classic European city with cobblestone streets, ornate lampposts, commemorative statues and a wide graceful river passing through the center of town. Crossing the Green Bridge over the river, we followed Zawalna Street toward the Tarbut High School. My father had walked this route every day to school and in doing so had unknowingly passed right under my mother's apartment window at Zawalna #2, just two buildings up from his school.

As we walked, my mother spotted the apartment building that she and her parents had lived in during the first twelve years of her life. "There it is!" she exclaimed as she pointed excitedly at a stately two-story building. We hurried up to what had been the front door, leading into a foyer. Mother showed us what had been their large, gracious apartment with beautiful parquet floors and tall, spacious windows that allowed light to stream into their home. Today it is divided into business offices with many customers and office workers hurrying in and out. We peered into the glass doors of these businesses, trying to imagine a bright and spacious home with my grandmother waiting for her daughter to return home from school to a snack of strawberries and cream. My mother's home had frequent visits from her aunts and uncles as well as her own friends, Mira Jedwabnik and Nathan Bak. As we listened to my mother tell stories of her life in this apartment one could imagine it as a busy place. I could imagine my Uncle David Gerstein telling bawdy jokes in Yiddish to peals of laughter from the adults. A normal life, like I had in Connecticut with my family.

My father pulled us back outside and down the street. "Come on, let's find my high school!" he urged. Sure enough, a short walk down the street led us to #4 Zawalna, the site of the former Tarbut High School. The school today is a Jewish museum documenting the vibrant Jewish community that

vanished half a century before. My father, standing in the front door and
then exploring the halls and classrooms, was hit by a flood of memories. In
his mind's eye he could see crowds of students, laughing and joking, teachers and administrators hurrying to their classrooms and offices. He remembers:

> We had school six days a week, seven hours a day, and they gave us
> lots and lots of homework. If you couldn't keep up, that was too bad;
> there was no coddling of students back then. I was lucky. My best friend
> was Berel Kamenmacher, a real genius, and we studied together. He had
> an open mind, he understood anything that he looked at, and with his
> help, I was able to get through all the work. Our high school was re-
> nowned for its level of teaching, and the graduates of this school went on
> to become leaders in their fields, many joining the faculty of the Hebrew
> University in Jerusalem. We were Zionists, ardently working to re-estab-
> lish a Jewish homeland in Palestine. We spoke only Hebrew while at
> school; Yiddish was the language of the ghetto, and we were very dedi-
> cated to the revival, the rebirth of the Hebrew language.

My father showed us around his school, showing us where he had sat in
a large sunny classroom with tall windows. Downstairs he showed us where
the door to a dentist's office had once been, and told us how he and his
friends had tormented the office receptionist by repeatedly ringing the bell
and running away (until she caught them and gave them a thrashing). He
remembered a teacher, Dr. Liber, who was a genius at languages, speaking
over fifteen fluently. After the Russians occupied Vilna in 1939 and declared
Lithuanian to be the official language, Dr. Liber learned Lithuanian in a few
short months. By the following school year, he was able to teach his students
perfect Lithuanian. Neither Berel Kamenmacher nor Dr. Liber survived the
war.

After leaving the Tarbut High School, my mother took us to the Vilna
Ghetto, where in September 1941 the Germans relocated thousands of Vilna's Jewish residents, including my mother and her extended family, into a
few square blocks. In the ghetto we walked through cramped, claustrophobic streets, crowded by the run-down, deserted buildings, which still sat
abandoned fifty-five years after the war. The buildings were so close together
that only a small section of sky could be seen from the streets. My mother
told us that during the two years that she lived in the ghetto, she did not get

to see the sun shine once, nor did she lay eyes on a green leaf or a blade of grass. She shared a one room flat on Strashuna Street with twenty-six other people and tried to avoid a slow death by starvation or disease. As we walked through the ghetto together, my mother found the apartment at Strashuna #1, which had been her unhappy home from 1941 to 1943 before she was moved to the HKP labor camp. We stood silently in the street looking at its boarded-up windows. Strashuna Street, along with the rest of the Vilna Ghetto, was still deserted fifty-five years after the war. Empty apartments, broken windows, sagging roofs; it seemed to me that the terrible memories of what had occurred here lingered, working like an invisible but unbearable toxin, keeping away any would-be newcomers.

The next day we traveled to Niemenczyn, my father's hometown. Packed into a mini-van, we passed beyond the city limits and drove twenty kilometers through heavily forested countryside to the resort community where my father had lived as a child. There we met with Lila Paszkowski, whose parents had helped warn the Gduds of impending danger in September 1941, when the Nazis were coming to kill the Jews of Niemenczyn. Lila had been eight years old at the start of the war and remembers being told by her parents not to let anyone know about the Gduds, who often hid in the family barn. She says that during those years of waiting, my father taught her to play the mandolin, which she still plays to this day. After viewing my father's old elementary school, we drove to the now deserted meadow where the Gdud home had once stood. There is virtually no sign of his old house or the adjoining turpentine factory. The area was beautiful, with broad meadows filled with wild flowers, tall evergreens standing against the horizon, and birds singing in the trees. My father could point out the fields he played in, the trees that he swung from and the rivers that he kayaked on. As my father talked of his childhood here, Sue walked through the meadows, tall flowers brushing up against her skirt, and my children laughed in the background as they skipped through the forest looking for wild strawberries. I wondered how long it had been since these woods had heard the sounds of Jewish children laughing?

From the meadows around his old house, we moved down the road to yet another grim reminder of local history: a memorial to the 403 Jews of Niemenczyn, including my father's mother and brother, who were killed by the Nazis and their Lithuanian collaborators on September 20, 1941. We stood around the memorial marker that stands in the middle of a forest, as the songs and whistles of songbirds echoed hauntingly through the trees. My father recounted how he and his father had escaped execution, but how his mother and brother, who had initially hidden after the Paszkowski's warning, were later captured and killed at this spot. As he spoke, Lila burst into tears, sobbing into her handkerchief. Her tears were infectious, soon all of us stood around the mass grave wiping our tears, listening to my father tell the story of the last days of the Jews of Niemenczyn.

After the visit to the graveside memorial, we traveled further into the woods to a small cluster of farmhouses, the home of Ghenia Gasperowicz, a local farmer whose family had helped my father and grandfather during the war. Ghenia is my father's age and was a teenager when she and her family sheltered him along with his father at great risk. Ghenia was in her garden when we arrived, peeling off her dirty gardening clothes. Her face glowed in happiness as she kissed my father warmly and viewed his family as we emerged from the van. My father recalled how he and his father had once hid in a small space above the stove when a teenage boy, trying to court Ghenia, had arrived unexpectedly. She had to light the stove to make tea for him while my father and grandfather stood above the stove in danger of roasting alive. They all laughed as they remembered how she had tried to get rid of this unwanted visitor, and how the hidden Jews had staggered out of their hiding place sweating and smoking when he finally departed.

The Gasperowicz live today just as Polish peasant families have lived for centuries: raising much of their own food and livestock, slaughtering animals in the barn, canning vegetables for the winter. My children were wide-eyed as they looked at the dirt floors of a farmhouse with no running water, bumping their heads against home cured hams and cheeses hanging in the pantry. By American standards, the Gasperowicz live in poverty, but their home was rich in goodwill and laughter as we sat down together for a sumptuous homemade farm feast.

We found such strange contrasts as we explored my parent's world. Tragic tales from the Holocaust juxtaposed with the faces of families who bravely opened their homes to my father in 1942 and warmly welcomed him back 57 years later.

Throughout our time in Lithuania, as we walked the picturesque cobblestone streets of Vilnius, or wandered through the forests around Niemenczyn, it seemed that the ghosts of the 70,000 Jews who perished there during the war followed us. Vilnius has not been able to replace its Jewish residents.

Their absence lurks at every corner, at the synagogues now used for secular purposes, at the apartment buildings once filled with friends and relatives but now occupied by strangers. Yiddish, the language of the Jews, has vanished; it no longer echoes down the streets in the calls of vendors, it is not heard on the stages of theaters, nor is it read in newspapers or in novels. Wherever I went the question loomed: how is it that our family is alive? How did we survive when so many thousands died? The ghosts of Vilna's lost Jews haunt me. Long after the ashes of the Holocaust have blown from view, the ghosts of Vilna ask me: how can you be here?

The Holocaust

2

THE DESTRUCTION OF
THE JEWS OF VILNA

On September 6th, 1941 the Lithuanian Police chased us out of our apartment with only the few things we could carry. Father carried a huge pack in a bedspread. I wrapped a pillow, an electric cord and many other odds and ends in my bedspread. As they chased us down Zawalna Street toward the ghetto whose previous inhabitants had been killed, we were hot and sweaty from running in our winter clothes . . . The Gestapo, with yells and threats chased us to Strashuna Street . . . Tall brick walls blocked off all the outlets of the streets connecting the ghetto with the rest of the city. The Germans placed a placard on the gate bearing a large warning to the rest of the population which said "DANGER of CONTAGION."[1]
—Memoirs of Pearl Good

During the long flight to Vilnius in June of 1999, I finally read my Grandfather Samuel's memoirs. They are contained in a massive volume 434 pages long, and as they sat perched on my lap, they weighed heavily on me. I had been avoiding them for almost a decade.

My family always claimed that I was my grandfather's clone. I looked like him, I had the same interest in history and politics as he did, I even waved my hands just like he did when arguing politics. My grandfather's nickname was "Munya" (short for Shmuel or Samuel), and within our family, I was called "little Munya." My grandfather was born in 1897 and lived through World War I, the Russian Revolution, the Holocaust, and the Cold War. After my grandmother Ida's death in 1975, in an effort to help him break out of a deep depression, my mother urged my grandfather to write his life story. After many months of delay, he began this work, which would take the last ten years of his life to complete. The manuscript was written in elegant Russian and wove our own family's story into the historical backdrop he

1. Memoirs of Pearl Good, http://members.aol.com/michaeldg/MemoirsP.rtf, 28.

created. After his death in 1984, my mother translated his work into English, so that his grandchildren could read what he had written, a difficult task that took her five years to complete. However, even after the years of effort that my grandfather and mother had put into this great work, I could not read it. I tried many times. I would read about his childhood in Czarist Russia, his student days in Saint Petersburg during the Russian Revolution, and his time in Germany during the 1920s. Then I would reach the Holocaust and find myself unable to continue. The section on the Holocaust begins with the following paragraph:

> Even though forty years divide me from the ensuing events, I approach their description with the feeling of shivering horror—the earth opened under our feet and swallowed a huge part of the surviving members of the Jewish community, including almost all of the members of my family.[2]

Whenever I tried to move forward, the story of the merciless Nazi killing machine would unfold, enveloping my grandparents, aunts, uncles, and extended family in its voracious jaws. After several pages of my grandfather's clear and lucid description of the Holocaust and the horrible toll it had on each of the people whom he had previously described in loving detail, I froze, unable to continue. I have similar experiences whenever I try to read books on the Holocaust. The topic is so evil, the images so overwhelming, that I rarely can read a whole book, managing merely to read small parts in bits and pieces, as vivid Holocaust images form an anxiety-filled montage in my unconscious mind. Yet now, on the way to Vilnius, I began to read again, and even though I still broke out in an anxious sweat, I was successful in reading the entire section on the Holocaust. Through his memoirs, my grandfather taught me both how the Holocaust was planned and carried out by the Nazis as well as what happened to my extended family during the war. With this knowledge imparted to me by my grandfather, I was able to understand and fully appreciate my parents' stories during the time we spent in Vilnius. While writing this story, I have realized that I too must try to impart certain basic outlines of the Holocaust in Vilna to those readers who are new to the subject. Without some understanding of the vocabulary and details of the Holocaust in Vilna, the miracle of my parents' survival and the

2. Memoirs of Samuel Esterowicz, http://hometown.aol.com/michaeldg/memoirs smesterowicz.doc, 295.

subsequent tale of Karl Plagge's startling actions becomes unintelligible. So, even though I am one who for years could not read Holocaust histories myself, I have found it necessary to include a brief history of the Holocaust in Vilna. I hope that those who read it will be able to swallow it quickly like a dose of bitter medicine and be better off for having braved the experience.

World War II began on September 1, 1939, when Hitler's armies attacked Poland. Having signed a nonaggression pact with the Soviet Union, Hitler and the Soviet dictator Stalin agreed to divide Poland in two. As Vilna was in the eastern half of Poland, it was occupied by Soviet forces, while cities to the west, such as Warsaw, were under German control. Vilna had historically been under the varying control of Russia, Lithuania, and Poland, with all three nations claiming the city as their own. When the Russians invaded Poland in 1939, they returned Vilna to Lithuanian control while making all of Lithuania a Soviet Republic. Thus, citizens of Vilna had to contend both with a forced imposition of Communism in their economic world, as well as a change in official language from Polish to Lithuanian, as the city was forced to change from being a Polish city to a Lithuanian one. For two years, beyond the stresses of living under imposed Communism, and becoming part of Lithuania, relative calm prevailed.

For the Jews of Eastern Poland, the Holocaust started on June 22, 1941, when Germany, in a sudden betrayal of its nonaggression pact, launched an overwhelming attack on the Soviet Union. The fury of the German war machine rapidly destroyed the Russian army on the eastern front, throwing the Soviets into a chaotic retreat. The German air force bombed and strafed the streams of retreating Russian soldiers and refugees clogging the roads leading east, killing thousands and causing complete panic among the survivors. The mechanized armor of the Wehrmacht (German army) stabbed deep through the Soviet lines and rapidly reached Minsk, cutting off hundreds of thousands of Russian troops and civilian refugees, depriving them of an escape route out of German-controlled territory. On June 24, 1941, just two days after the war started, the German army occupied Vilna. For the Jews of Vilna, unprecedented catastrophe would soon follow.

From my modern American vantage point, looking 60 years into the past, it has always been hard for me to understand how the Germans were able to carry out their acts of genocide. I used to wonder, "why didn't all those Jews resist, why didn't they arm themselves and fight back? If armed resistance was not possible, why didn't they run away from their homes and go into hiding? Didn't they know what the Nazis were going to do?" The answer, of course, is that the Jews of Europe had no idea what was in store for them; the Holocaust was beyond anything they could have imagined in their worst nightmares. In the Nazis, the Jewish civilians of Europe faced an enormously powerful enemy who secretly planned to destroy a whole people.[3] The world may have viewed the Germans as aggressive and imperialistic, but certainly, everyone thought they were civilized. The savagery that was to be unleashed against the Jews was unimaginable to everyone, including the victims themselves. It is due to this element of surprise and the continued use of the "big lie" that the Germans were able to carry out genocide in communities throughout Nazi-occupied Europe.

Across Europe, including in Vilna, the Nazis carried out the killing of the Jews in a carefully planned manner. It started with the widespread deception of the occupied populations, who were told that Jews were being taken for use as laborers. This deception was followed by the rapid destruction of any possible source of resistance from their victims through the killing of young Jewish men and community leaders. The Nazis planned the logistics of capturing their prey and then transporting them; they calculated the most efficient ways of executing them and then disposing of their bodies. Most importantly, the psychological manipulation of their victims was carefully conceived and orchestrated. Divide and conquer, give hope that those who

3. The question of when exactly the Nazis decided to embark upon the systematic annihilation of European Jewry remains a matter of historical debate. Some scholars feel that the Nazi hierarchy had decided in early spring 1941 at the onset of Operation Barbarosa (the attack on the Soviet Union) to carry out a "final solution to the Jewish problem" by physically killing all the Jews in Nazi-controlled Europe. Others feel that while there was widespread killing of tens of thousands of Jews in former Soviet-controlled territory by the Einsatzgruppen (mobile killing units) during June through September of 1941, the actual decision to kill all the Jews of Europe did not coalesce into formal policy until late fall and winter of 1941, culminating in the Wannsee Conference in January 1942, where it is generally accepted that Nazi leadership outlined the Final Solution. Two excellent references regarding this historical debate are The Holocaust in History by Michael R. Marrus (University Press of New England, 1987), 31–55; and The Nazi Dictatorship by Ian Kershaw (Arnold Publishers, 2000), 93–134. For the purposes of my narrative, I feel that regardless of what decision had been made with respect to all the Jews of Europe, it is clear to me that those Nazis occupying Vilna in June and July of 1941 clearly had a plan to kill and enslave the Jews under their jurisdiction.

cooperate will survive and use ruthless brute strength against even the slightest hint of disobedience or resistance. Additionally, in their Jewish victims, the Nazis were dealing with a population that had almost no military tradition. European Jews saw themselves as "people of the book" and largely applied themselves to intellectual pursuits in religious, academic, or scientific realms. Most Jewish families in Poland had no family members with any military experience. The traditional Jewish tactic when faced with persecution, even violent persecution, was to lay low, try to be inconspicuous, and wait for the storm to pass. While these tactics had worked well enough during the spasms of anti-Jewish violence that flared with some frequency throughout Eastern Europe during the nineteenth and early twentieth centuries, it would prove to be a catastrophically inadequate response to the Nazi genocide that was soon to devastate the Jews of Europe.

It is hard for modern people living in free societies to remember that 60 years ago no one had the word genocide in their vocabulary; there had been no killing fields of Cambodia, no slaughter in Rwanda, no ethnic cleansing in Bosnia. In order to understand the stories of Perela Esterowicz, Wowka Gdud, and Karl Plagge, we must pause and go back to the summer of 1941 and learn about a world that was about to be enveloped in evil, the extent of which had yet to be encountered in modern history.

Barely a week after the Wehrmacht occupied Vilna, the Gestapo arrived to start work on their high priority task of "securing the occupied territories" from the threat of "Communist Commissars and Jews." Vilna was under the administrative command of Hans Hingst, who was assisted by his deputy for Jewish affairs, Franz Murer. With the arrival of Hingst and Murer came a series of edicts aimed at the Jewish population. Jews had to wear an identifying armband with the letter J (later a yellow star), they could not walk on the sidewalks, and they were allowed to move about only in the gutter. Soon a curfew was imposed so that Jews could only venture out for a few hours a day. These measures were taken to humiliate the Jews and also to make them easily identifiable, to restrict their movements and isolate them from the rest of the population. Violations of any of these anti-Jewish edicts were punishable by immediate execution.

These anti-Jewish laws made performing the daily necessities of life extremely difficult—going to work, shopping for food, moving about the city became excruciating. But at this early stage, it was the altogether new sense of humiliation that was most painful for Vilna's once proud Jewish community. A fourteen-year-old boy from Vilna, Yitskhok Rudashevski[4], kept a diary during these difficult days. He recalls how he felt when he first looked out his window and saw his fellow Jews adorned by the identifying badges:

> It was painful to see how people were staring at them. The large piece of yellow material on their shoulders seemed to be burning me and for a long time I could not put on the badge. I felt a hump, as though I had two frogs on me. I was ashamed to appear on the street not because it would be noticed that I am a Jew but because I was ashamed of what (they were) doing to us. I was ashamed of our helplessness. We will be hung from head to foot with badges and we cannot help each other in any way. It hurt me that I saw absolutely no way out . . . Now we pay no attention to the badges . . . We are not ashamed of our badges! Let those be ashamed who have hung them on us. Let them serve as a searing brand to every conscious German who attempts to think about the future of his people.[5]

During the first week in July, the Germans executed the Jewish leadership and young men of fighting age at a secret execution ground in the forest of Ponary, 10 km outside of Vilna. There, Jewish victims would be taken to the edge of large pits and shot. Their bodies would be covered with lime, and then a new group of victims would be brought in for execution. During the month of July, Lithuanian policemen and German SS (short for "Schutzstaffel," or defense squad) officers roamed the streets and arrested young able-bodied Jewish men, who were told that they were needed for labor details but were actually taken to Ponary and executed. The SS was the paramilitary force of the Nazi Party, headed by Heinrich Himmler; they ran the concentration camps and both oversaw and carried out the Nazi's policy of genocide.

4. Yitskhok Rudashevski was a teenager from Vilna who chronicled ghetto life in his diary. The diary was found after the war. It had been left behind in Yitskhok's hiding place after the final liquidation of the Vilna ghetto in September/October 1943. At that time Yitskhok and his family were discovered and they were captured by the Germans. He was presumably killed at the execution ground of Ponary soon thereafter. Excerpts from his diary can be found in a new book called *Salvaged Pages: Young Writers Diaries of the Holocaust* by Alexandra Zapruder (Yale University Press, 2002). His whole diary has been published in a volume called *The Diary of the Vilna Ghetto*, by Yitskhok Rudashevski (Ghetto Fighters' House, 1973)

5. Zapruder, *Salvaged Pages*, 199.

Other police organizations within Nazi Germany included the Gestapo, or political police, and the SD, or security police.

During the first week of July 1941, 300 community leaders and over 500 young men were thus captured and killed. My grandfather comments on the these tactics and the inability of the Jews to comprehend what was happening to them:

> During the first couple of months we stubbornly refused to give credence to those few who managed to return from Ponary, declaring their tales of what was happening there the sign of psychotic delirium—so much did it seem monstrous and impossible. When one of the two survivors of Ponary, my future son-in-law Vova Gdud, reached his home only his parents believed him; all the neighbors thought him insane. One should note that in our case this procrastination was deadly—before we got oriented to what was going on in reality, our enemies had time to annihilate a large part of those who would have been able to put up some resistance.[6]

By August 1941, having executed the leaders of the Jewish community as well as many of the young Jewish men, the Nazis had deprived the Jewish community both of its political leadership as well as its practical ability to put up any physical resistance. On August 31st, after falsely proclaiming that German soldiers had been fired upon by Jews, the Nazis began what became known as the "provocation *aktion*," surrounding the old Jewish quarter and taking 8000 of its Jewish residents to Ponary, where they were executed. The provocation *aktion* was the first large-scale extermination effort by the Germans that included the elderly, women, and children. It accomplished both the goal of decreasing the swollen number of Jews in Vilna (estimated at 100,000 by the end of June 1941 due to influxes of refugees) and also cleared a predominantly Jewish section of town of its inhabitants in preparation for the formation of the Vilna Ghetto.

Throughout the summer of 1941, the Germans were greatly aided in their genocidal efforts by the active cooperation of newly arrived Lithuanian paramilitary units. In September 1920, following the turmoil that surrounded Russia's exit from World War I, a Polish general named Zheligovsky gained

6. Memoirs of Samuel Esterowicz, 280.

control of Vilna in a sudden land grab that made Vilna a Polish city, sur-rounded by hostile Lithuanian territory. When the Russians invaded Poland in 1939, they returned Vilna to Lithuanian control while making all of Lithuania a Soviet Republic. However, given the twenty-year history of Polish control of the city following the First World War, Vilna had relatively few Lithuanians; its population consisted almost entirely of Poles, Belarussians, and Jews, with less than 10% of the city having a Lithuanian heritage. The Germans, wanting to retain the goodwill of their new Lithuanian subjects, also put Vilna under the auspices of a Lithuanian civilian government. Within the Lithuanian population, they found many willing allies in their war against the Jews. While there had been deep anti-Semitism in both pre-war Poland and Lithuania, hatred of the Jews exploded in Lithuania once Russian forces were pushed east in June 1941, even before the Germans had established control of many parts of the country.

Many Lithuanians felt that local Jewish socialists and communists had supported the Soviets, who had occupied their country for two years. This perception led to widespread attacks against all elements of the Jewish popu-lation when the Soviets fled ahead of the German onslaught. Pogroms (anti-Jewish riots) and mass killings swept both the countryside and cities, with resulting waves of Jewish refugees flooding Vilna trying to escape the killings throughout the rest of Lithuania. When the Germans began organizing their genocide against the Jews, they had no trouble enlisting the help of the Lithuanian police force and right-wing paramilitary units, many of whose members were eager to help them in their task. Use of local Lithuanians aided the Germans in identifying Jews and then arresting them.[7] In Vilna

7. My parents have always insisted that Poles and Lithuanians could readily iden-tify someone as a Jew, even at a distance. They claimed that the Poles and Lithuanians had a "sixth sense" that allowed them to tell a Jew from a Gentile. I never believed this, as here in America most of us cannot tell a person's ethnicity and/or nationality by looks alone. We often cannot tell a Jew from an Italian or a Pole, etc. Of course, if a male in Vilna was under suspicion, the SS or Lithuanian police could always check to see if he was circumcised. However, when we traveled to Warsaw during our 1999 trip, within minutes of arriving, we were approached first by a taxi driver, then a bus driver, and then a bellboy, who all asked whether we wanted any help in arranging for a tour of the Auschwitz concentration camp. When I asked my parents why every-one was asking us whether we wanted to go to Auschwitz, my father replied that it was because they knew we were Jews and assumed we wanted to go to the place where our relatives had been killed. When I asked how they could possibly know that

proper, Lithuanian police (called "*Khapuny*" or "grabbers" by the Jews) carried out most of the arrests of Jewish men. At Ponary, the officers of German *Einsatzgruppe* (mobile killing squads) organized the mass executions, but Lithuanian volunteers under the direction of German officers performed much of the actual killing. The Jewish population thus had to contend not only with the murderous actions of the occupying German forces, but also with the enthusiastic support of those actions by many members of the surrounding civilian population. The local Polish population, while not friendly toward the Jews, also found themselves in the role of being persecuted by the Nazis, who considered them to be racially inferior Slavs.

Having successfully eliminated the leadership and many of the young men of the Jewish community, the Germans then began the next phase of their plan to destroy the Jews of Vilna; the formation of the Vilna Ghetto. Throughout Eastern Europe, the Nazis formed over 400 Jewish ghettos, walled-in areas where Jews were forced to live. By putting all the Jews from a geographic region in a ghetto, the Germans were able to concentrate and trap their victims, separate them from the local non-Jewish population and keep them from communicating with other Jewish communities. Conditions in the ghettos were squalid, with insufficient food supplies, lack of urban infrastructure, and only rudimentary medical facilities. Infectious epidemics swept through the ghettos killing thousands in spite of the efforts of Jewish physicians who cared for their brethren under very adverse conditions. Throughout Europe, deaths due to starvation and infectious diseases took a large toll of the Jewish ghetto communities even before the beginning of Nazi "*aktions*" during which Jewish victims would be captured and taken to be liquidated at execution grounds or death camps.[8]

By the autumn of 1941, due to a summer of killings and deportations, the Jewish population of Vilna had fallen to 48,000. On September 6, 1941, the Germans proceeded with their plans to force the remaining Jews of Vilna into two ghettos recently cleared of their inhabitants by the "provocation *aktion*," which had been carried out the previous week. There was the "large

---

we were Jewish, and not a family of American Gentiles, he replied, "It's because they have the sixth sense!"

8. Much of the information regarding the formation of Eastern European Jewish ghettos was obtained from the Holocaust Memorial Museum Web site, http://www.ushmm.org.

ghetto," which consisted of a four-block area between Zawalna street and Niemiecka street, and the smaller "second ghetto" near Gaon street. In the early morning hours, Lithuanian police units went out into the city and surrounded all apartments with Jewish residents. Policemen went door to door, and Jewish families were given a half hour notice to gather what belongings they could carry. They were then forced to walk, carrying bundles and often wearing several layers of clothes, to their designated ghetto area, a journey that was several miles in length for those who lived far from the ghettos. The Lithuanian police made them march without any chance to stop or rest. The streets were lined by Polish and Lithuanian civilians, some showing signs of sympathy, others catcalling and jeering. Most watched the procession in silence. Approximately 30,000 Jews were packed into the large ghetto and 10,000 into the smaller second ghetto, and 8,000 were taken to Lukishki prison as a temporary stopping point on the way to Ponary, where they were killed during three days of executions between September 10th and 12th. In a display of remarkable German "efficiency," the Jewish population was gathered, segregated, and confined to two tiny ghettos in less than a day.

Once the Jews were moved to the ghettos, the Germans appointed a five-member Jewish city council (Judenrat) to replace the community leaders they had executed over the summer. Additionally, they ordered the formation of a Jewish police force to create order within the ghetto. In the Jewish police, the Germans had a tool that they skillfully used to manipulate the Jewish population of the ghetto. The Nazis emphasized to the police, and the population in general, the importance they placed on order and cooperation. The Jews were told that strict adherence to Nazi edicts and rules would greatly increase their chances of survival. The example of the "provocation *aktion*," which had resulted in the deaths of 8,000 Jewish men, women, and children, was graphic evidence of what would happen if there were disorder or resistance of any kind to German rule. They gave the Jewish police responsibility to enforce German rules and, for the policemen and their families, the Germans offered safety from the terrifying and deadly *aktions* being carried out by the SS and the Lithuanian police. Over time, the Jewish police became more and more enmeshed with their German masters, becoming more like the oppressors as each German edict and order was dutifully carried out. In the following passage, young Yetskhok Rudashevski comments on the appearance of the Jewish police in the ghetto:

Soon we notice the first Jewish policemen. The are supposed to keep order in the ghetto. In time, however, they become a caste that helps the oppressors in their work. With the help of the Jewish police, the Gestapo accomplishes many things in the course of time. The Jewish police help to grasp their brothers by the throat; they help trip up their brothers . . .[9]

To the Jews in the ghetto, the Germans offered the illusion of safety, using them as laborers in war related workshops and giving the impression that such work was essential to the German war effort. The Germans promised that this war-related work would offer protection from arrest and execution. When the Nazis wanted another group of victims, they used the Jewish police to round up the required number of Jews, under the pretense that they were being transported to labor camps elsewhere in Eastern Europe. It is clear from today's historical vantage point that the Jewish police understood the true destination of those they captured for the Germans. It is to their everlasting shame that they failed to warn their fellow Jews of the German deception in an ultimately futile attempt to save themselves.

The Judenrat appointed a Jew from Kovno to command the Jewish police, a man named Jacob Gens. Gens, a former officer in the Lithuanian army, was an enigmatic figure who sparks heated controversy within the survivor community to this day. To his detractors (of whom my grandfather was a vocal member), Gens was a power-hungry megalomaniac who cooperated with the Germans in exchange for being given the power of life and death of his fellow Jews. To his defenders, Gens was a tragic figure, thrust against his will into the impossible situation of having to mediate between the Nazis and their victims. The defenders think that Gens did his best to delay and minimize the killing by using the limited means at his disposal. To speak for the detractors, here is my Grandfather Samuel Esterowicz's indictment of Jacob Gens:

I personally do not belong to those of the survivors who, looking back, see Gens not as he was in reality, but rather as we all in the beginning so passionately desired him to be: a leader who was doing his best to save at least some of us. I came to the conclusion (as did many others) that Gens was a man stripped of any moral standards long before his treacherous role became obvious to most of us.

9. Zapruder, *Salvaged Pages*, 201.

Faced with the demand of the Germans to furnish them with victims, without hesitation Gens seized the right not given to anybody—to decide who of us should stay alive and who should die and then to deliver the victims to the executioners. In similar circumstances, the head of the Warsaw ghetto, engineer Adam Czerniakow, faced with a task unthinkable to any decent person, committed suicide.

But that was not all: Gens faced us with the fact that both he and his ruling clique (mostly Lithuanian Jews from the Kovno area), including the police and his mistresses, were exonerated from the duty of contributing their blood to our horrible sacrifices as we all had to do. While taking away our mothers—supposedly in the name of saving the young—they shamelessly protected their own mothers.

Following in the footsteps of Stalin, Gens had created a class of those privileged (even if only temporarily so) who, to protect their own survival, helped him by exonerating his frequently obvious treacheries; they, as did the Jewish police, actively helped Gens to successfully carry out the role of the "Trojan Horse" for which he was designated by the Gestapo.

In any event, the destiny of the Jewish community was sealed—the forces were much too unequal. I lingered in some detail on the description of the deeds of Yakov Gens, and will return to it more than once, since in Gens we may find the reason why the Wilno Jewish community wrote the most brilliant pages of its chronicle during its life, rather than at its death.[10]

Having anticipated that his detractors would later judge him as a traitor and collaborator, Gens left us these words given in a speech at a gathering within the ghetto:

> Many of you consider me a traitor. . . . I, Gens, lead you to death; and I, Gens, want to save Jews from death. I, Gens, order hideouts to be blown up; and I, Gens, seek to create permits, work and benefit for the ghetto. I TAKE STOCK OF JEWISH BLOOD AND NOT OF JEWISH HONOR. When asked for 1,000 Jews—I give! If we, Jews, do not give, the Germans will come and . . . the whole ghetto will be chaos. With hundreds, I save thousands. With a thousand, that I give, I save 10,000.
>
> You, the people of spirit and pen, you don't touch the dirt of the ghetto.

10. Memoirs of Samuel Esterowicz, 295.

You will go out of the ghetto clean. And if you survive the ghetto, you'll say "we come out with a clean conscience."

But I, Jacob Gens, if I survive, I will come out dirty and blood will flow from my hands. And yet I shall place myself before the bar. To the judgment of Jews. I shall say: I did everything in order to save as many Jews as possible from the ghetto and lead them to freedom. In order to preserve a Jewish remnant, I was compelled to lead Jews to death. And in order to allow Jews to go out with a clean conscience—I am compelled to be stuck in dirt and deal unconscionably.[11]

To this day, there is no agreement on how to judge Jacob Gens.[12]

In the grim ghetto reality created by the Germans, the key to survival was a job in a German war-related workshop. These jobs paid no wages, but the precious worker identification papers gave its holder and his family protection from arrest and execution. Initially, a heterogeneous mix of Jews populated the two ghettos. However, throughout September of 1941 the Germans made efforts to transfer all Jews with work permits to the Large Ghetto and move nonworkers and their families either to the Small Ghetto or to Ponary.

11. This quotation of Jacob Gens was found by Salomon Klaczko (whom the reader will meet in Chapter 5) in a program of the play Ghetto by Joshua Sobol. The program presented several historical documents and speeches, including this one by Gens. This speech was apparently given during a "literary evening" event in the ghetto. This same speech is also found being given by Gens in the play Ghetto itself. While I have not been able to verify its authenticity, I do think that it likely portrays how Gens would have defended himself when confronting his detractors.

12. After much contemplation on the issue of Gens, I have decided that I join my grandfather as one of Gens's detractors. My main objection to his actions and deeds is that throughout his tenure as chief of the ghetto police, ostensibly to prevent panic and chaos, he continued to deceive the ghetto Jews as to the true intentions of the Nazis. Initially he covered up and countered rumors of the executions at Ponary and later when this was widely known, he would assure those who were rounded up for deportation that they were being sent to a labor camp when he often knew that this was not the case. It is this deception of his fellow Jews that I hold against him, as without clear understanding of what they were facing, the Jews of the Vilna ghetto were not able to decide for themselves and their families which path was best to take in their quest for survival. As we will see in the next chapter, it was this clear-eyed understanding by my father and grandfather that enabled them to escape Vilna and survive the war. That being said, there still is no consensus in the historical community on how to view Gens.

By the end of September, their task was complete with those remaining in the small ghetto consisting of either nonartisans (i.e., professionals, intellectuals) or the infirm. Starting on the Jewish holy day of Yom Kippur on October 1, 1941, and through the first three weeks of October, the Germans carried out a series of *aktions* against the Small Ghetto until all of its remaining inhabitants, approximately 7,200 people, had been killed at Ponary.

In order to further reduce the number of Jews remaining in Vilna while also preserving a Jewish slave labor force, the Germans issued "work permits" on yellow paper, which, if possessed, would allow a Jewish worker, his spouse, and two of their children to be protected from execution. These precious documents became know as "Yellow Life Certificates" ("Gele Shain" in Yiddish) and were issued to only 3,500 workers and their families, about 15,000 people in all. When it was realized that anyone not protected by a yellow life certificate was doomed, rapid efforts were made within the populace to ensure that any holder of one of the documents had a "wife" and two children whether in reality this was actually the case or not. For some families with more than two children there was a desperate search to find a certificate holder who could "adopt" their third or fourth children. If an adult in a family was not issued a life certificate, all were doomed. If issued a certificate, one was not allowed to save a mother, father, or in-laws, only a spouse and two children.

On October 24, 1941, all Jewish workers with yellow life certificates were ordered to appear at the gate of the large ghetto with their families. There, Martin Weiss, head of the Security Police (SD) and Franz Murer, adjutant to *Gebietskommissar* Hingst, inspected their papers. Anyone whose papers were not in order was sent immediately to Lukishki prison; the rest were allowed to proceed with their families to their workplaces. For a whole day, the Lithuanian police and the SS scoured the ghetto in search of Jews without the life-preserving yellow certificates. However, unlike earlier *aktions* where their victims were unaware of the German intentions, the surviving Jews now understood what would befall them if captured. During the days before this *aktion*, those ghetto dwellers who could not obtain protection of a life certificate had been frantically trying to escape from the ghetto, or preparing hiding places (called "*malines*") in order to avoid arrest. In spite of a thorough search of the ghetto, the Germans and Lithuanians were able to find only 3,700 Jews, who were taken to Ponary and killed.

The Germans were very disappointed in the results of the first "Gele Shain" *aktion* and thus changed tactics. First, they made efforts to stop any aid that Jews may have been getting from Gentiles outside of the ghetto. This aid usually consisted either of hiding Jews or holding money or possessions for their Jewish friends to use when needed. On October 29, *Gobietskommissar* Hingst issued a decree, signed by Murer, ordering the Gentile populace of Vilna to report Jews and half-Jews living outside the ghetto. They were also informed that if they were found hiding a Jew or their possessions, the offending homeowner would face severe penalties. My grandfather describes how this was carried out:

> We should take note the following occurrence which forced our Gentile friends to think twice before they gave shelter to the Jews:
>
> Shortly before the "yellow life certificate *aktion*" Franz Murer came to the ghetto gate and summoned my childhood friend Victor Chelem. Victor and his sister Eugenia, the heirs of Isaac Chelem, were owners of a wholesale glass business and sizable real estate in the commercial center on Niemiecka Street and were thought to have become very rich after World War I. Murer demanded that Victor give up to him the gold that he had hidden outside of the ghetto. Nothing would happen to Victor if he complied, Murer said, but if he refused, he would be shot immediately.
>
> Victor could do nothing else but take Murer to his former apartment house and ask the caretaker, Nikolay Ordu, to give the gold to Murer. Murer kept his word and let Victor Chelem go—but he ordered Nikolay Ordu hanged. The body of Nikolay Ordu was hanging in Cathedral Square with a board fastened to him announcing that this was what awaited all those who hid Jewish property or who gave shelter to the Jews.[13]

Having made hiding outside of the ghetto much less likely due to the severe penalties that would befall any family helping a Jew in any way, the Germans proceeded to segregate the certificate-holding workers and their families from the "illegals," those without life certificates. On November 4th, all certificate-holding workers and their families were again ordered to appear at the ghetto gate. There they were inspected by Jacob Gens and the Jewish police who carried out the check of their papers under the supervision of German officials.[14] The "legals" were then taken to the recently emptied

13. Memoirs of Samuel Esterowicz, 299.
14. Yitzhak Arad, *Ghetto in Flames* (Holocaust Library, 1982), 154.

Small Ghetto, where they stayed for three days while the large ghetto was systematically searched for hiding places. The second ghetto was eerily quiet, its inhabitants having been taken by the Germans only days before. Here again is my grandfather:

> The lifeless streets of the second ghetto were horrifying—the room we entered was deathly quiet, there was an unfinished meal on the plates on a table, opened prayer books and prayer shawls spoke about a suddenly interrupted life, about people who were caught unawares when taken to their deaths.[15]

After three days, the "legal" workers were allowed to return to the first ghetto where they found all of the apartments ransacked, with cupboards and walls smashed open by three days of searches for hidden Jews. The Germans had found an additional 1,400 victims during this second "yellow life certificate *aktion*." There now remained only 15,000 Jews in Vilna.

After this *aktion*, Jacob Gens was confronted by a group of Jewish rabbis who told him that he had no right to select Jews and hand them over to the Germans. Gens replied that by surrendering some, he was saving others from extinction. To this the rabbis replied with a quote from Maimonides who had said, "better all be killed than one soul of Israel be surrendered."[16] This is one of the deep, tragic memories that Jewish survivors carry with them from the Vilna ghetto. Not only the story of the genocide carried out by the Nazis, but the painful specter of fellow Jews helping the oppressors in an attempt to save themselves. Within the Vilna Ghetto, Yitskhok Rudashevski wrote in his diary:

> That Jews in uniform drive their own brothers to the ghetto, distribute certificates, and keep order with the knout . . . How great is our misfortune, how great is our shame, our humiliation! Jews help Germans in their organized terrible work of extermination![17]

Between October 1941 and Christmas two more *aktions* were carried out in the ghetto, first one directed against family members of Jews who worked in the Gestapo offices and a second against "illegals" who persisted in the

---

15. Memoirs of Samuel Esterowicz, 300.
16. Yitzhak Arad, *Ghetto in Flames*, 156.
17. Zapruder, *Salvaged Pages*, 210.

ghetto without proper work certificates. However, as the year drew to a close, world events would intervene for a time on behalf of Vilna's remaining Jews.

Hitler had originally planned for a rapid summer assault on the Soviet Union, expecting that his eastern campaign would be finished by fall of 1941. However, in spite of early successes, the war did not go entirely as planned and, as winter approached, the Germans were unable to capture Moscow, Leningrad, or Stalingrad. The Germans had not prepared for a cold-weather campaign, and the winter of 1942 turned out to be exceptionally bitter. With their troops dressed in light summer uniforms and their vehicles ill equipped for subzero weather, the German advance ground to a halt. The Wehrmacht's generals realized that they required significant support for an ongoing war effort and for this they needed the slave labor of the Jews of Lithuania, including those in the Vilna ghetto. Throughout Lithuania, Jews were put to work as furriers, mechanics, and seamstresses making fur coats, repairing vehicles, and sewing damaged clothing for the German Army. After the second "Yellow Certificate Aktion," when 2,200 of the Wehrmacht's skilled Jewish workers were killed, a bitter dispute broke out between the Wehrmacht and the SS over the fate of the remaining Jews of Lithuania. Wehrmacht commanders complained that they could not replace Jewish artisans, who were being killed en masse to the detriment of the German war effort. They began to intervene to stop the killing of skilled Jews and their families by the Einsatzkommando mobile killing units. Holocaust scholars have examined memos from both Wehrmacht and SS commanders in Lithuania during this period. They reveal a fascinating glimpse of the bureaucratic infighting that occurred over the fate of Eastern Europe's Jews. For example, after SS and Einsatzkommando commanders complained to their headquarters about the interference from a Wehrmacht officer named Gewecke in Schaulen, Lithuania, Gewecke wrote the following defense of his actions:

> When all the deportation aktions have been completed, 4,000 Jews including members of their families who are need as skilled workers, will remain in the Schaulen region . . . It is impossible to carry on work without Jews. This is especially the case in the leather tanning industry. Every single artisan in this industry is Jewish . . . On the basis of the conversation I had with you and in light of this report, you may be convinced that we have acted in the Jewish question in the Schaulen region with necessary intensiveness and with National-Socialist stubborness.[18]

18. Arad, Ghetto in Flames, 166.

Another officer reported the following:

> On November 7, 1941, Mey, an officer in the Quartermaster General's Command in the Ostland, appeared before me and swore that Jewish artisans employed in workshops and other armament factories of the Wehrmacht were being liquidated in Vilna, and that it was impossible to replace them by local workers. In these factories vehicles of combat units are being replaced.[19]

Additionally, Wehrmacht officers reported that the mass extermination of civilians was causing morale problems within the army's ranks. In this memo the *Gebietskommissar* of Latvia complains of the effects of the killing on his men:

> The liquidation of the Jews, which resumed last week is arousing resentment . . . especially the shooting of women and children, which stirred general opposition . . . Even the officers ask me whether it was necessary to liquidate the children.[20]

At the insistence of the Wehrmacht war planners, the mass extermination of Vilna's remaining Jews was temporarily halted, much to the dismay of the Gestapo and SS executioners. In the following memo, *Standartenfuehrer* Jaeger, the commander of *Einsatzkommando* 3 and head of the Security Police in Lithuania, writes a summary of his activities to his superiors in Berlin:

> I can state today that the goal of the solution of the Jewish problem in Lithuania has been reached by Einsatzkommando 3. There are no longer any Jews in Lithuania except the working Jews and their families which total 4,500 in Schaulen, 15,000 in Kauen, and 15,000 in Vilna. I intended to kill these working Jews and their families too, but met with the strongest protest from the civil administration (Reichskommisar) and from the Wehrmacht, and I received an order prohibiting the murder of these Jews and their families. I consider the bulk of the aktions against the Jews to be finished as far as E.K.3 is concerned. The working Jews and Jewesses left alive for the time being are badly needed and I presume that even when winter is over this Jewish labor force will still be badly needed . . .[21]

19. Arad, *Ghetto in Flames*, 168.
20. Arad, *Ghetto in Flames*, 167.
21. Arad, *Ghetto in Flames*, 170–171.

This tension between the Wehrmacht, which wanted more slave labor for the war effort, and the SS, which for ideological reasons wanted to kill all remaining Jews, continued for much of the remainder of the war. These memos show that the Germans in Lithuania were not entirely uniform in their views or motivations regarding the fate of the Jews. The ardent Nazis wanted to kill every Jew no matter what the cost to the war effort. Less politicized officers were more concerned with winning the war, using Jewish labor if necessary. Some were upset by the aktions and methods of their SS colleagues. Regardless of their personal feelings, given the political climate of Nazi Germany, no one wanted to appear as a protector of Jews or seem to disagree with National Socialist sentiments. As we will see later, it was because of this tension between the Wehrmacht and the SS that Karl Plagge was able to protect the Jewish workers under his command through much of the war.

Starting in January 1942, there began a period of relative stability for the Jews of the Vilna ghetto. No further aktions were carried out, and for the next 18 months they were rarely subjected to mass killings. Within the walls of the ghetto, the Jews began to organize basic social structures. Physicians representing all specialties staffed the ghetto hospital and took vigorous measures to prevent deadly epidemics from spreading among the ghetto populace. Two bathhouses were built, and all residents were required to bathe twice a week in order to get their food rations. While at the bathhouse their clothing was vigorously deloused and disinfected. The Gestapo allowed only starvation rations for Jews, intending to kill the remaining Jews through disease and starvation. However, the Judenrat organized food smuggling operations, bribing the Lithuanian police to allow carts of food to enter the ghetto. They also utilized the services of a group of chimney sweeps to help smuggle essential goods into the ghetto over the rooftops and between buildings adjacent to the ghetto walls. Workers who left the ghetto in work brigades to go to workshops outside the walls were also an important source of smuggled food. They were able to buy goods from Gentile co-workers and then smuggle these rations back into the ghetto for their families. Orphanages were established to care for the large number of children whose parents had been killed during the previous summer and fall. The community allocated supplemental food rations for these orphans and efforts were also made to make food available to those Jews who did not have the means to buy food on the black market. As a result of these efforts, Vilna's ghetto was able to avoid the widespread death by hunger and disease that was seen in other Jewish ghettos throughout Europe. In addition to securing food and medical care for its inhabitants, the Judenrat also helped form schools, theaters, and libraries, hoping that these cultural institutions would help stave off despair and hopelessness among the surviving ghetto inhabitants.

Even though they had gained a respite from the constant killings of the previous year, the remaining Jews in the Vilna ghetto no longer had doubts as to what the Germans intended their fate to be. While the Nazis had hidden their deadly intentions and activities with great success for the first six months of their occupation of Lithuania, by 1942 their deceptions were no longer believed. Within the ghetto, resistance groups were formed, most coalescing under the umbrella organization called the "United Partisans' Organization" (Fareinikte Partisaner Organizatie-FPO). The FPO gathered what remained of the various Jewish youth groups that had existed before the war and tried to coordinate resistance against the Germans. The FPO began to buy small arms and made plans to begin armed resistance should the Germans try to liquidate the ghetto. While the military capabilities of the resistance movement within the Vilna ghetto were pitifully small compared to the overwhelming armed might of the German army, psychologically the resistance movement was very important to the wretched Jews trapped under Nazi occupation. The existence of an armed resistance movement gave the Jews of the ghetto the feeling that some of their people were capable of fighting back. Even though the odds for surviving the war were stacked against them, the remaining Jews had not given up hope or the will to resist the Germans in whatever manner was at their disposal.

Listening to the resistance songs popular in the ghetto, one can feel the emotional impact that fighting back had for the oppressed Jews both in Vilna and in ghettos across occupied Europe. Here are the lyrics to a popular song written in the Vilna ghetto. This song, "Zog nit keynmol" (Never The Last Journey), subsequently became the Jewish resistance anthem during the war:

> Never say that there is only death for you
> Though leaden skies may be concealing days of blue
> Because the hour that we have hungered for is near,
> Beneath our tread the earth shall tremble: We Are Here!
>
> We'll have the morning sun to set our day aglow
> And all our yesterdays shall vanish with the foe

And if the time is long before the sun appears,
Then let this song go like a signal through the years
—Composed by Hirsch Glick[22]

In addition to joining the resistance groups, increasing numbers of Jews were trying to escape from the ghetto into the surrounding forests where they hoped to hide or join partisan groups fighting the Germans. The Germans were aware of these developments and took vigorous measures to eliminate these threats to their plans. To prevent runaways, they instituted a policy of mass killing of family, friends, and co-workers among those left behind by the runaways. For instance, in one of the work camps assigned to cutting firewood for the ghetto, some of the workers escaped into the forest in July 1943. In retaliation, Bruno Kittel, the head of the Secret Police (Gestapo) in Vilna, ordered the rest of the members of these work details into wooden sheds where he had them burned alive.[23] The knowledge of what one's escape would mean for loved ones left in the ghetto was a great deterrent for any able-bodied Jew who considered fleeing.

To combat the formation of armed resistance units, the Nazis ordered Gens and the Jewish police to turn over the leaders of the FPO, which, to their everlasting shame, they did. One FPO leader, Isaac Wittenberg, was arrested by the Jewish police, only to be freed by members of his FPO unit.

22. From Remember.org (http://www.remember.org/hist.root.music.html) comes the following explanation:

"Of all the songs of all the ghettos, the one which spread like wildfire, almost from the moment that it left the poet's pen, was the marching song by Hirsh Glik, "Zog nit keynmol az du geyst dem letstn vet" ("Never Say that You Are Trodding the Final Path"). Set to a tune by the Soviet composers, the brothers Pokras, it became the official hymn of all the Eastern European partisan brigades and was subsequently translated into Hebrew, Polish, Russian, Spanish, Rumanian, Dutch, and English. With almost magical speed it was caught up by all the concentration camps, and by the time the war was over, it was being sung by Yiddish-speaking Jews the world over and by a score of other peoples as well. Composed in Vilna, it is most often related to the Warsaw ghetto uprising, which began in the morning hours of April 19, 1943." More information on this song (including a recording) can be found at the Holocaust Memorial Museum Web site at http://www.ushmm.org/museum/exhibit/online/ music/never.utp. This particular translation was found in "A Family Haggadah" by Shoshana Silberman (Kar-Ben Copies, 1987), 21.

23. Memoirs of Samuel Esterowicz, http://hometown.aol.com/michaeldg/mem oirssmesterowicz.doc, 331.

The Germans threatened to start an *aktion* that would capture thousands of Jews if Wittenberg was not delivered to them. Gens appealed to and then threatened the FPO members, to no avail. He then rallied the ghetto populace against them, saying that the hotheads of the FPO would be to blame for the deaths of thousands of innocents that would follow if the Jews did not comply with German demands. Reluctantly, the FPO asked Wittenberg to surrender voluntarily, which he agreed to do. After surrendering himself, Isaac Wittenberg committed suicide by swallowing cyanide before he could be interrogated by the Gestapo. By using tactics of mass retaliation for the acts of resistance or escape by individuals, and the continued policy of dividing the Jewish community with threats of death of one group or another, the Nazis succeeded in keeping the vast majority of Vilna's Jews trapped in the ghetto.

By the end of August 1943, rumors began to circulate that the Germans intended to kill the remaining Jews in Vilna, to "liquidate the ghetto." On September 1st, the Germans started a widespread *aktion* to capture ghetto inhabitants for transport to the slate mines of Estonia. Over the next week 7,000 of the ghettos most able workers were captured and transported. For the remaining Jews, it was understood that the end was upon them. The FPO had originally intended to make a military stand when the Germans came to liquidate the ghetto and to call for mass resistance by the populace. Unfortunately, due to betrayal by a member of the Jewish police, the FPO was taken by surprise when the Germans entered the ghetto on September 1st. One half of their fighters were captured and deported on the first day of the "Estonia *aktion*," and the remaining fighters were thrown into disarray. A small fire fight broke out between the remaining FPO fighters and the Germans. The building in which the FPO fighters were hiding was blown up, and most of the fighters were killed.

On September 14th, the Gestapo called Jacob Gens to their headquarters and summarily executed him. Gens had been warned earlier of his impending arrest and execution and had been advised to flee. Though he had the ability to arrange an escape, Gens reportedly told his associates that his escape would bring calamity down upon the ghetto, and he therefore presented himself to the Gestapo and met his unhappy fate. Having eliminated a leader they no longer needed, the Germans proceeded to empty the ghetto on September 23, 1943; 5,000 Jews were sent to slave labor camps in Estonia and Latvia. Five thousand elderly, women, and children were sent to the gas chambers at Maidanek concentration camp or shot at Ponary. The destruction of Vilna's Jews was almost complete.

By September 25, 1943, only 2,300 Jews remained in Vilna: 1,200 were in a protected furrier's camp called "Kailis," 70 worked in a military hospital, and 70 worked at Gestapo headquarters. Additionally, just one week before the liquidation of the ghetto, 1,000 Jews were moved out of the ghetto to a small camp located at 37 Subocz Street, due to the insistence of an obscure Wehrmacht officer named Plagge who was in charge of Vilna's vehicle repair unit (HKP). There, the HKP workers were able to continue their work repairing army vehicles for the German war effort. My mother and her parents were among the lucky few transferred to the HKP camp. We will now rejoin my parents and hear how they came to escape from the Nazi death machine, a tale that will soon lead us to the discovery of a hidden rescuer who wore the uniform of those who did Hitler's bidding.

THE GDUDS

When I told them what had happened to me at Ponary, none of the Jews who lived in our apartment building believed me—they said I was crazy. They thought I must have had a nervous break-down . . . but my father believed my story and he said: "they are out to kill us all—we are not going to the ghetto, we are not going to let them lock us up, we are getting out!"
—Memoirs of William Good

On the first morning of our visit to Vilnius, Susan, Jonathan, Rebecca, my parents, and I all departed from the Hotel Palaite and walked toward the Green Bridge over the Vilya River.

"What is today's date?" asked my father.

"June 22nd," I replied.

"You're kidding," he said. "Today is the 58th anniversary of Operation Barbarossa, the German surprise attack against the Soviet Union." As we stood overlooking the Vilya River, my father remembered the events of that day more than half a century ago. He recalled that he had gone out kayaking on the river with four of his friends. The group paddled up the river and outside of town. At about ten in the morning, they saw that the sky was filled with planes. At first they thought it was a military exercise, but before long they could see that the planes were bombing the city. At first they wanted to return home, but decided to wait until the aerial bombardment had ended. When they returned to Vilna in the afternoon, they found the city in chaos and the Soviets in retreat. It was clear that the Germans would soon be in control of the city.

My father had heard that the Germans were committing atrocities against Jews, namely that they were castrating Jewish boys. As a young teenager, this was too terrible for him to even contemplate. He wanted to flee from the advancing Germans by following the retreating Russians. After consulting with his parents, it was agreed that he would try to run away from the German occupation. He and Abrasha Lipman, a friend from school, packed supplies and rode their bikes to the east, hoping to get to Minsk. The roads were packed with refugees fleeing the Germans. Russian soldiers, Communists, Jews—anyone who feared the Nazis was trying to escape. Suddenly, German planes flew low over the road and began to fire their machine guns into the crowds. Abrasha, who was only an arm's length away from my father, was hit and killed. My father miraculously escaped injury. After his friend's death, my father continued biking to the east. However, he did not make it to Minsk. The Germans advanced faster than he could pedal his bike. He soon heard that the Wehrmacht was already ahead, occupying Minsk and surging further into Russian territory. Reluctantly, he turned around and headed back to Vilna. On the way home, peasants who were emboldened by the arrival of the Germans pounced on a lone Jewish teenager as easy prey and robbed him. They took his bike, his backpack, his shoes, and even his shirt. Soon he was trudging barefoot, wearing only his pants. It took him ten days to get back home to his parents' apartment; he arrived dirty, hungry, and tired on July 8.

Even though he had only been gone two weeks, my father found that life for the Jews of Vilna had already changed dramatically. Due to anti-Jewish German edicts, he now had to wear an armband with the letter J on it when he went out in public. He could not use the sidewalks when walking through the streets; Jews could only walk in the gutter. Still, he was alive and living safely with his family once again. Two days after his return, he decided to get a haircut at the neighborhood barbershop. As he walked in the street, he saw a German army jeep driving toward him. Nervous, he sped up and ducked into the barbershop, hoping that his white armband had not been seen. Moments later a German officer came into the shop, "You! Come with me!" he yelled, and hauled my father out and put him in the jeep. They then proceeded down the street, picking up several other young Jewish men as they went. They were taken to St. Bernard's Park, where several hundred young Jewish men waited under guard. The Germans told them that they would spend the night in the park and then be taken to clear rubble in Molodeczno, a nearby town damaged in the recent fighting. This sounded plausible, as there had been much destruction both in Vilna and the surrounding towns during the rapid German attack. My father and the other Jews spent a quiet night in the park under loose guard. He is sure they could have slipped away during the night, but no one felt any urgency to run away. In the morning a convoy of canvas covered trucks arrived and the young Jews filed into them, 30 to a truck. However, their journey did not take them to Molodeczno, but rather to the nearby forest of Ponary.

When the covers over the back of the truck were thrown open, my father and the other Jews looked down the barrels of two machine guns manned by Lithuanian police. "No one is to move or speak, if anyone disobeys the machine guns will open fire," they were told. Behind the machine guns was a large open grave, with many bodies in it. Under the direction of a German officer, the Lithuanians took the Jews out of the truck one by one, walked them up to the grave, and shot them in the back of the head. The remaining Jewish teenagers and men watched in shocked silence. Staring at the machine guns, they dared not speak or move. They could not believe what was happening. Soon an armed Lithuanian in civilian clothes grabbed my father by the arm and led him toward the open grave. My father could tell that his executioner was drunk. Off to one side, he could see a German officer taking pictures of the operation. Even as he was led forward toward the grave, he could not believe that he was about to die. As he was pushed toward the grave he stumbled and fell forward toward the grave. At the instant that he tripped, a shot rang out as the drunken Lithuanian fired the bullet meant to kill him. It missed. My father fell to the ground just in front of the grave and lay still. His executioner thought he was dead and went back to the truck for his next victim. For the next several hours my father lay perfectly still, terrified but unharmed. Truck after truck drove up, and their occupants were shot. The bodies of other executed men soon covered my father; he was drenched in their blood. Some of the Jews were not dead; moans and cries came from the mass grave. Having shot approximately 15 truckloads of victims, the machine guns were turned around and fired into the grave in order to finish off the wounded. In spite of the fusillade of bullets around him, perhaps because the bodies on top of him protected him, my father was unharmed.

After a time, all became quiet. My father arose to find the Germans and Lithuanians gone. All the Jews lying in and around the mass grave were dead. Incredibly, he was alive and totally unscathed! The area around the grave was surrounded by barbed wire; my father ran down the road toward the gate that the trucks had entered upon arriving at Ponary. The gate was guarded by two soldiers, who soon spotted him. One fired a shot at him, but he ducked down and ran back to the mass grave. My father was filled with panic. He was sure the guards would soon come looking for him. He was desperate to escape this horrible place before they could find and shoot him. He began to dig frantically under the barbed wire with his hands. Having made a shallow hole under the barbed wire, he squeezed underneath the fence, ripping his clothes and cutting his back as he passed. He leapt to his feet and ran into the woods. He ran on and on, and after a time he came to a small hut occupied by a Polish peasant family. Stumbling into their home, crying hysterically, he told them what had just happened to him. He does not know whether they believed him, but says they were kind to him nonetheless. They helped him wash off the blood and gore that covered him and gave him a new shirt to wear. They then showed him the way back to Vilna. In a daze, he then walked all day back to his parents' apartment in the city.

Upon his return home, he immediately told his parents and his Jewish neighbors about his experience, warning them that the Nazis were killing innocent Jews they picked up off the street. While his mother and father believed his tale, the neighbors in the surrounding apartments did not. They thought he had gone insane and become psychotic. When confronted with such a story told by a traumatized seventeen-year-old boy, they could only conclude that he had lost his mind. They told his father that the journey to Minsk and the loss of his friend Abrasha must have been too much for his son to withstand.

But, after listening to his son's story and thinking about the virulent anti-Semitic edicts that had been enacted with the arrival of the Germans, my grandfather quietly said, "They mean to kill us all." With that, he started to make preparations to leave Vilna and go into hiding. They decided to go to Niemenczyn, where the family knew the lay of the land and all of the neighbors. Before leaving Vilna my grandfather entrusted some money and valuables to some Gentile friends. When rumors began to circulate that the Germans might force all the Jews into a ghetto, my grandfather said, "No ghetto for us! We're not going to be trapped in a place like that!" So, during the third week of July, one week after my father had escaped from Ponary, my grandfather led his family out of Vilna and headed for Niemenczyn.

In Niemenczyn, for two short months life reverted back to what it had been before the German occupation. There were no German troops in the countryside, and the only sign of the anti-Semitic edicts so prevalent in Vilna was the arrival of a twenty-four-year-old Lithuanian named Stephan Neras, who was appointed by the authorities to be "in charge" of the family turpentine business. His arrival was arranged and ordered by the Nazis, who declared that they would not allow Jews to be in a position which caused them to supervise Gentiles. Stephan was totally inexperienced in the running of a turpentine factory, so he needed guidance in all things from Grandpa Dov. To make things even more comical, Stephan spoke only Lithuanian, not Polish, Russian, or Belarussian, the languages of the factory workers. In order to talk to either my grandfather or the workers he needed the services of my father, who spoke Lithuanian, Polish, Russian, and Yiddish. Thus, during the summer of 1941, the family turpentine factory was run by a young, inexperienced Lithuanian who gave orders through my father, after consulting my grandfather on what was to be done.

Because of their time together, Stephan and my father became friends. They kayaked on the river together, had wrestling contests and danced to folk tunes played on the violin by my father's brother Mot'l. The summer passed uneventfully. The Gdud family heard of the formation of the ghetto in Vilna, but in Niemenczyn, things were quiet. Nonetheless, Grandfather Dov prepared for the worst eventuality. In back of the turpentine factory was a huge yard filled with mounds of tree stumps waiting to be processed into turpentine. In the middle of this field, he created a small room underneath the piled up logs where he stockpiled food, water and blankets. Additionally, he took many of the family's valuables, such as good clothing, furs, and leather goods, and entrusted them to the safe keeping of some of his workers. Having made their preparations, the family waited. Two months later their waiting ended. My father describes what happened next:

> On the night of Friday, September 20, 1941, we were asleep when suddenly the dog started barking—he was on a leash on a wire running across the property and he was furious, barking madly. My father got up, opened the window and saw the figure of a woman.
>
> He asked, "who is it"?
>
> She whispered—"Josefowa" [Joseph's wife].
>
> "Listen," she whispered, knowing that there were Lithuanians in the house, "our husbands have been mobilized to dig graves for the Jews of Niemenczyn. They will all be killed at dawn, get out of the house immediately!"
>
> "Did you hear me?"

"Yes!"

"Did you understand?"

"Yes, thank you!"

It turns out that all the local peasant men had been mobilized to dig graves for the Jews of Niemenczyn, who were to be killed by the Lithuanian militia in the morning. Joseph Paszkowski, a neighbor, was among the peasant men who were being forced to dig the graves. When he understood what was going to happen, he pretended to step into the woods to relieve himself and then ran quickly to his home, where he instructed his wife Felicia to warn the Gduds. She traveled through the night to warn them, even though she knew that Stephan and other Lithuanian overseers slept at the Gdud house. If she or her husband's actions were discovered, they both could have been executed.

Following Felicia's warning, the Gdud family quickly left the home and went into hiding. My grandfather had originally planned to have the whole family enter the hiding place under the stump pile. However, on further reflection he decided they should split into two groups. My grandmother Hannah and her youngest son, Mot'l, went into the prepared hiding place, while my father and grandfather went to hide in the forest. His reasoning was that many of the turpentine factory workers knew of the hiding place and also of the family valuables hidden with some of the workers. If all the Gduds were in one hiding place, one of the workers might be tempted to betray them and, following their arrest, take their valuables. However, if only half the family was discovered, those responsible for their arrest would have to worry about the threat of retribution from the members of the family who remained at large.

After spending the night in the forest, my grandfather told his son to travel two kilometers to the farmhouse of a peasant family named Gasperowicz, while he would go back to the house to dig up some guns he had buried on the property. My father departed, emerging from the forest into a large field shortly after dawn. On the far side of the field he saw his Lithuanian friend Stephan Neras walking with a rifle slung over his shoulder. Stephan waved to my father, inviting him to join him. My father could have slipped back into the woods but was embarrassed to show a lack of trust in a friend, so he joined up with Stephan and they walked to the Gasperowicz farm together. Upon arriving at the farm, Stephan turned his gun on my father and ordered him into the barn. My father pleaded with him to let him go, saying they were buddies, but Stephan replied, "do as I say or I'll kill you right now." He locked my father in the barn, throwing a thick wooden bar across the entrance. To the Gasperowicz family members who were watching, he said in broken Russian, "If Gdud escapes, you will die."

With that warning, he left to join the other Lithuanians who were gathering to execute the Jews of Niemenczyn. My father, locked in the darkness of the barn, called out to Vincent Gasperowicz, a teenager who was his friend, "Vincent, let me out!" To which Vincent replied, "You heard what he told me; if I let you out, it will come to me what is coming to you." After a moment Vincent suggested that my father break down the door from the inside, "Just knock down the door, throw yourself against it!" My father frantically began to hurl himself against the sturdy door. Initially, it did not budge, but after getting a running start across the barn, he was able to throw himself with sufficient force to burst through the barn door. Stephan, hearing the commotion as he was leaving the property, returned to the barn just in time to find my father emerging from behind the shattered barn door. My father describes what happened as he emerged:

> If I had only waited five minutes, Stephan would have been gone to mobilize the peasants, but he heard the first knock, so he came back and there he was standing pointing his rifle at me.
>
> There was a dog running on a leash between us, barking furiously.
>
> A neighbor was calling to me in Polish:
>
> "Vovka [William], throw yourself at him! kill him!"
>
> I looked at him and thought "I can kill him, I'm sure I can kill him, but how do I get to him? He has a rifle!" In a split second I knew I couldn't do it; he could kill me before I reached him, so I just dodged the dog and ran. I ran behind the barn and into the field away from the village. Stephan was afraid of the dog and went the long way around the barn to chase me. I threw off my sheepskin in order to run faster and gave a glance back. I saw Stephan leaning his rifle on the fence and aiming—the very same moment that he fired, I threw myself down to the ground. Immediately after the shot I jumped back on my feet and ran, ran, ran, zigzagging—I threw myself down each time a shot was fired. The moment I would swerve or fall, a shot would go off. This happened seven times. I tried to pull off my high boots to run faster but it was too

time consuming—this was lucky for me because these were my boots for the next three years and I would need them to survive. I ran through the field and into the forest out of his sight. I continued to run until I was totally exhausted and totally breathless; then I fell and just cried and cried and cried.[1]

At the same time that my father was escaping from his traitorous friend Stephan Neras, my grandfather was also facing life-threatening difficulties. He had gone back to the family property to try to dig up some handguns that he had buried behind the house. After observing the area and thinking it free of intruders, he began to dig up the weapons. Suddenly, a concealed Lithuanian policeman emerged from hiding with his gun drawn and arrested him. Pleading and attempts to bribe the policeman were to no avail; he was marched to the town jail, where he joined the rest of Niemenczyn's Jews. They were told that they were going to be taken to the Vilna Ghetto. Each one carried a large bundle of belongings. My grandfather said to them, "Fellow Jews, don't bother to pack and drag all your belongings; they are going to kill us." Nobody believed him. The 700 Jews were guarded by 250 armed Lithuanians and marched down the road toward Vilna. However, about seven kilometers outside of town they came to a large meadow between two thick areas of forest and were turned off the road. It became apparent that they were not going to Vilna.

Suddenly all the Lithuanians moved to one side of the Jews and upon the cue of their leader began to fire their weapons into the group of Jews in front of them. Pandemonium ensued. Most of the Jews in the crowd were shot and killed or wounded in the initial volleys. After the shock of the first moments, those who had not yet been hit began to run for their lives. The shooters began to fire primarily at those who were running away from them, trying to pick them off before they could escape into the forest on the far side of the clearing. My grandfather initially stood straight up, hoping to be killed outright instead of being wounded and having to endure a prolonged agonizing death. However, after a few moments, in spite of the bullets whizzing around him, he found himself unharmed. He realized that the shooters were primarily firing at those Jews who were running away from them. So

1. Memoirs of William Good, http://www.hometown.aol.com/michaeldg/mem oirs_of_william_good.doc, 12.

he began to run toward the shooters and soon placed himself among them. Once he was in their midst, the shooters were unwilling to shoot at him for fear of hitting one of their own. As he ran he heard someone yell, "Mr. Gdud, wait for me!" It was Ester Bernstein, the pharmacist's wife. "Ester, follow me, run for your life!" he yelled. A teenager, Yankel Leifer, also followed him as he ran behind the shooters and into the woods. Together they ran through the forest and away from the executions. All three of them would ultimately survive the war. Yankel made his own way into hiding, while Ester, who had no prepared hiding place, stayed with my grandfather, who provided for her during the ensuing three years of Nazi occupation.

Over the course of the war, my grandfather would provide the logistics and financing for hiding several of the surviving Jews of Niemenczyn, enabling them to survive. After the war, Yankel Leifer would immigrate to America and settle down in Colchester, Connecticut, half an hour from where I now live. He and my father had an emotional reunion at the time of my wedding in 1983, 42 years later. Yankel told my father that if it hadn't been for my grandfather's cool example, he never would have survived the execution.

My grandmother Hannah and uncle Mot'l were not to be as fortunate as my father and grandfather Dov. After being warned by Felicia Paszkowski, they went into the hiding place prepared by my grandfather in the stump field. For two days they remained in hiding and escaped detection during the time when the rest of the Jews of Niemenczyn were captured and taken away for execution. However, fourteen-year-old Mot'l became increasingly restless and claustrophobic in their cramped hideout. It appears that he left the concealed space to look around. He was spotted by a passing shepherd, who, when asked by a Lithuanian policeman later in the day whether he had seen any Jews, replied, "Yes, a young one near the Gdud's place." The police soon came and captured Mot'l, taking him to the Niemenczyn police station. When he did not return that evening, my grandmother came out of hiding and asked some of the factory workers if they knew what had happened to him. They told her that he had been captured and was being held at the police station. He was with about 20 other Jews who had been captured after running away from the previous day's execution. She was told that they were to be killed in the morning. My grandmother could not bear the thought of her son being alone and surrounded by his murderers during the last night

The haunting visage of the HKP Labor Camp shortly after liberation in 1944.

Standing in the courtyard of the HKP labor camp in June 1999, Pearl Good tells the story of how Major Plagge, the German commander of the camp, saved her life during the Holocaust. A local film crew, grandson Jonathan, daughter-in-law Susan, and granddaughter Rebecca look on. Today, these buildings are used as low-income housing. Note the boy riding a bicycle in the background, unaware of the events that occurred here fifty-five years before.

Pearl Good, age seven, circa 1936.

Pearl Good three years after liberation in 1947.

Pearl's parents, Ida and Samuel Esterowicz. Samuel's scrupulous business practices created ties that would save his family. Ida's social grace and tact helped soften his brutal honesty.

The Gdud family in 1941, shortly before the German occupation. Left to right: Mot'l, Hannah, Dov and Vovka (William). This is the last known photo of the family together.

Having survived three years of living in the forests and swamps outside of Vilna, Vovka and Dov Gdud pose for a portrait in 1945, one year after liberation.

Ghetto Fighters' House

A Jewish woman is questioned by an SS man at the gates of the Vilna ghetto. Note how she stands rigidly at attention when addressing a German officer.

Pearl Good guides her grandson Jonathan through the ghostly streets of the Vilna ghetto, still uninhabited fifty-five years after the war.

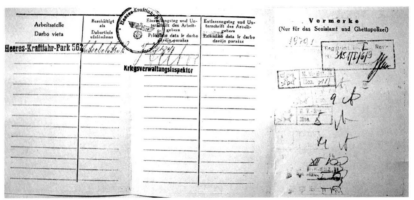

The above photos show both sides of a precious HKP "Ausweis" or work permit. Such a work permit, supplied by Major Plagge to his Jewish workers, protected a Jewish man, his wife and two of his children from lethal SS Aktions. The middle section on top contains the following regulations:

1. The owner of this identity card must carry it on his person

2. The assigned work has to be accepted immediately.

3. Leaving the workshop without authorization is punishable.

4. Orders of the social assistance office and the authorized employment department are to be obeyed.

5. Dismissals and changes of address are to be registered immediately.

6. Failure to follow these regulations will be punished.

This particular Ausweis protected Abraham Malkes, his wife, and his son Simon. Simon has preserved it to this day.

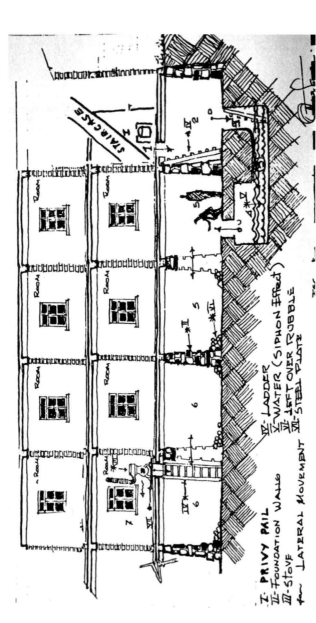

I - PRIVY PAIL
II - FOUNDATION WALLS
III - STOVE
IV - LADDER
V - WATER (SIPHON EFFECT)
VI - LEFT OVER RUBBLE
VII - STEEL PLATE
↞↞ LATERAL MOVEMENT

Transverse architectural view of the HKP "malines" number one and two as they were in July 1944. This drawing was prepared by Pearl's cousin Gary Gerstein, who hid in the maline as a child of eight, survived the war, and became an architect in Mexico City.

1 - Entrance to Maline #1 (privy in cubby hole under stairs)
2 - First Foundation space
3 - Tunnel
4 - Original Maline #1
5 - Enlarged Maline #1
6 - Maline #2 (previously unknown to Jews of Maline #1)
7 - Entrance to Maline #2

Jacob Gens, the enigmatic chief of the ghetto Jewish Police.

SS-Hauptscharführer Martin Weiss was in charge of the killing units at Ponary. He oversaw the Children's Aktion in March of 1944.

Known as "The Liquidator of the Vilna Ghetto," SS man Bruno Kittel had a reputation for committing acts of sudden savagery. He was a handsome film actor, and my mother remembers him smiling at her as he stood with his SS guards surveying the women of the HKP camp. After inspecting his victims he abruptly ordered that thirty-six of them be taken for execution.

William Good is reunited with the Paszkowski family, who helped him to survive three years of hiding in the forest.

Searching through the mists of time. The author at his computer in Durham, Connecticut.

of his life. She walked to the police station and turned herself in so that she could join him on his final journey. The next day they were taken along with the other Jewish prisoners down the road out of Niemenczyn. Lila Paszkowski recalls seeing them being led down the road under guard. She says that Hannah's face was bruised, her mouth bleeding after having been beaten at the station. As they walked past their neighbors, Hannah turned and said, "You see what has become of us?" These were her last known words.

On September 23, 1941, my father was hiding in an abandoned World War I bunker in the forest outside of town. He heard a prolonged burst of gunfire in the distance. He looked down at his watch; it was 1:10 PM. It would be two weeks before he learned from local peasants that this fusillade of gunfire marked the death of his mother and brother.

I have often wondered why my father never talked of his brother in a warm way. He seemed to remember his brother in negative terms: he was a klutz; he was a poor student; he was immature. This is not how one usually describes a sibling who died tragically at a young age. But now, as an adult, I realize that my father was only a teenager when he lost his beloved mother. He blames her loss on his brother, whose impatience and lack of street-smarts caused his capture and, indirectly, his mother's death. Although he does not often speak of it, my father also harbors anger toward his own mother. It was she who sacrificed her life in order to spare his brother from one night of pain. In doing so, she condemned her older boy to live out the rest of his life without her.

During the first months of hiding, my father and grandfather were separated and unable to find each other. My grandfather hid with Ester Bernstein in the home of a friendly worker, Stas Konsiewicz, whose home was isolated and far from town. My father hid in the forest during the day and would emerge at night and beg from local peasants for food. Those who knew him would gladly feed him. If they did not know who he was, he would tell them, "I'm Gdud's son," and then he was always generously fed. He could not stay with anyone for long, however, because he did not know who to trust and also because he did not want to endanger their families. Anyone caught hiding a Jew was killed along with all of their family members by the Nazis. My father describes his plight, hiding by day, begging at night:

It was dangerous for me to move—I didn't have my sheepskin and I was so cold, so cold. Once I planted myself somewhere it was hard to move. Some nights I was afraid to go out if it was very rainy and foggy—I was afraid of getting lost, so I wouldn't eat for two days.[2]

As the autumn progressed and the nights grew colder, my father was in increasing danger of freezing to death. He saw that the Paszkowskis were building a new house on their property. No one lived there, but the shell was complete and weatherproof. He started to live in the attic without anyone's knowledge. During the day he would hide in the attic and from the window observe all that went by. Farmers and their families, Lithuanian police, Stephan Neras and his friends (always armed—they knew that my father and grandfather were alive and hiding in the area). At night he would emerge and forage for food. He tried not to frequent the same farmhouses for fear of being ambushed if he followed a nightly routine. He was always on the move. A month passed and the winter cold deepened. As it got colder, it was harder to move about without freezing to death. My father did not know how long he could go without eating and still stay alive. He was caught between these two dilemmas: freezing to death if he ventured out into the forest in search of food, starving to death if he remained in hiding.

My grandfather heard through the grapevine that his son was intermittently appearing at different farmhouses asking for food. He wrote a letter and entrusted it in the care of one of his workers, who delivered it to my father the next time he appeared at their door. The letter instructed my father to go to the Paszkowskis' house on the night of All Saints Day. It told him that Stas Konsiewicz's stepdaughter Genia would be there and could be trusted. My father followed these directions and was led by Genia to the Konsiewicz house in the forest, where he was reunited with his father.

For the next two and a half years my father and grandfather stayed on the run, moving from hideout to hideout during the winter, living in remote snake-infested swamps during the summers. During those years, my grandfather supported a total of seven other Jewish escapees. He found them hiding places and paid for their food and supplies from his own meager cash reserves. Once in 1943, an old friend named Moishe Beckenstein and the four members of his family contacted my grandfather, saying that they had run out of money. They asked for a loan so that they could stay in hiding.

2. Memoirs of William Good, http://www.hometown.aol.com/michaeldg/mem oirs_of_william_good.doc, 16.

My grandfather decided to give them half of all the money he had. My father recalls that he was furious, saying:

"What do you mean, we are going to split our money with Beckenstein? Listen, we are two years into the German occupation, who knows how long it will go on! What about us, what about me? You are also paying for Esther and Libka. Who knows how long this war will go on?"

My grandfather's response is one my father was never to forget:

My father looked at me and said: "My son, do you know whether a month from now, a week from now or even a day from now you or I will be alive—do you have any assurance that we will need that money—ever? We have no right to gamble on the presumption of our survival and keep the money for ourselves—we may be dead tomorrow. This money can buy five lives today." The fact was that we survived, the two women survived and the five people of the Beckenstein family survived; they are all in Israel. That was a lesson I never forgot. It had an incredible impact on my life in many, many ways.[3]

As a young man, it was very difficult for my father to lay low and hide. He carried a tremendous anger at the Germans and the Lithuanian police, who had killed his mother and brother. He wanted to fight back. There was a constant struggle between father and son, with the elder trying to steer a careful, low profile and cautious path of survival, while the son hungered to strike back against their enemies.

During their days in the forest, he encountered escaped Russian prisoners-of-war who would, on occasion, perform acts of sabotage against train lines used by the Germans. My father began to accompany them on these missions. During the summer of 1942, while sabotaging a rail line with some Russian soldiers, he was captured by German troops and taken to Lukishki prison. Initially the Germans did not realize he was not a Russian, but the Lithuanians working with them recognized his nationality immediately and identified him as a Jew. He was sent to a cell with other Jews who were to be transported for execution at Ponary the next day. One of the Jews being forced to work in the prison as a translator for the Gestapo was the father of

3. Memoirs of William Good, http://www.hometown.aol.com/michaeldg/mem oirs_of_william_good.doc, 22–23.

his best friend and schoolmate, Berel Kammenmacher. Mr. Kammenmacher managed to tell my father that his only chance of survival was to claim to be a skilled craftsman during roll call. The next morning, the Germans asked all skilled craftsmen to step forward. My father joined them, saying he was a shoemaker. These prisoners were marched out of Lukishki and toward the Vilna ghetto. As the line of men walked under guard, my father saw an opportunity and ducked into a courtyard. He rapidly scanned the area for a hiding place and spotted an outhouse. Quickly he jumped into the outhouse and climbed under the seat, where he perched, pinned to the sidewall of the privy hole. In spite of the horrific smell and the traffic of visitors using the facility, he managed to cling to his perch without moving for ten hours until nightfall. After curfew he emerged and crept down the city streets, listening for the sounds of steps as German patrols passed nearby. To return to his father, he had to cross the Vilya River. The bridges were guarded, so he carefully traveled down the banks of the river, moving away from guard posts, and plunged into the rapidly moving water. The Vilya River is quite wide with a powerful current, but being a strong swimmer, he was able to find his way across successfully and then travel through the night to rejoin his father.[4]

In the spring of 1944 the war was turning against the Germans as the Red Army advanced toward Poland and Lithuania. Realizing that there would be fighting in the area, my grandfather prepared a hidden bunker in the forest stocked with food and supplies where they were able to wait out the battles that ensued between the retreating Germans and the advancing Russians. Finally, in July of 1944, they saw Soviet tanks approaching their bunker. They emerged from their underground hiding place, filthy with matted hair and tattered clothes. The Russians stared at them as if they were creatures from another world, but my father and grandfather were filled with joy. They were liberated! They had survived!

4. A 2004 documentary film, "Out of the Forest" by Limor Pinhason and Yaron Kaftori, chronicles the miraculous escape from Ponary by my father and three other Jewish survivors. Information about the film can be found at www.outoftheforest.net.

4

THE ESTEROWICZ

Toward the early evening—about seven o'clock—on July 1, 1944, it
was still light and Major Plagge gathered a group of the HKP inmates
and proceeded to speak. It was not an official speech, people just
gathered around him. Plagge said "You all must have heard that the
front line is moving west and that HKP's assignment is to always be
a certain number of kilometers behind the front line. Therefore, HKP is
being moved away from the front. As a result, you the Jews and
workers will also be moved. It is natural to think that since all of you
are highly specialized and experienced workers in an area of great
importance to the German Army, you will be reassigned to a HKP unit.
I cannot assure you that it will again be my unit, but it will be a HKP
unit.

You will be escorted during this evacuation by the SS which, as you
know, is an organization devoted to the protection of refugees. Thus,
there's nothing to worry about . . ."

This is my recollection of the speech. I have repeated it to myself
hundreds of times over the years. I remember thinking that this overt
warning to us that we were about to be killed (by mentioning the SS
as an organization for the protection of refugees) was made with a
human stroke of the pen, so to say, because- and I repeat—because he
didn't have to say it at all.[1]

—Testimony of William Begell, HKP survivor

On the second day of our stay in Vilna, my mother led us out
of our hotel toward the old Jewish Quarter of Vilna. She wanted to show us
the Vilna Ghetto. As we walked past her old home, she began to tell us
how the Lithuanian police had chased her family into the Vilna Ghetto on

1. Testimony of William Begell, http://members.aol.com/michaeldg/plagge
testimony-begell.doc.

September 6, 1941. Recalling how she had only moments to grab a blanket, a pillow, and a few possessions, she asked her grandchildren what they would quickly gather to take with them if they were forced to make such an exodus from their home. My daughter Rebecca said she would take pictures of her friends and her dog. My son Jonathan said that he would quickly take his computer hard drive, which held all his writings, his school projects, and his music collection. Listening to my mother and children talk, it seemed that surely more than one lifetime must have passed from those distant days to our modern electronic age. Yet, there they were, grandmother and grandchildren earnestly trying to imagine changing places in time.

My mother led us down the street and to the streets of the ghostly, deserted Vilna ghetto. It is still without inhabitants to this day. As she told her story we were all transported fifty-eight years back in time.

When the Germans first invaded, many of our family members thought that things might actually get better compared to life under the Communists. Because they were businessmen, my grandfather Samuel and many of his family members had been labeled as capitalist enemies of the state by the Russian Communists. Their businesses had been taken from them and nationalized, their bank accounts frozen, and they had lived in danger of being deported to Siberia by the NKVD, the Soviet secret police. Just one week before the German invasion, several members of the family went into hiding during a NKVD sweep of Vilna. My Aunt Rachil and her husband, Yermasha Cholem, ran out the back service door when the NKVD knocked on the front door of their apartment in the middle of the night, intending to arrest them. Little did they know that in a few short weeks the ones taken to Siberia would soon be considered fortunate by their brethren back home.

The first brush with death came to my grandfather Samuel on June 29, five days after the Germans first occupied the city. At night there was a strict curfew and blackout. Anyone showing a light risked being shot as a Russian spy. My grandfather was quite scrupulous in maintaining the blackout; he even took the fuse out of the apartment fuse box at bedtime to prevent anyone from accidentally turning on a light in the middle of the night. Apparently, one of the Lithuanian neighbors, a man named Mr. Labanauskas, was not as careful; a beam of light showed from his window and attracted a passing patrol of Lithuanian police to investigate. Fearful of punishment, Labanauskas told the policemen and the German officer leading the patrol that it was not he who showed a light, but the "Jewish Communists across the landing." Soon my mother and her parents were awakened by the thunderous noise of rifle butts pounding on the front door. Upon opening the door they were confronted by the German officer, who led a unit of Lithuanian guardsmen. The German ordered all the men in the apartment to dress, whereupon they were arrested and taken to the local police precinct house. At the police station they were assailed by Lithuanian fascist students who were beating Jews arrested in the city, shouting, "This is what you get for your Daddy Stalin." (This referred to the alleged collaboration with the Communists by Jews during the Soviet occupation—something of which my grandfather and his family were entirely innocent.) Unexpectedly, one of the Lithuanian guardsmen came forward and told his superiors that it had not been these Jews, but the neighbor Labanauskas who had been violating the blackout. He explained that it was the German officer, in his eagerness to arrest Jews, who had believed this story, but in fact it was clear that they were falsely accused. Because of his declaration, my grandfather and the others were told that they were free to go home but would have to wait in the station until dawn, when the curfew ended. Sitting in the precinct house, my grandfather witnessed a parade of Jews who were arrested and subsequently beaten by the students.

To their horror, shortly before dawn, a group of German SS officers entered the station. The SS was newly arrived in Vilna, and its fanatical National Socialist troops were eager to begin their work of ridding the city of Jews. Upon learning that the group in the corner of the precinct house was Jewish, the SS men leapt rabidly upon them, pummeled them, pushing them up against the wall with pistols pressed against their heads as they were searched. In the pocket of Mr. Kaplanski, a man sharing my grandfather's apartment, they found a scrap of paper with some Lithuanian writing on it. Threatening to kill the Jews, they demanded that these scraps of writing be translated for them. My grandfather stepped forward and readily interpreted the harmless newsprint into impeccable German. One of the Nazis stared at him and asked, "Where did you learn to speak such German?" My grandfather replied that he had studied Political Economy at the University of Berlin. The SS man asked if he knew of the coffeehouse named Krantzler, to which my grandfather responded that he had been there many times and gave a description of its exact location on Friedrichstrasse. The Nazi broke into a smile as he proudly proclaimed, "I was the violinist at the Café Krantzler." After a short silence, the SS man turned to him and proclaimed loudly,

"But you are not a Jew, you are not a Jew!" He then set them all free. The group stumbled home to their families, who greeted them as miraculous survivors from the land of the dead.

The ensuing weeks were full of fear and confusion for the Esterowicz family and the Jews of Vilna. After they were ordered to wear yellow Jewish stars[2] while in public, my mother and her family members had to modify all their clothing to comply with the new German edicts. My mother, even at age 12, was too proud to openly admit that the yellow stars were a sign of humiliation. Talking with the son of her building's Russian superintendent, she told him that she might embroider them to make them more fashionable.

During that first summer, several family members were captured by the Khapuny (the Lithuanian "Grabbers") and never seen again. My grandfather Samuel was one of the few lucky ones. After being captured by the Khapuny he spent a day loading cement bags onto railcars, but was then sent back home unharmed. The Jews soon learned that the only thing that could prevent such abductions were certificates authenticating that the bearer worked in a workshop considered by the Germans to be vital to their war effort. Fortunately for my grandfather, his friend Poddany's car repair workshop was co-opted by the Germans and integrated into the Wehrmacht war machine under the command of the HKP unit in the Vilna area. From the first days of the German occupation, Poddany assured my grandfather that he could be counted on to protect him and his family. The HKP unit had car workshops dispersed throughout the city. A civilian owner ran each workshop with some supervision by a German overseer. In Poddany's workshop, there were about 60 Polish and 20 Jewish workers, who were overseen by Poddany himself and a German noncommissioned officer. My grandfather was put to work in the stockroom keeping track of inventory and helping to supply the workers with car parts necessary for their vehicle repairs.

Over the summer the Esterowicz and Gerstein families suffered their first casualties. My grandmother's beautiful sister, Rachil Cholem, lost her hus-

2. During the course of the summer of 1941, there was a series of orders from the Nazis regarding how the Jewish population was to be marked—first with an armband with the letter "J," then with armbands with a Star of David, and finally with yellow stars sewn onto their clothing.

band, Yermasha Cholem, who had just escaped deportation by the NKVD. He was taken during the first week of July to Ponary when the Germans eliminated 300 of the Jewish business leaders of Vilna. My grandfather's brother Yeffim Esterowicz, his sister Anya's husband Sasha Minz, and his cousin Kola were all taken by the *Khapuny* to Lukishki prison and from there to their deaths at Ponary. My grandmother's brother Nochem was killed on June 22nd, when his house was hit by a German bomb during the capture of Vilna. This was the beginning of a steady attrition of family members that would continue for the next three years. Out of thirty-three members of the Gerstein and Esterowicz families alive in 1941, only eleven would survive the war.

On September 6, 1941, the Lithuanian police and Gestapo chased my mother and her parents into the Vilna Ghetto. In spite of their planning, the Germans did not have a clear idea of how many Jews would fit into the small area designated as the Jewish ghetto. By the end of the day, unbearable congestion ensued and no more Jews could physically fit into the two ghettos. My mother describes what she and her family found on arriving to Strashuna street:

> Since we were one of the early arrivals into the designated Ghetto, we and the Zlatins were able to occupy a room on the second floor of the first house on the right side—Strashuna #1. Standing in the street Father finally saw Grandmother, aunt Anya with her daughter Shela and aunt Emma with her daughter Eva and son-in-law Lolek. They all squeezed into our room with their packs
>
> The number of people who lived in our modest size, narrow, elongated room of about 6 by 24 feet grew to 26 by evening. The following nights we had to sleep huddled on the dirty floor, some lying down, some sitting since there was not enough space for everybody to stretch out on the floor at the same time; the grownups had to take turns, but I was able to lie down on the pillow that I had brought in with such effort. Sleeping next to me was a teenage girl crippled by polio; she must also have had epilepsy. One night she had a seizure, made scary noises and kicked me.
>
> The apartment we were in had another room, which was full of the Jewish criminal element, "the strong ones," whom everybody was scared of. There was only one coal-burning stove in the apartment which the "strong" women appropriated, letting the "intellectuals" cook only dur-

ing the Sabbath, a time when it was forbidden to cook by the Jewish religion. The "intellectuals" meekly stayed away from the kitchen during the week, but not my Grandma Esterowicz—she was not about to transgress against her religion! When she entered the kitchen she was menaced by one of those "strong" women, but far from being intimidated, she pushed a frying pan into the other's face, leaving a black soot-mark on her nose. From then on they let Grandma cook during the week.[3]

After arriving in the ghetto, my mother and her parents initially thought that at long last they would be safe from all the abductions and killings. However, these hopes were soon dashed; by September 15th the Germans began to move nonworkers to the "little ghetto" and then to Ponary. When the "Yellow Life-Certificate" *aktions* began on the eve of the Jewish holy day of Yom Kippur on October 1, 1941, the Jews began to realize the horrible nature of their situation. Here my grandfather describes the moment when he first understood his predicament:

> With the liquidation of the second ghetto is connected the memory of an event which opened my eyes to the full horror of our situation. In front of the windows of our workshop the Lithuanian police were driving down the street to the Lukishki prison a multitude of Jews from the second ghetto—men, women and children. In the passing crowd, I recognized some of my acquaintances—the successful criminal lawyer Smilg; my customer Rachmiel La; Sergey Smorgonsky with his wife, the actress Winter. The scene of these innocent people, my fellow Jews, being driven to their death shocked me to the depth of my soul. This became even more horrifying when I realized that the Polish workers in the workshop looked at this terrible injustice not with sorrow but with yells of joy and satisfaction. "Look," they were jumping for joy. "The Jews are taken to be killed."[4]

Yet, even as the enormity of their horrible situation dawned on my grandfather, there were glimmers of hope that not everyone was intent on their extermination. My grandfather's friend, Boleslaw Poddany, at great risk, took many of the family valuables for safekeeping. His assistance in this matter assured that my grandfather and his family would have a source of

---

3. Memoirs of Pearl Good, 30.
4. Memoirs of Samuel Esterowicz, 290.

goods for barter that would protect them from destitution and starvation during the next three years. Even at the moment when he watched his Polish co-workers rejoice at the sight of his friends and neighbors being led to their deaths, there was a hint of their future salvation in the reaction of the German sergeant overseeing the HKP workshop:

> I encountered some exceptions, i.e. Gentiles who were not infected with the burning Nazi anti-Semitism (even among the Germans). Even though they were subjected to the hate mongering propaganda of Goebbels and the "Stuermer" some were openly indignant about the horrors committed against the Jews.
>
> One of the above was a German soldier named Berger who had been assigned to our automobile repair workshop and with whom I became friendly. A common worker from Chemnitz in Saxony . . . Berger exclaimed while watching the Jews being driven to their deaths: "Was diese Lumpen im Namen des Deutschen Volkes hier herumtreiben—Jahrhunderte werden wir uns nicht reinwaschen koennen." (What this scum perpetrates here in the name of the German nation—centuries will not suffice for us to cleanse ourselves!)[5]

In retrospect, this expression of horror by a German noncommissioned officer of the local HKP unit is a clue that standing apart from the vicious actions of their peers, there were some Germans who disagreed with the murderous crowd. In Sergeant Berger one can see that at least in one unit, HKP 562 of Vilna, there were soldiers who opposed the genocide being committed against the Jews. What could account for attitudes such as these? Were they the thoughts of a single soldier, or were there others who harbored similar thoughts? Did his superiors have any notion of how he felt about the Nazis? As we will see, it would be attitudes such those expressed by Sergeant Berger that would ultimately lead to the salvation of a small fraction of my family.

Through October and November, the Esterowicz and Gerstein families suffered losses along with the rest of Vilna's Jews. My mother's cousin, Zhenia Gerstein, was caught trying to sneak some food to a sick Jew in the ghetto and was executed. During the "Yellow Life Certificate *Aktions*" my mother lost seven family members: both grandmothers, three aunts and two

---

5. Memoirs of Samuel Esterowicz, 293.

cousins. It seemed that the Nazi killing machine would soon consume the entire family. Then suddenly, at the beginning of 1942, the mass killings stopped. Unbeknownst to the hapless Jews of Vilna, the Wehrmacht had temporarily prevailed over the SS in preserving the remaining Jews as a slave workforce. During the next eighteen relatively bloodless months, my mother and her family adapted to the dreary and harsh reality presented by life in the ghetto.

My mother was twelve and thirteen years old during her time in the ghetto, a confusing time for any adolescent girl. She and her friends used to walk through the ghetto, dreaming of life as it used to be:

> As a thirteen-year-old at that time, I would pace the congested, trun-cated alleys of the ghetto with my friends Lubka Kantarowicz and Ninka Kaplinska. We would look up at the sky, try to find some of the rare sunny crevices and dream about walking outside, looking up at the leafy trees (there was not a blade of grass in the ghetto), swimming in the river, inhaling the breeze, going to school. School seemed glorious, learning a privilege I aspired to rather than the drudgery it used to be. I could not imagine how people free to enjoy all these wonders could possibly be unhappy—life would be so beautiful![6]

My mother tells me that more than anything else, the lack of privacy at home and in the streets weighed on her constantly. She and her parents shared the apartment on #1 Strashuna Street with surviving members of their family. She could never be alone, never talk with her parents in private; she always had to be polite. Some of the family members grew short tempered and mean toward each other. In my mother's case, it was her Aunt Vera who was particularly nasty. Before the war, she had always considered this aunt's saccharine sweetness toward her to be fake, and under the harsh conditions of the ghetto any such pretense dissolved. She recalls a day when her parents did not come home from work on time from the HKP workshops (my grandmother was now working as a cleaner in Poddany's office). When an hour passed beyond their usual arrival time, my mother became frantic with worry. Perhaps the Germans had taken her parents! Vera, seeing her apprehension, taunted her "Now you'll be all alone!" My mother confesses that at that time she hated her Aunt Vera more than the Nazis.

6. Memoirs of Pearl Good, 49.

My mother and her parents spent a total of two years in the Vilna ghetto, from September 1941 until September 1943. After the terrorizing *aktions* of the fall of 1941, the ghetto inhabitants gradually fell into a grim routine of ghetto life and slave labor. My grandfather worked in the vehicle repair shop originally owned by his friend Poddany which was now under the control of a German engineering unit, HKP 562. He and the other Jewish workers left the ghetto as a group, and after being checked by the Jewish Police at the ghetto gate, walked to work on Wilenska Street. He worked twelve hours a day, six days a week. While he manned the storeroom at the workshop during the day, he had the opportunity to barter for food and other essentials with Gentiles in and around the workshop. On days when he carried illegal items back to the ghetto, he ran the risk of a surprise inspection by the SS at the ghetto gates. Sometimes as the line of Jewish workers approached the ghetto, word would travel down from the front that the SS was searching prisoners at the ghetto entrance. The men would immediately drop all items of food that they carried in order to avoid detection by the SS guards. On such days the snowy streets would be littered with foodstuffs dropped by the workers, depriving hungry families of a meal for the night.

During 1942, the Judenrat established cultural institutions such as libraries, literary groups, and theaters within the ghetto. My mother especially recalls the liberating experience of checking out books from the library. As a teenager trapped in the midst of war, books allowed her to fly free into the imaginary worlds created for her by their authors and soar above the horrors of ghetto life. She remembers craving books incessantly, like a drug that allowed her to escape from the pain of day-to-day life in the ghetto. Today she remembers with irony the time that, with the help of a Polish-English dictionary, she read *Gone with the Wind* and cried over the hardships suffered by poor Rhett Butler! With regards to the musical and theatrical productions happening in the ghetto, my grandfather refused to let his family members attend, declaring: "You don't go dancing in the cemetery."

As the months passed into the summer of 1943, increasing rumors began to circulate throughout the ghetto that the Germans were intending to liquidate the ghetto's remaining inhabitants. Some ghetto dwellers made preparations for a final liquidation of the ghetto, preparing "*malines*" (hiding places) or making counterfeit documents and searching for safe havens outside of the ghetto on the Gentile side. During the last days of August, the Germans began to deport Jewish male workers to the slate mines of Estonia.

From September first to the third, Estonian troops surrounded the ghetto and began to capture Jewish men for deportation. My mother remembers those harrowing days:

> The cataclysm was upon us in full force on September 1st, 1943. When we woke up at dawn to go to work, we heard from our neighbors about the panic reigning in the ghetto; everybody was looking for a hiding place. During the night Estonian soldiers surrounded the ghetto and wouldn't let anybody out. We next heard that the Estonian patrols had entered the ghetto and were seizing men. When we and the Zlatins rushed outside, looking for a place to hide, we passed the gate of the house across from ours on Straszuna 4. The inhabitants of that house (Mother's cousin Jasha Shapiro among them) motioned for us to go in before they would clang the gate shut. We hurried in—the Estonian patrols were closing in. One of the basements of the house in the back of the yard was transformed into a "maline," a hiding place. Jasha Shapiro took us in and we hid for two days. During the two days in the malina, Ninka Kaplinska and I were holding hands, squeezing them to give each other courage in the darkness, and the listening for the incessant knocks which would signify that our hiding-place was discovered.[7]

Two days later, the family emerged from hiding and returned to their apartment on Strashuna 1, thinking it safe as it had not been raided by the Estonian troops. This turned out to be a miscalculation. The apartment was soon surrounded by troops. In the apartment courtyard stood the chief of the Jewish Police, Jacob Gens, and his assistant Salek Dessler. Standing beside them was the head of the Vilna Gestapo, *Obersturmfuhrer* Rolf Neugebauer. They ordered all male inhabitants to pack their belongings and to ready themselves for transport. At first my grandfather resigned himself to his fate and began to prepare to leave. However, my grandmother noted that most of the apartment's inhabitants being taken had been workers assigned to the Gestapo headquarters, while her husband worked at HKP—this might make a difference. She ran into the courtyard where Neugebauer and Salek Dessler stood surrounded by SS officers. She begged Dessler to let her husband remain, since, unlike the others, he was a HKP worker, not a Gestapo worker. Initially Dessler shrugged her aside, but then Neugebauer suddenly

7. Memoirs of Pearl Good, 51.

demanded to know, "What does this woman want?" Dessler told him that she was asking for permission for her husband, a HKP worker, to stay. Neugebauer then shrugged and remarked: "This one can stay for the time being." Thus my grandfather was saved.

On September 14th news swept through the ghetto that Jacob Gens had been killed. He had been ordered to Gestapo headquarters and personally executed by *Obersturmfuhrer* Neugebauer. With the killing of Gens, the head of the Jewish Police, the Jews of the ghetto knew the end was near. Anyone who had prepared a hiding place now stocked it with provisions so they could enter it quickly when the liquidation of the ghetto began. Those with false documents who had contacts outside of the ghetto tried to escape to the Gentile side (my mother's uncle David and his wife Mera escaped into the countryside, where, for some remuneration, they were hidden by a peasant). For those without a prepared hiding place or escape plan, my mother and her parents included, there was nothing to do but wait for the final calamity to fall upon them. My grandfather tells what happened next:

> During the ensuing dismal days, while we feared for our lives, there came a sudden ray of hope: tidings came to the ghetto that Major Plagge, the chief of HKP 562, had succeeded, after many requests to contrive a work camp for the Jews working in his establishment.[8]

For the lucky Jews working for HKP 562, it appeared that Major Plagge, the Wehrmacht commander of the vehicle repair unit in Vilna, had performed a miracle. It was said that he had traveled first to Kovno and then all the way to Berlin to demand that his workers be spared from the approaching liquidation. He had arranged for them to be transferred to a freestanding camp on Subocz Street, separate from the rest of the ghetto. The camp was situated in what had previously been a subsidized housing complex on the far edge of town, near the railyards of Rossa. Originally built for the Jewish poor, these large apartment houses standing in the middle of large grassy fields, were now a refuge for the HKP workers who came from all segments of Jewish society. On September 16th, 250 HKP workers and their families, a thousand people in all, left the ghetto and traveled to the newly formed HKP camp. It was none too soon. One week later, on September 23, 1943, the SS began the final liquidation of the Vilna ghetto. During the ensuing

8. Memoirs of Samuel Esterowicz, 336.

week, almost all of the remaining members of the Esterowicz and Gerstein families were taken to their deaths. The few survivors included my mother's uncle David and Aunt Mera, who were in hiding in the countryside, as well as my mother and her parents at HKP. My mother's uncle Mula Gerstein and aunt Nina, along with their son Gary, hid in a *Maline* during the liquidation of the ghetto. After many close brushes with death, Mula and his family eventually made their way into HKP with the help of my grandparents. Additionally, my grandfather managed to save his niece Eva and her husband Lolek by getting him inscribed on the HKP work list. Thus of the 33 members of my mother's family, eleven clung to life after the liquidation of the Vilna ghetto. Of those, eight were saved, for the time being, by Major Plagge's success in forming a camp for his workers.

While the Jews in the HKP camp were ultimately under the jurisdiction of the SS, the details of their day to day circumstances were delegated to Major Plagge and his HKP unit. Plagge himself was somewhat of a mystery to the Jews working for HKP. While death and murder seemed to descend from all sides in the Vilna ghetto, Plagge's workers always seemed to be spared. Many of the HKP workers attributed their good fortune to the efforts of Plagge himself, although how and why he managed to protect his workers was totally unknown. Interestingly, shortly before his own death at the hands of the SS, Jacob Gens advised our family friend and HKP survivor Bill Begell to try to get into the HKP camp as "Plagge can keep you safer than I can." My mother recalls seeing Major Plagge from a distance, a thin man who walked with a limp, always neat and proper in his Wehrmacht uniform. She thought that he was an older man as gray hair showed under his officer's cap. Even sixty years later, it is hard for HKP survivors to explain why, but they say they were never afraid when they were around Plagge; to the contrary, they actually felt safe.

The HKP camp consisted of two large, stone three story buildings which occupied a large parcel of land on the outskirts of town. My grandfather Samuel describes conditions in the HKP camp and the impressions that HKP prisoners had about Major Plagge:

> We were separated from the rest of the world by walls of barbed wire which were patrolled by the Lithuanian police. Our camp was under the administration and subjected to the Nazi "S.S.," embodied in a long-necked German named Richter whom we had nick-named "Golosheyka"

(little bare neck).The technical control of the workshops rested in the hands of the German army through two so-called "Schirrmeisters" subordinate to the chief of the HKP, Major Plagge.

As I mentioned before, it was thanks to the endeavors of Major Plagge, who was guided by his desire to protect his Jewish workers, that the thousand dwellers of HKP were able to avoid, at least temporarily, the fate of those Jews who remained in the ghetto. Therefore it was not surprising that Major Plagge, our protector, was much beloved and respected by us. According to those who had personal contact with him, Plagge was a man of the highest moral character—as we all ascertained later.[9]

Unlike the notorious conditions in concentration camps and slave labor camps throughout Europe, conditions in Plagge's HKP camp were relatively benign. Work hours were reasonable, and, in addition to the near starvation rations allowed by the SS, a black market for additional food was openly set up within HKP.

The sympathy toward us of Major Plagge, the chief of HKP, had put its stamp not only on our working conditions but on the whole way we lived. Personally I worked not too laboriously as the stockroom keeper of the workshop for vehicle seat-repair. We worked from 6 AM to 6 PM with a one hour interruption for dinner, which I ate in our room with my family.

In the room, which we shared with other prisoners, there was running water and a kitchen stove. We slept in beds and were able to wash ourselves and to cook. We were frequently able to change our personal and bed linen and even had a carry-out privy which we placed in a cubbyhole under the staircase—thus we did not have to use the filthy, stinking enclosed pit in the courtyard. As in the ghetto, the HKP workshops serviced the needs of the German army. My wife worked in the workshop which repaired German army coats, and our fourteen-year-old daughter worked in the one where heels were knitted onto the torn and dirty socks of the German soldiers.[10]

During the first two months of their stay in the HKP camp, my mother and her parents were torn by mixed emotions: exhilarated by their survival,

9. Memoirs of Samuel Esterowicz, 339
10. Memoirs of Samuel Esterowicz, 339–43.

but mourning for their lost family members in the ghetto. The HKP Jews initially felt safe under the protection of Major Plagge. They set up a system of smuggling food and essentials, which the Wehrmacht guards tolerated and benefited from monetarily. Within a few weeks, a camp routine complete with black market economy was established. However, the prisoners were soon reminded that while they were working for the Wehrmacht, the SS had ultimate control over their fate. My grandfather describes an event that showed them that not even Major Plagge could always protect them:

I do not remember the exact date, but it happened before the advent of frosts which usually come in November. After all the workers had been mustered out on the yard where the Jewish police had previously (upon the command of the Germans) built a gallows, the gate suddenly opened and three Gestapo-men, led by Bruno Kittel, the liquidator of the ghetto, drove in, riding in an open car. They brought with them two fugitives from our camp whom they had caught—a woman nicknamed "Pozhar" (Fire) and her common law husband, a man named David Zalkind (whom I had known as an employee of the stationary store of Zhabinski on Nie-miecka Street).

A deathly silence reigned as the Gestapo-men moved towards the gallows with the two condemned prisoners. This silence was broken by the piercing cry of "Mama!" which suddenly sounded from a window on the upper floor of one of the buildings in which we saw a child's head. Before the passing of even one minute a little girl, maybe eight or ten years old, ran out from the building and rushed with a joyous cry of "mama" to embrace her mother (Pozhar). We witnessed a horrible, heartrending scene—the joy of the child who thought that she had found the mother she was longing for and the distorted, suffering face of the mother who was passionately embracing her child, knowing that she was walking to her death. When the whole group arrived at the place of execution, Kittel motioned with his hand for Grisha Shneider, the camp's blacksmith (the brother of Alexander Shneider, a violinist famous in the United States), to step forward from our lines and ordered him to be the executioner. However, when the man (whom they were hanging first) fell, the noose broke, twice. Kittel ordered him to kneel down and killed him by a shot in the back of his head. Afterwards, while he was killing the woman, one of the other Gestapo-men killed the child.[11]

11. Memoirs of Samuel Esterowicz, 345.

My mother describes what happened the next day when the SS decided to execute thirty-six women in retribution for the escape attempt, hoping to forestall any further flights from the camp:

The next morning, after the men had gone to work, the Gestapo ordered the Jewish police to chase all the women and children out of the rooms onto the huge yard adjacent to the buildings.

When the policeman Miganz, a man my parents knew, chased us down onto the yard, we were immediately surrounded by rifle-wielding Lithuanian police. Kittel mustered us out into rows and stood before us with his arms crossed. My mother and I were in the first row, Kittel was standing just in front of us. He was very handsome, like a film actor. I will never forget his standing before us, regarding us for a very long time—I had nightmares long afterward imagining huge, flashing, fluorescent green eyes staring at me. Then Kittel smiled and, I guess on a sign from him, the Lithuanian police started to club us, herding us around the side of the building, toward where they were grabbing and dragging women into the black van standing in between the two buildings. My mother said: "Let's go, why be beaten up before we die?" But I wanted to live so passionately; I was looking at the tiny barred basement windows and wishing I could squeeze through them. I pulled my mother away from the side from which they were dragging women to the black van, at the risk of being clubbed. My Mother was anxiously repeating: "I have the golden cigarette case on me; dad will have nothing to live on after they take us!" Then, suddenly, my father broke through the clubbing Lithuanians to join us. He was the only man who came to stand with his family. . .

When the Germans had fulfilled their quota of victims, they let the rest of us go. We ran like arrows to the upper floor of the building—the ecstasy of being able to do this simple thing was indescribable! Through the high window we looked down on the yard—the black van was still there; we saw a frenzied man in a paroxysm of anguish next to it, vainly begging on his knees for the Germans to let his wife out.[12]

My grandfather remembers the reaction of Major Plagge to these deadly episodes:

12. Memoirs of Pearl Good, 64.

Major Plagge, came to encourage us after these events. Obviously embarrassed about the latest "achievements of his fellow Germans," he told us, among other things: "Regrettably, the war has destroyed moral values as well as the material ones."[13]

With this intrusion by the Gestapo, the atmosphere in the camp changed. The Jews could now see that while the SS was not a daily presence in the camp, when they wanted, they could assert their authority. Whereas there had previously been the opportunity to leave the camp to engage in black market trade or even to escape to the Aryan side, security was now tightened. Every week there was a roll call to ensure that all were accounted for. They now understood that if anyone ran away, an awful price was to be paid by those that remained behind.

Listening secretly to the BBC via a homemade radio during the winter of 1943–44, the inmates could tell that the war was turning against the Germans. Their advances into Russia had been stopped and now the Red Army was moving west. However, they also heard from the BBC that the Nazi policy of extermination of the Jews was accelerating even as the fortunes of war changed. Tension mounted as everyone tried to calculate whether there was a chance for liberation by the Russians before the SS finished off the final remnants of Vilna's Jews.

While in the early days of the German occupation there were high rates of suicide among the newly persecuted Jews, by early 1944, such suicides were very rare. Those who survived thirsted for life. They spent much of their energy trying to engineer plans of escape or preparing hiding places for the time when the SS returned to the camp. During early March of 1944, my mother was using the portable toilet that was placed in a cubbyhole under the staircase in their apartment building. She noticed a small opening in the floor in front of her. The next time she used the toilet, she found the opening had completely vanished. She then understood that this opening represented an entrance to a "maline" and noted its location for future reference.

On March 26, 1944, the Jews of the HKP camp celebrated the Jewish holiday of Purim, with the main celebration centering around skits and plays put on by the children for the benefit of the adults. Even the camp's two German Schirrmeisters sat in the audience and applauded the talented and

13. Memoirs of Samuel Esterowicz, 346.

heartwarming performances of the camp's children. The next day, on March 27, the SS instituted an *aktion* against all the Jewish children in the Lithuanian occupied territories. Early in the morning, shortly after the men had left for work, the SS commenced the Children's *Aktion* at the HKP camp. The *aktion* was heralded by the arrival of the Gestapo man Martin Weiss, who headed a large contingent of Gestapo officers and Lithuanian policemen. The Lithuanian police fanned out across the camp and began to drag all children and teenagers up to the age of fifteen to large trucks that had been driven into the camp courtyard. Heartrending scenes ensued as children screamed for their parents and hysterical mothers tried to break through the lines of armed policemen to get to their children. One mother, a woman named Zhukowski, had a young boy who was known for his innocent beauty. After her son was taken, she ran up to Martin Weiss, spat in his face and called him a murderer. Weiss pulled out his gun and shot her dead. Some mothers refused to leave their children and joined them in the trucks taking them to their deaths. Over 250 children were taken from the HKP camp; only a dozen or two escaped capture. My mother saved herself by hiding in her newfound *maline* under the toilet. On the morning of the Children's *Aktion*, when she heard the camp was surrounded, she ran to the cubbyhole and saw her neighbor, an attorney named Zmigrod, going down through the hole into the cellar. She ran and got her mother, and together they went down into Zmigrod's *maline* where they hid for the rest of the day. My mother's cousin, eight-year-old Gary Gerstein, also managed to survive. The Lithuanian police were taking him down the stairs when he squirmed out of their grasp, slid down the banister and ran to his father's workshop. There his father, Mula Gerstein, managed to hide him until the danger had passed. My grandfather describes the mood that enveloped the camp following this horrible day:

> The "Children's *Aktion*" shook the camp to its very foundations. The air was filled with moans of the disconsolate mothers; people moved around the camp like shadows. I ran into Borys Beniakonski who had lost his daughter. In a state of anguish he declared "we are worms, you hear, we are nothing but crushed worms!"
>
> There was a multiplicity of reactions to the loss of their children in the "Children's *Aktion*." Some mothers confined themselves to inconsolable grief, but there were quite a few others whose grief drove them to hatred

of the surviving children. We took Gary, my wife's nephew, to stay in our room to preserve him from fits of hatred from Gurvich, a woman who shared their room and who had lost her child.[14]

Whenever there was a hint of danger, my mother and her cousin Gary would be spirited into the *maline* under the toilet. During this period, a disagreement arose between the "owners" of this *maline* (i.e., those neighbors who intended to use this hiding place themselves when HKP was in danger of liquidation) and my grandfather over allowing young Gary Gerstein to hide in the *maline* whenever danger presented itself. Gary's mother Nina had a reputation for being a gossip. Those who planned to use the *maline* feared that she would not keep its location a secret from others in the camp, including Gestapo-planted informants. However, my grandfather was adamant in insisting that Gary must be saved. With the same ethical logic that my paternal grandfather Dov Gdud used when he insisted on sharing his money with other Jews in hiding, Samuel said, "We don't know whether she will disclose the secret—this might cost us our lives in a few months. The child's life is in peril now; we have no right to deny Gary life now, on the chance that it could imperil our lives later." Again this was life-saving. Gary, who survived the war, became an architect, and the father of three children. He lived in Mexico City until his death in 1991.

As spring progressed, the BBC news brought word of the Red Army's advance toward Vilna. The HKP dwellers were aware that in areas where the Russians had overrun German concentration camps, they found all the Jewish inmates dead, killed by the SS before the retreating Germans evacuated the area. The HKP workers thus understood that when the Russians took Vilna it would be a time of grave peril for the camp's inmates. After the Children's *Aktion*, lawyer Zmigrod's *maline* became the agreed upon hiding place for all the residents of my parents' landing in the HKP apartment building, a total of about twenty-five people. All the men worked feverishly at night enlarging and improving the hiding area. My grandfather and Lolek Szelubski (his niece Eva's husband), who was an engineer, worked diligently to make the *maline* more secure from discovery. The original *maline* beneath a small space under the stairs was enlarged. This small space under the floor beneath the portable toilet could only hold a few people and was relatively

14. Memoirs of Samuel Esterowicz, 351.

insecure from diligent searches. Using metal tools the men dug through the foundation wall adjacent to this area in order to enter the underground space around the building's concrete footings. This second space was larger and much harder to find, being covered by a camouflaged trap door. Their experience from the Vilna Ghetto told them that they needed to hide their *maline* not only from the Germans, but also from their fellow Jews. This was because they had seen, during the ghetto *aktions*, that those without a prepared hiding place would flee to any *maline* that they were aware of. Soon the *maline* would overflow and the crowd at its entrance would doom all the inhabitants to capture and death.

As the front-line fighting between the Russians and Germans approached Vilna, tension mounted within the camp. No one knew exactly what the military situation was. The Jews could not tell when the precise moment would be that they should go into hiding before the SS arrived. Having provisions to last only a few days, timing was of essence if they were to survive. Once again, just as before the liquidation of the Vilna Ghetto, Major Plagge acted in a lifesaving manner. My mother recounts what happened next:

> On Saturday, July 1st, 1944 Major Plagge, the kind head of the HKP 562, came to talk to us. We clustered around him, eager to hear what he would tell us about what lay before us. Major Plagge warned us that the German army was leaving Vilna and our camp would be evacuated westward in connection with the nearing of the Russians. To emphasize his warning Major Plagge informed us in his speech that we would stop being a HKP work camp and would be entirely in the hands of the S.S.—he then carefully commented: "And you all know how well the S.S. takes care of their Jewish prisoners." This speech of Major Plagge aroused terrible fear in us. According to the British Radio station BBC, before retreating, the Germans had shot without mercy all the Jewish inmates of the camps [to the East]. The vast majority of us understood, especially after Major Plagge's veiled warning, that for our camp the moment had come which we all feared and for which the dwellers of our landing had made feverish preparations.[15]

Plagge indicated that the evacuation would occur on Monday, July 3. To prevent any escape, the SS posted more guards around the camp. Those

---

15. Memoirs of Pearl Good, 75.

inmates with prepared *malines* tried to slip into them without attracting attention. About thirty young men, who worked in the blacksmith's shop on the second floor of the HKP building, stole into the shop on Sunday night. Using blowtorches, they cut the bars covering a window at a spot remote from most of the guard posts. In the dead of night they jumped out the window, climbed over the barbed wire fence, and ran into the surrounding fields away from the camp. Several dozen succeeded in escaping before the guards spotted this escape route and shot anyone subsequently emerging. By the end of the night, a pile of dead lay under the smithy window. Those without the ability to flee or a prepared hiding place anxiously awaited their fate.

Attorney Zmigrod was trying to find an opportune moment to enter the *maline*. He soon discovered that he was being followed by a group of young men without a hiding place. After wandering for several hours, trying to lose them, he found himself cornered by these young men. They had heard that he had a *maline* and demanded to know its location. When he refused to reveal its hidden entrance they gave him a savage beating, bringing him to the edge of death. Having no choice, he had to tell them of his *maline's* location. Soon, in addition to the original inhabitants, another 80 prisoners descended into the hiding place. As a result, almost 100 prisoners were packed into the *maline*, more than three times the number that it had been intended to hold. My mother describes the scene within the overcrowded hiding place:

> A small electrical bulb connected to a stolen car battery barely illuminated the space where about one hundred of us were lying down on the bare ground. With the coming of morning and the moment when the Germans would discover that a few hundred people did not appear at the inspection, our tension increased. Fearing that the Germans would blow up the building, we began to thrust ourselves against the outside walls assuming that this would give us a better chance to survive.
>
> Added to the fears of discovery by the Germans, or that we would perish under the ruins of the building, came excruciating physical suffering from lack of fresh air. We had not appreciated the importance of and thus did not arrange for sufficient ventilation. Because of the unforeseen crowding, our hiding place was rapidly becoming ever more stifling. Being faced with death by suffocation, our leaders, Zmigrod and Mintz

(one of the newcomers) broke through the outside walls with pickaxes to make some tiny openings (risking that this would bring us to the attention of our enemies).

The scanty trickle of air thus generated saved us from suffocation but was insufficient to protect us from the effects of severe oxygen deficiency of the air we breathed (a candle could not burn). To our misfortune, this severe oxygen deprivation together with the terrifying psychological burden we were subjected to evoked (as we had later learned) many cases of insanity. As a result truly infernal scenes were enacted among those of us suffering in the maline. As Father now remembers, feeling that he might find more oxygen in the layer of air near to the ground he was stretched out breathing heavily with his face to the ground when the strained silence in our shelter was interrupted by a piercing scream of a male voice repeating, "But why, why do you want to slaughter me?" seconded by a woman crying, "Such a brilliant future would await our children, after all." The screams were emitted by a couple named Gutman who had forcibly pushed themselves into our maline with their two girls. Father knew Gutman from the times before the war. Gutman was the owner of a bicycle repair workshop with the reputation of being a hard working and honest craftsman. Hearing these screams Father rushed to the Gutmans. Imploring them not to cause the deaths of all of us with their screams and assuring them that none of us intended to kill them, he succeeded in quieting down the Gutmans. "Yes, Mr. Esterowicz, you are a decent man, you will not slaughter me." Gutman tried to shake off the nightmare persecuting him and tried to let himself be talked out of it, only to resume his piercing screams a little while later. This scene was repeated several times, but each time Father was able to quiet Gutman down. But then one event brought on a series of tragic happenings. Our leader Zmigrod declared that since we needed to conserve the energy in our battery (after all we did not know how long we would have to hide), he decided to turn off the light. Nobody objected to this decision and wanting to be near Gutman to be able to quiet him if needed, Father sat down next to him on his left. On the right side of Gutman sat a man named Malkes dressed in his heavy winter coat.

Unexpectedly, soon after our shelter was plunged into darkness there came sudden desperate calls for help. When the light was put on the following picture stood before our eyes: Gutman was standing up, wild-

eyed with a bloody pocketknife in his hand, on the ground before him lay
Malkes, saved from death by his winter coat but bleeding from the numerous wounds inflicted on him by Gutman. Gutman's reaction to darkness
soon brought on angry exclamations from Zmigrod, "This is our blood"
pointing his finger at the battery he addressed the Gutmans, "And we
want to live, do you hear. We want to live!" he repeated furiously. This
was followed by events which shook us to our depths. After a short consultation, the bunch of youths who had attacked Zmigrod killed the Gutmans, braining them with some bricks which lay on the ground nearby.
This did not end the horror: with every passing moment I realized that
my Mother was also hallucinating. Her speech was becoming ever more
irrational and pointless. I remember that my despair, related to Mother's
delusions, was deepened by the realization that if she should start to
scream she would be killed. The events in our maline had demonstrated
that when people are caught in the situation of hunted animals, their lust
for life (sharpened in such cases) frequently converts them into merciless
killers. Two young girls, the sisters Arluk, were hiding in our maline.
When one of the girls began to show signs of violent insanity, our leaders
strangled her before our eyes. This terrible moment was made even more
terrifying for my father and me by Mother's mental state. Not understanding the cause of her condition, Father took her onto his lap and with his
whole heart tried to inspire her to the "last effort." "Idochka, darling,
this is our last battle, the last obstacle we have to overcome—we have to,
do you hear me, we have to overcome to survive!" He kept whispering to
her, thinking that she had temporarily broken down emotionally because
of the horrifying scenes she witnessed. To our despair, Mother didn't
regain her senses. I kept asking Father, "Tatus (Daddy) is this for always?" Mother continued her demented babble, providentially in a gentle
and quiet voice which did not invite attention to her.

Mama was stroking the face of the raven-haired Lizka Persikowicz repeating, "What a beautiful baby, what a beautiful blonde baby, so blonde
and darling." This must have been July 4th, or maybe July 5th, 1944 . . . I
remember that my mother fell asleep with her head in my lap. Since I
seemed to have had a rock lodged under my spine the position was very
uncomfortable but I couldn't move because if she woke up, my mother
could have called attention to herself with her delirium.[16]

16. Memoirs of Pearl Good, 78–80.

Outside the *maline*, the liquidation of the camp ensued. Special SS troops wearing black uniforms and wearing a skull insignia on their caps arrived for roll call on Monday, July 3. The 500 inmates who, having no where to hide, appeared at roll call were taken to Ponary and killed. Seeing that there were almost 500 missing prisoners, the Germans began a systematic search and captured an additional 200 Jews, who were executed in the camp court-yard. Included in this number were my mother's cousin Eva and her husband Lolek. Lolek had obtained a gun, joined a resistance group within the camp, and insisted on leaving the hiding place in order to fight the Germans. Eva reluctantly accompanied her husband. Both Lolek and Eva were killed in the ensuing fighting.

For those hiding in the suffocating conditions in the *maline*, uncertainty reigned. Unable to stand the inhuman conditions below, some emerged from the hiding place too soon and were killed by the German troops who were scouring the camp. Those hidden in the *maline* suffered not only from lack of oxygen, but also from thirst. Becoming dehydrated, they were forced to drink sewer water strained through a handkerchief. Finally on the evening of Tuesday, July 4th, they sent some scouts out of the hiding place. The scouts found that the Germans had abandoned the camp, but remained in control of the city of Vilna. The scouts went to the camp boundaries and began to cut a hole in the barbed wire toward the rear of the camp. Learning that the Germans had left, the surviving Jews began to emerge from their hiding place. However, soon after they began to emerge, some of those who had ventured into the camp rushed back, saying that the Germans had returned. The Jews thus beat a hasty retreat and returned to their infernal hiding place.

Another day passed. Outside the camp, the Gentile population had heard that the Jews of HKP had been killed and came to the camp to loot their belongings. Taking clothes, bed linens, comforters, pots, and kitchen utensils, the Poles were disappointed that they were unable to find any of the gold and jewelry that they anticipated finding among the possessions of the "rich Jews." Groups of looters began to tear up the floors of the camp buildings in search of the hidden treasure. After a time, they found and removed the cover to the hidden *maline*. As the light streamed into their hideout, the Jews cringed, fearing that the Germans had discovered them. But when the voices demanding their emergence spoke in Polish, they knew that their worst fears had been avoided. Upon exiting from the hiding place, the dirty, exhausted prisoners were robbed of any valuables they carried by the Polish mob.

Staggering out of their hiding place and extricating themselves from the looters, my mother and her parents quickly exited the HKP building. In the camp courtyard they passed the partially buried bodies of their neighbors and family members who had been captured and killed by the Germans the day before. They decided to leave the camp and try to get to their old apartment building on Zawalna 2, where they knew the janitor was trustworthy. Traveling across the fields that surrounded the camp, they encountered Poles who informed them that the center of town was still under German control. They were at a loss as to what to do, when suddenly a Lithuanian man appeared, offering to shelter them at his apartment in town. Frightened at the prospect of trusting a stranger, but having no other options, they decided to go with him. Before they could proceed, they tried as best they could to wash their filthy clothes, which were covered with mud and water from their stay in the hiding place over the previous three days. They then followed the Lithuanian into town. Seeing German patrols, the Lithuanian went ahead to reconnoiter the route to his apartment. Waiting for him to return, my mother and her parents experienced waves of anxiety—would he betray them and return with the Germans? They made escape plans for such an eventuality. However, their fears proved to be unfounded. The Lithuanian proved to be benevolent and soon brought them into his home. Lying on the floor, they fell into a deep and exhausted sleep.

Having found temporary shelter, the family now had to ascertain how to obtain food. With much trepidation, my grandparents sent my mother out to their old apartment at Zawalna 2, hoping that their old janitor Nikolai and their friend Poddany could provide some food for them. This mission was successful, but as she was procuring the provisions a neighbor ran in and said that the Germans were grabbing people and forcing them to go to the front to dig trenches. Not wanting to endanger her hosts by her presence, my mother beat a hasty exit into the suddenly deserted streets. As she walked down Zawalna Street, now devoid of any pedestrians, she could hear the measured steps of German guards making their way towards her. Suppressing her desire to run, she trudged doggedly onward, clutching her packages of food. The German guards passed by her without incident. She scurried back to the apartment door where she had left her parents, holding her breath as she knocked and waited for them to open it. Outside their window, the family was able to see a steady stream of German army units retreating in good order to the West. They left behind a rear guard, which was to defend the city against the advancing Russians. As the Red Army reached the city limits, heavy fighting broke out and the Russians began to bombard the city. Many of the residents fled into bomb shelters, but my mother and her parents were afraid that the Gentiles would betray them to the Germans who still controlled the city. My mother describes these final days under occupation:

> The Russian army came close to the city during the night from Friday to Saturday and the artillery shelling began. Father was standing next to a window Saturday morning when an artillery shell hit our house. The air-pressure created by it impelled the window frame into the house and threw him into the next room. The sequential deafening roar of a near-by explosion forced us all to look for a bomb-shelter. Directed by the janitor, we ran to the bomb-shelter situated in the basement of a many-storied building at No 5 Kwiatowa Lane connecting Zawalna to Sadowa street which led to the railroad station. The large bomb-shelter was overfilled by people seeking refuge from the bombing, which was getting worse with every minute. The people were lying on the floor on comforters; many had also brought pillows for sleeping. What was particularly useful to them, since we were stuck in the cellar for five days, was the food they had brought with them. We, on the other hand, had no food and had to sleep on the bare ground, using an arm as pillow under our heads.
>
> Having ended up among a crowd of Gentiles, in addition to the physical privations we were also afraid that our neighbors might learn that we were Jewish. Since the center of the town was still in German hands, this put our lives in great danger. At first, everything was going smoothly. We thought that we were able to deflect the suspicions evoked by our unusual appearance, our lack of belongings and my parents' less than perfect Polish. We explained that we were Russian and we had to run out of our house because of a bomb explosion. My Polish was good and I became friendly with a Polish teenage girl.
>
> The ceaseless roar of the shelling shook the walls of our shelter. To make matters worse, Monday morning, on our third day in the shelter, it dawned on the Poles that we were Jewish; one of the Poles suddenly said that he remembered having encountered Father before the war and knew

he was a Jew. We were made aware of their conclusion when an old lady suddenly asked me: "How was it in the ghetto?" The news about our being Jewish spread like wildfire through the shelter and evoked different reactions, from reserved coolness to expressions of outright hostility. My young "friend" would have nothing to do with me. Most horrified was a religious woman who was ceaselessly praying, crossing herself and demanding that we should be handed to the Germans. She was sure that we would be the death of them all—we would be throwing bombs and the Germans would kill everybody in retaliation. We were saved by the lady janitor of that house who promised to keep us under strict observation and suppress any attempts by us to attack the Germans. I also remember a gesture of sympathy from a Russian peasant from Smolensk who, learning that we were Jewish, sent us a bowl of hot soup which he had managed to cook right there in the cellar. The stubborn fighting continued in the city without letup. We had to spend two more unbearably slow days in this atmosphere poisoned by the hostility of those around us. The first patrol of the Red Army appeared in the yard of our bomb shelter in the morning of July 12, 1944. Their coming proclaimed the end of the three years of our torment.[17]

17. Memoirs of Pearl Good, 88.

The Search for Major Plagge

5

SEARCHING THROUGH
THE MISTS OF TIME

To Whom It May Concern:

My name is Michael Good. I am the son of two Holocaust survivors from Vilna, Poland. I am writing to ask for any help that you can give as I try to discover the fate of a German army officer named "Major Plagge" who was instrumental in saving the lives of my mother and her family during the Holocaust. . . . If you or any of your family members have information that could help me track down Major Plagge and his descendants, I would appreciate any help you can give me. Specifically, I am looking for his first name and his town of origin. This information will allow me to attempt to contact his family and let them know what a good man he was and how grateful the children and grandchildren of his workers are for his good deeds.
—From my "Plagge search letter," e-mailed hundreds of times.

Our family journey to Vilnius made a deep impact on me. Upon returning home, I found myself frequently thinking about our trip, going over different parts in my mind, trying to digest all that I had seen and experienced. I had heard my parents tell their stories in the places where dramatic events had happened to them. I had seen with my own eyes the places I had been trying to imagine since I was a child. The trip made what had seemed like ancient tales from the distant past come alive with vivid intensity. The stories were real, the places were real, and most of all, the people were real. Meeting the Paszkowski and Gasperowicz families who had helped to hide and save my father was especially emotional. As we stood before them, I could see the satisfaction in their eyes as they looked at the three generations of our family visiting their home. We were the fruits of their bravery and their joy made a profound impression on me. My father's story was important to our family because it explained our very existence. But I could see that it was also very important to the Paszkowski and Gasperowicz families. Our survival was due to the risks they had taken and the success of their good deeds gave them a feeling of pride that continued through the decades and generations.

As I contemplated the effect that the war had on all our families, I also began to wonder about the character repeatedly mentioned by my mother and maternal grandfather, the mythical commander of the HKP unit, Major Plagge. Both my mother and grandfather felt certain that he had saved their lives on at least two occasions. The first time was in September 1943, when, just before the Vilna Ghetto was to be liquidated, he created the HKP camp on Subocz Street and transferred his Jewish workers there, days before they were to be killed. The second instance was when he warned the inmates about the impending arrival of the SS before the German retreat in July 1944. A myriad of questions ran through my head. Who exactly was Plagge? Why did he try to protect his Jewish workers when the rest of the German war machine seemed so intent on killing them? What had happened to him after he left Vilna? Had he survived the war? Did he have a family? I was particularly concerned with whether his family knew of his role in saving over 250 Jewish lives in Vilna. I worried that he may have been killed during the final months of the war. Maybe all his family knew was that he was in charge of a concentration camp for Jews in Vilna. Perhaps they even thought that he had participated in the genocide! This latter thought was particularly galling and gnawed at me. After pondering over these thoughts during the summer of 1999, I decided to attempt to uncover the full identity and fate of Major Plagge. My hope was to try to contact his family and make sure they knew of his role during the war and to express our family's gratitude for his good deeds.

I do admit to some doubts in the beginning. I did not know if it was possible to find someone who had vanished into the chaos of war over half a century in the past. I also did not know exactly who or what I would find even if successful. While I knew that my mother and grandfather felt strongly that Plagge had saved their lives, it was not clear to me how he had helped Jews, nor why. I wondered if perhaps chance played a role in the survival of the HKP Jews. Was it possible that the Germans merely needed their labor to repair vehicles and that this group of Jews was at the right place at the right time? Maybe the HKP prisoners' preparations and hiding places were larger and better concealed than in other similar camps. Who really knew how big a role this Plagge character played in the survival of such a large number of HKP Jews? In spite of all these questions, the fact remained that my mother (who is not exactly sentimental when it comes to Germans) was quite adamant that Plagge had saved her life along with her parents and many other Jews. In the end, it was my blind belief in what my mother told me that carried me forward to begin a search spanning thousands of miles across continents and half a century into the past.

I began by talking to my mother and reading my grandfather's memoirs, looking for clues as to Plagge's identity. I did not find much to go on. His workers knew him only as "Major Plagge," the commander of the HKP unit in Vilna. My mother remembered him as an older man; she could see that under his officer's cap he had gray hair. She did not know of anyone who had actually conversed with him, but she did note that, unlike the other Germans, the Jewish workers felt safe in his presence. My grandfather specifically mentioned in his memoirs that Plagge, ". . . according to those who had personal contact with him, was a man of the highest moral character." Yet no one knew for sure what he was his thinking when he formed the HKP camp or when he made his speech to the prisoners informing them of the coming of the SS. What were his motivations? Some of our survivor friends could think of self-serving reasons for his actions. The HKP unit was safe, far behind the front lines away from the fighting. Perhaps Plagge formed the HKP camp in order to keep his cushy job repairing vehicles? Perhaps he warned the workers because he knew the war was lost and wanted to garner favor from his prisoners after the war. My mother did not agree with these hypotheses. She thought Plagge was motivated by a true desire to help his workers. She remembers that when some older women were discussing Plagge in the camp, they said they wished they could repay his kindness. Perhaps, they said, giving him a foot massage and pedicure would be a small token of appreciation that bespoke their warm feelings toward him. These were not the feelings that Jewish prisoners would have had toward a conniving, self-serving German.

In September of 1999, when I began my search, I knew that I was looking for an older man who was in charge of a vehicle repair unit in Vilna from 1941 until 1944. I knew he was a major in the Wehrmacht and that his last name was Plagge. I did not know his first name, where he was from or the exact name of his unit. Where to begin? I saw several possibilities. First, it was possible that Holocaust historians knew the story of HKP and Plagge; if so, different Holocaust museums and historical institutions might be able to help me. Another possibility was that there were archival records in Germany about the Wehrmacht, with records of what personnel were stationed in

Vilna during the war. However, without a full name or unit designation it would be difficult to make a query to the military archives in Germany. Finally, it was possible that one of the HKP survivors might know more about the camp commander than my mother and grandfather. I thought that tracking down and talking to Jewish prisoners who had survived HKP might yield some bits of information that could give me some good leads.

I began by composing the following email to the research department of the US Holocaust Memorial Museum in Washington, DC:

Subj:Help with Research
Date:9/9/99
To:archives@ushmm.org
CC:pearl good

To Whom it may concern,

My name is Michael Good. I am the son of two survivors of the Holocaust, Pearl and William Good, who survived the Vilna Ghetto and the killing grounds of Ponary. My parents, my wife, children and I recently returned to Europe to retrace my parents life before the war and to relate the story of their survival to another generation. During our visit to the HKP slave labor camp in Vilnius where my mother spent the last year of the war, she related the story of a certain Major Plagge, the German commander of the camp who tried to protect the Jews under his command from the murderous intent of the S.S. (for more detailed information about this please see "Pearl's Story" at the website I made about our trip at http://hometown.aol.com//michaeldg/).

During the months since our return from Vilnius I have begun to wonder what happened to Major Plagge; specifically, did he survive the war and is his family aware of his exemplary conduct during the Holocaust? I would like to undertake an attempt to locate Major Plagge's descendants in order to make them aware of his good deeds. I was wondering whether the Holocaust Museum had any researchers or facilities which would be of assistance in this quest. Any help or advice you could give would be greatly appreciated.

Sincerely,
Michael Good, MD

I also wrote to Yad Vashem, the State of Israel's Holocaust Museum, the Simon Wiesenthal Center in Los Angeles, and the Jewish Museum in Vilnius, Lithuania. Most of these queries came up empty. However, the US Holocaust Memorial Museum wrote back quite promptly:

Subj:Re: Help with Research
Date:9/10/99 1:11:37 PM Eastern Daylight Time
From: archives@ushmm.org (Archives) To: Michael Good

Dear Dr. Good:

When I searched the electronic descriptions of the collections held in the Museum Archives, I did not get any "hits" on the word/surname "Plagge." Therefore, I cannot answer your question about his fate.

The National Archives and Records Administration contains microfilmed copies of the Nazi Party and SS Membership Files for thousands of individuals. The originals of these are held in the Berlin Document Center, but under the German privacy law (a.k.a. Datenschutz), access to files relating to individuals is perhaps not as easy as one would wish. A researcher using the copies of the identical files that are held in the American National Archives and Records Administration does not have to worry about the German privacy law and, as a result, access is much easier. The microfilmed files at the National Archives contain a Party Membership File (Party Member Number 785,656) and an SS Membership File (SS Member Number 31,158) for a Hans Plagge (This is the only individual I found who had the surname of Plagge).

I hope that the above is of help to you. If I may be of further assistance to you, please let me know.

Sincerely,
Aaron T. Kornblum, Reference Archivist
Archives Branch,
United States Holocaust Memorial Museum

So, the hunt was on! I was heartened by the fact that Mr. Kornblum chose to respond so quickly and that there appeared to be considerable archival resources available for use by a trained researcher. I was fairly certain that the Hans Plagge found by Mr. Kornblum was not the Plagge in question, as I was sure that our Plagge had not been a member of the SS. It also became apparent that I had to somehow come up with Major Plagge's first name. Without it one would come up with too many possible leads and have no way of knowing which thread to follow.

I asked my mother to contact the HKP survivors that she knew, both to ask if they knew Plagge's full name and also to ask that they write their recollections of their HKP experience. Most of the survivors who were still living had been children and teenagers during the war and were now scattered across the globe in the United States, Canada, France, and Israel. Several HKP survivors agreed to try to write down their memories of their experiences at HKP and, over the next year, I gathered several moving accounts of their wartime memories. Unfortunately, none could recall ever having heard Plagge's first name. It seemed that as camp commander, he was such an authority figure that none of the prisoners would have referred to him in terms less formal than his official title. Even if some of the adults at the camp had known his first name, they apparently did not use it in the presence of their children.

After several months, having had no success with either the museums or the living HKP survivors, I pondered what other avenues were available to explore. Having had some exposure to genealogical research while working on my family tree, I thought that it might be possible to use the burgeoning world of online genealogical resources to help with my research. While I was unable to plumb genealogical websites in Germany due to my inability to speak German, there are a large number of German-ancestry genealogy websites in the United States. I began to do searches at German genealogy websites, looking for the name Plagge. Fortunately, it was not a common name, and eventually I came across a handful of sites that listed it. I then wrote to the webmasters of those sites, telling them of my search for a German Wehrmacht major named Plagge. None of my queries resulted in any breakthroughs, but I did get several helpful and encouraging letters from the webmasters and some of their correspondents. A patient of mine with extensive experience in genealogical research recommended that I visit a particularly good site covering the Windheim area of Germany. Its webmaster wrote me back with some particularly helpful advice:

Subj:Re: Plagge Surname
Date:12/30/99 11:17:23 AM Eastern Standard Time
From: (Richard Scheimann)
To: Michael Good

Dear Michael

I have a great interest in your project, and will keep it in mind during the coming months. Here are some preliminary observations:

1. Plagge is not a surname indigenous to the Windheim area. The Plagges were not farmers, but millers. Millers moved from place to place. The Plagge surname disappeared from the area rather early.

2. It would be possible to do a search for the Plagge surname in all the sections of present-day Germany. I am not sure how fruitful this would be.

3. In the political climate after World War Two it is not likely that Major Plagge talked about his lenient treatment of Jewish workers. It is possible that he might have made a cryptic remark or two to members of his family before his death. If he had a family!

4. We do not know whether he was from "East Germany" or "West Germany." That might make a difference in the preservation and availability of military records. If Major Plagge was in charge of vehicle repairs in Poland/Lithuania during World War Two he ought to be identifiable even if we do not know his first name.

I would suggest that you write to Jim Eggert (one of my correspondents) for further suggestions.

Cordially
Richard Scheimann

Mr. Scheimann did perform a search of all the phone directories in Germany and came up with a total of 250 people named Plagge in Germany. While this was a manageable number, the question remained, how to contact them and how would I know when I had the right family? Presumably, many of these families had men who had served in the Wehrmacht during the war. If I came upon a family that said that their father or grandfather had served

on the Eastern Front during the war, how would I know if their relative was
the man I was looking for?

At Richard's suggestion, I wrote to his acquaintance Jim Eggert who
worked at MIT. I received the following response:

Subj:Re: [MichaelDG@aol.com: Searching for
Major Plagge]
Date:01/04/2000 11:56:43 PM Eastern Standard Time
From: (Jim Eggert)
To:MichaelDG@aol.com

Hello Michael,

Your note about Major Plagge was very interesting. I hope the following
suggestions might help you a little. First a note of encouragement: I can't
imagine that there were very many Major Plagges in the German
Wehrmacht. A major is a staff officer, so he shouldn't be too hard to find.

The first book I would consult to find Major Plagge would be
AUTHOR: Germany. Heer. Personalamt.
TITLE: Rangliste des deutschen Heeres 1944/45 : Dienstalterslisten T und
S der Generale und Stabsoffiziere des Heeres vom 1.Mai 1944 mit amtlich
belegbaren Nachtragen bis Kriegsende und Stellenbesetzung der
hoeheren Kommandobehoerden und Divisionendes Deutschen Heeres
am 10. Juni 1944, hrsg. von Wolf Keilig.
PUB. INFO: Friedberg : Podzun-Pallas, [1955?]
DESCRIPTION: 408 p. ; 22 cm.
LOCATION: Widener: Harvard Depository KE 33367

Not having used this book, I don't know what the T and S mean in the
title. I hope it doesn't mean only officers with names beginning with T or
S. In any case, you should be able to get this on interlibrary loan if your
local library doesn't have a copy. I know Harvard has it. Or you could call
the reference desk at Harvard and see if they would be willing to look up
Major Plagge for you and fax you anything found. The reference telephone
number is 617–495–2411.

You can check the online list of German war cemeteries to see if your
Major Plagge is listed:
http://www.volksbund.de/

This would only help if he is buried in one of the listed cemeteries.

Finally, another word of encouragement. I think you are doing a good thing. I wouldn't stop, however, with merely a personal attempt to contact the Plagge family. I would write up the story as you know it and submit it to the Wiesenthal center, the US Holocaust Museum, and whomever else you might consider important. I know it cannot erase the terrible blot presented by the Holocaust, but uncovering a little corner of light in a dark chapter of history and documenting it for future generations is nonetheless important for future generations.

—Jim Eggert

I was very encouraged by these contacts, especially that they thought my search was of historical interest, and also that they thought it could end in success. I began to follow their suggestions one by one. First I called the Harvard reference library, and over the course of two days their librarians tracked down the book mentioned by Jim Eggert listing all Wehrmacht officers between the years 1944–45. The librarians then found a research assistant who spoke German and who agreed to look through the book for an officer named Plagge. Unfortunately, there was not a single Plagge listed. There was a Col. Plagemann, but nothing closer. The German-speaking research assistant kindly read the book's foreword out loud to me. It stated that as of the date that this volume was compiled (1955) the Wehrmacht records were very spotty, many documents having been destroyed or confiscated by the allies at the war's end. He suggested that just because a major named Plagge was not listed in this particular book, it did not mean that there was no record of such a person somewhere else in either German or American military archives.

In January 2000, I did find one small piece to the Plagge puzzle—his unit name and number. Searching through my grandfather's voluminous memoirs, I did find a reference to the unit that Plagge commanded. My grandfather said it was called HKP 562, or military vehicle repair park 562. My father wrote to the Jewish museum in Vilnius to ask if they had any information about Major Plagge. While they couldn't offer much, they did confirm that the unit he commanded was indeed HKP 562.

I next turned to query military archives in Germany, starting with the war cemeteries registry in Germany and *Wehrmachtauskunftstelle* (a.k.a. W.A.S.T.)

archive, which contains information about Germans who served in the military during WW II. As I made queries into the German archives, I often saw notices such as this one at the W.A.S.T. archive:

> Please state your reasons for your application (Relationship, future use of the information obtained . . .) and provide further details, insofar they are known to you, about the person you are tracing.

After sending out many queries, I did not receive a single response from any of the German archives. Being a novice researcher, I did not understand that unlike American archives, which are generally open to the public, strict privacy laws cover German records. Military records are generally open only to family members or recognized official researchers. One is not given access to these records unless you are identified as someone that the archival staff thinks has a "right to know." By the summer of 2000, in spite of much helpful advice and good wishes, I had not made any tangible progress. Plagge's full name and town of origin and all the other details of his identity were still mysteries.

Frustrated by the lack of response from Germany, I turned to the National Archives in Arlington, Virginia, which I hoped might have copies of German military records captured at the end of the war by the victorious allies, but returned to Germany after reunification in 1992. While I encountered some friendly archivists who were quite helpful, none of them was able to find a trace of a Major Plagge in charge of vehicle repairs in Vilna. They suggested that I contact the German National Archives, called the Bundesarchive, in Aachen, Germany, for further information regarding the personnel files of the Wehrmacht during World War II. Having had little success to date with German archives, I decided to try a new tactic and make my inquiry in German. Maybe all my previous failures were due to a German clerk's inability to understand English? Maybe it was typical American chauvinism that led me to think that my inquiries made in English were understandable to whoever received them. I began to look for someone who could translate my "Plagge Search Letter" into German. One night at dinner I mentioned that I was looking for such a translator, when my son Jonathan piped up to say that he was sharing a locker at his high school with a German exchange student. What a stroke of luck! He carried my letter to this exchange student, a boy named Marcus Schneider, who promptly translated the letter, which Jonathan carried back to me the next day. I sent off both the English and

German versions of my letter and began to wait. However, there was no reply from the Bundesarchive.

I was beginning to run out of options. In spite of my initial optimism, I had gotten nowhere in over a year of searching. I began to wonder if it was really possible to track down a man whom no one had heard of in over fifty-five years. In a somewhat desperate ploy, I began to send blind emails to anyone in Germany who had an email address with the name Plagge in it. While several people named Plagge in Germany responded, none of them knew of any relatives who fit my description of a German Wehrmacht major stationed in Vilna during the war.

In the meantime, my Plagge search letter continued to circle the globe, passed on by friendly genealogists to their contacts. In October 2000, 13 months after I had started my search, I received an innocent-appearing note from a Jewish genealogist specializing in the Vilna area named Joel Ratner, who forwarded an email from a man in Hamburg, Germany:

Subj:S. Klaczko
Date:10/09/2000 10:03:45 PM Eastern Daylight Time
From:Joel Ratner
To: Michael Good

Dear Michael,

It looks like this gentleman may have some promising avenues you can pursue. I think his partner with the military background might be a good place to start, especially with his knowledge of logistics.

Please keep in touch—I'm interested in how this proceeds.

Joel

Monday, 09 October 2000
FROM: "Dr. Salomon Klaczko-Ryndziun"
TO: "Joel Ratner" AND: "Dr. Michael Good"

Dear Joel,

I read the letter you sent prepared by Dr. Michael Good on behalf of his family. I am living and working in Hamburg, were I own a small hi-tech company . . . One of my co-owners is a retired lieutenant colonel of the German army and he teaches at the Hamburg Military Academy. Since he is a specialist in Logistics, he may know how to approach the military archives in Germany, in order to localize MAJOR PLAGGE. I will try also at the national telephone directory of Germany, to look, if there is somebody there with the same family name. Maybe, we will succeed in localizing a son or daughter or grandchild of Major Plagge. There are not too many people in Germany who really risked to help Jews during the Nazi times. These few people are the real heroes of the German nation. I will therefore do my best in order to help.

Sincerely yours,
Salomon Klaczko

I immediately wrote to Mr. Klaczko, thanking him for his offer to help and telling him I would very much appreciate any assistance that his business partner could offer. I soon heard from Joerg Fiebelkorn, Klaczko's business associate:

Subj:your request—Maj. Plagge
Date:10/13/2000 10:01:10 AM Eastern Daylight Time
From: Joerg Fiebelkorn
To: Michael Good

Dear Sir,

I have forwarded your request to the "Bundesarchiv—Zentralnachweisstelle" (Federal Archive—Central Bureau) in Aachen/Germany, where all personal files of the Wehrmacht are registered. If the name and unit is correct, you will have an answer about the where and when and further personal details such as the original address of Major Plagge within the next weeks. Then it should be no problem to trace his family—if he had one. I wonder, why there has not been any report about Major Plagge before? Especially in these days such an example of individual courage and humanity seems to be of some interest to the German public.

With kind regards
J. Fiebelkorn

At this point, having exhausted all other avenues of research that I could think of, all I could do was wait and hope that these two businessmen in Hamburg knew what they were doing. I was kept busy during this period by a fascinating development at nearby Wesleyan University in Middletown, Connecticut. Wesleyan's Jewish Studies Department had chosen the fall of 2000 to present a lecture, film, and drama series on Vilna and its central role in European Jewish culture. In addition to films and lectures, the drama department was putting on Joshua Sobol's play *Ghetto*, about the Vilna Ghetto. Mr. Sobol himself had come to Wesleyan to direct the production. My parents and some of their Vilna friends traveled to Connecticut to participate in the panel discussion that followed the play's opening night. The student members of the cast were astounded to find survivors of the Vilna Ghetto sitting in their audience. These survivors were fully engaged in the discussions inspired by the production and were themselves amazed to find their own history being portrayed by a young generation of American actors. The discussion ranged from questions of the morality of producing theater in the ghetto to history's judgment of Jacob Gens. Following the production, we had a joyous reunion of Vilner Jews at our home in Durham. Yiddish jokes brought peals of laughter, frequently followed by a second round of mirth after the older generation translated the jokes for their children and grandchildren.

On November 13, 2000, the day after our Vilna guests had departed from our home, I received an electrifying email from Joerg Fiebelkorn:

Subj:Plagge
Date:11/13/2000 5:31:52 AM Eastern Standard Time
From: Jörg Fiebelkorn
To: Michael Good

Dear Mr. Good,

There has been a positive response from the Bundesarchiv about Major Plagge. They have found—as you may have heard from them as well—the date of birth, the home-address in Darmstadt and the correct name of his unit in Wilna. The letter from the Bundesarchiv will need a few days more to reach the US than to me. So, here is a brief translation:

Dear Mr. Fiebelkorn,

Following the research as done here, the person sought is Major (Reserve) Karl Plagge, born July 10th 1897. A place of birth is not mentioned. Since 1941 he was the commander of the "Heeresfuhrpark 562" (Army RepairShop).

The home address was: Hoffmannstrasse 22, Darmstadt. The archive notes that he was married. Further details, especially about children, are not noted. To his further life we are unable to give any details. For this reason we suggest another request to the "Deutsche Dienststelle, Eichborndamm 179, D-13403 Berlin" (see attached form) and contact the personal register in Darmstadt as well.

I have sent a copy of this letter to Mr. Michael Good, in Durham, CT USA, who has contacted us directly as well. I assume you will proceed with your research and wish you all the success.

Now it is the question how to proceed:

I would suggest to write to the town mayor of Darmstadt directly, as this would be the most promising way to get more informations about his family. Another request should be made to the "Deutsche Dienststelle" in Berlin, where the personal files of all Wehrmacht personnel are kept. But here only family members are usually authorized to get information—exceptions could be from a very formal request by one of the major Jewish organizations or—via the Darmstadt town mayor—or by the family, if there is any. It would be a great honor for me to assist in the further research, and it may be easier for me to correspond with German public institutions. The Jewish community in Hamburg has signaled some interest in the case and a Hamburg Journalist—member of the community—is interested as well.

Please do send me a note

With kind regards
Joerg Fiebelkorn

At long last, a major breakthrough! For fourteen long months I had come up empty-handed. Now with the help of some strangers in Hamburg, Germany, I had taken a giant step forward, finding Plagge's name and hometown. I quickly wrote to Joerg, thanking him profusely on behalf of my mother and myself and urging him to move forward. I thought that it was particularly telling that the Bundesarchiv had had my request sitting on their desks for months, but only chose to respond when contacted by Joerg. It would appear that he would be much more successful than I would in maneuvering through the German bureaucracy.

Even so, I did request that Joerg proceed with caution, taking care to protect the privacy of any Plagge family members from the general public's

attention. We had no idea how they would react to stories about their relative's conduct during the war.

Agreeing with this strategy, Joerg wrote to the mayor of Darmstadt asking
on behalf of our family that efforts be made to open the city archives in
search of information about Karl Plagge and his family. While we waited for
the city of Darmstadt to reply, Joerg and I corresponded, trying to discover a
bit more about each other. We had, after all, only met via email, a medium
that was new to us and to the rest of the world. I directed him to a website I
had made during the summer of 1999, chronicling our family's journey and
my parents' survival stories.[1] He began to read both my mother's and grandfather's memoirs. Our exchange of emails gave me more insight into his
background and motivation for assisting me, and I'm sure he felt the same
way about me:

Subj:Re: Plagge
Date:11/27/2000
From: Michael Good
To: Joerg Fiebelkorn

Hello Joerg,

I hope that you have had a good week. My parents and I have been very
excited about the progress in finding Major Plagge's family. My parents
are contacting the survivors of the HKP labor camp that they know and
we are trying to gather as many stories and recollections about him as is
possible. My hope is to gather these tales together in a coherent way and
use it to build a memorial to Major Plagge, first at my website, and later
perhaps at a "brick and mortar" site somewhere. We are also interested
in documenting his story so that we can submit his name to Yad Vashem
in Israel as one of the "Righteous Among Nations," a designation which
we hope he would qualify for.

I am very hopeful that his family can shed some light on his own
perceptions of his actions. Did he feel that he was taking risks, did he

1. Following my return from Europe in 1999, I created a Web site called "Family
Journey," http:// www.hometown.aol.com/michaeldg, which served as a travelogue
of our trip for family and friends. Over time, I added sections regarding my search
for Major Plagge, including a document repository that contained my parents' and
grandfather's memoirs.

feel that he was markedly different from other Germans around him (as his prisoners strongly feel)? While I have heard a lot from his former subjects, understanding a little of how he viewed himself and his actions would help me to understand how it is that some people choose the path of genocide while others choose the road that opposes it. In my mother's story, two German officers stand in opposite camps. On the one side is Bruno Kittel, the SS officer who liquidated the Vilna Ghetto and lined the women and children of the HKP camp up to choose 36 to be killed in retaliation for two escapees. On the other is Major Plagge, who treated his prisoners humanely and protected them as much as he could. Understanding how these two men came to travel their respective paths of genocide and righteousness is the question that I am constantly hoping to answer when pondering the Holocaust.

Best Regards,
Michael Good

Re: Plagge
Date:11/27/2000 11:43:08 AM Eastern Standard Time
From: (Jörg Fiebelkorn)
To: Michael Good

Hello Michael,

Thanks for your mail. I have sent the letter to the Darmstadt town major last week and intend to call him tomorrow and ask, whether he received it. But more to your remarks about the different behavior of the Germans: It puzzles me as well. I know definitely that no German, who resisted the killing orders, had to face any punishment. There are enough such cases, witnessed by soldiers themselves as well as by the victims. So all those, who claim their obligation to "discipline" and "orders to be obeyed" are liars. I have asked my mother (who is 96 by now), how she has seen the Third Reich. To cut it short, she admits that she has "closed her eyes." There is much more to tell about . . .

Within her memoirs your mother is telling about a certain "Schirrmeister Berger," who worked together with Major Plagge. As far as I understood, this Sergeant Berger behaved similar to Plagge. If so, we should try to trace him as well. It is of such importance to publish these examples of courage and humanity especially to shame the great majority, who claimed (and still claim) that they "did not know" and if they knew "could not do anything without danger to their life." I have served in the German Army from 1962 until '87. Of course, all my superiors in the sixties were former Wehrmacht officers. It is a long story to tell about my personal experiences with the convictions of that generation.

I will inform you as soon as I get any news from Darmstadt.

With kind remarks
Joerg Fiebelkorn

These emails were most illuminating, showing me that in Joerg Fiebelkorn I had met a man who pondered some of the same moral questions of conduct that I had been asking during the years since my return from Lithuania. Having served with veterans of World War II, Joerg obviously had had many episodes that had caused him to ask: What choices did the men who served in the Wehrmacht during World War II really have to make?

Soon the long awaited answer from Darmstadt arrived via Joerg Fiebelkorn:

Dear Michael,

The Darmstadt archive has responded. Here is the "raw" translation:

The requested Karl Plagge, borne 10.07.1897 in Darmstadt, by profession civil engineer ("Diplom-Ingenieur"), has died in Darmstadt on June 19th 1957. His wife Anke Dorothea, borne Madsen on February 15th 1905 in Trier, moved on June 12th 1969 to Widdersdorf, Leonhardgasse 32 (by now suburb of Cologne). Whether she is alive, is not known here. The Plagges had no children; the address known to you (Hoffmannstraße 22) is the address of the parents, where the Plagges lived before the war. He had a sister Marie Plagge, born September 28th 1893; to our records she stayed unmarried, had no children and was living in Hoffmannstraße 22 as well. Possibly she became one of the victims of the destruction of Darmstadt in 1944, when all buildings in the Hoffmannstarße were destroyed (by allied bombing).

I will send to you the complete correspondence

With kind regards

Joerg Fiebelkorn

This news from Joerg, while fascinating, was a deep disappointment. I had always imagined that the ultimate goal of my quest was to find Plagge's family and to thank them on behalf of my family and the other HKP survivors for Plagge's benevolence. During the long months of searching, I had been buoyed by visions of writing letters of gratitude, perhaps even traveling to Germany with my mother to thank them personally. It seemed too cruel to think that after all of these efforts that my journey would come to such a sudden end, empty of the warm exchanges I had eagerly anticipated. If the archives were right, he had no children, no nieces or nephews; it seemed that there was no one to carry on his family line and memory.

After several days of brooding, I decided that my work was not done. If Plagge had no family to carry on his memory, then it was the duty of the HKP survivors and their descendants to create some kind of memorial to carry his story into the future. I could certainly make a memorial to Karl Plagge on my website, and if I gathered enough material, a physical memorial could be erected in Germany, perhaps in his hometown of Darmstadt. I also decided to try to have him honored at Yad Vashem, Israel's Holocaust Memorial Museum, as one of the "Righteous Among the Nations." This is a designation given to Gentiles who risked themselves in order to save Jewish lives during the Holocaust. Being designated as one of the "Righteous Among the Nations" would assure that his actions would be recorded and preserved in Israel, where his story would be preserved for posterity. "Righteous Among the Nations" is a weighty designation, and, before bestowing the honor to someone, Yad Vashem considers the following guidelines, which are listed at their website:

> Who is considered a "Righteous Among the Nations"
> In order to arrive at a fair evaluation of the rescuer's deeds and motivations, the commission takes into consideration all the circumstances relevant to the rescue story, including the following:
> - The dangers and risks faced by the rescuer at the time.
> - The rescuer's motivations, in so far as this is ascertainable; e.g., friendship, altruism, religious belief, humanitarian considerations, or others.
> - The availability of evidence from the rescued persons (an almost indispensable precondition for the purpose of this program).

In general, when the data on hand clearly demonstrates that a non-Jewish person risked his (or her) life, freedom, and safety in order to rescue one or several Jews from the threat of death or deportation to death camps without exacting in advance monetary compensation, this qualifies the rescuer for serious consideration to be awarded the "Righteous Among the Nations" title. This applies equally to rescuers who have since passed away.[2]

Two key questions would be brought up by an application to Yad Vashem on behalf of Karl Plagge. First, what were his motivations, and second, what risks did he take? My mother could shed little light on these particular questions. She knew that Plagge had saved her life by forming the HKP camp just before the liquidation of the Vilna ghetto, but did not know for sure why he did so. Certainly, his prisoners attributed altruistic motives to his actions, but no one had actually heard firsthand what his motivations were. Similarly, the HKP survivors credit Plagge with having warned them about the coming of the SS shortly before liberation. While this warning proved to be life-saving for the HKP survivors, many questions remained. Why did he make the warning, and what risk, if any, did he take to pass this information on to his prisoners?

With these questions in mind, I decided to review the testimony of as many HKP survivors as possible about what they remembered of experiences during the war. Over the previous year my mother and I had contacted as many of them as we could to collect their memories about HKP, and Major Plagge in particular. The first HKP survivor to contact me was Bill Begell, a teenager during the war, now an engineer and publisher in New York who sent me the following note:

Dear Michael:

You may remember me from your baby days in NY or from your parents' stories. I was—together with your Mom—in HKP during the war. She hid out the last few days before liberation while I escaped through a window in the mechanical shop several hours after Plagge's speech on July 1, 1944. My personal knowledge of him is rather nonexistent. I believe that I hadn't seen him at all until that evening of escape. My only recall of him

2. From http://www.yadvashem.org/righteous/index_righteous.html.

is through "grapevine" of people who worked at HKP before the liquidation of the ghetto. They always said that Plagge was a decent German. Also, just before the liquidation of the ghetto, my father was killed and Gens—the Jewish head of the ghetto—told my aunt that Plagge will be able to keep his Jews longer than he (Gens). He then arranged to have my mother, grandmother and me shipped to HKP, thus saving my life.

His famous speech is essentially the same as your Mom remembers it but if you wish I'll repeat it. Please let me know

Best regards,
Bill

Soon Bill joined my mother, Joerg Fiebelkorn, and Solomon Klaczko in an email group that we called the "Plagge Research Group." We continued to collect whatever testimony and documents from the HKP survivors we could find. This was difficult, as these survivors were aging; many had health problems to contend with or were caring for spouses who were ill. Trying to find the time and energy to write down their memories was a large undertaking. Some did not want to think of those times. Others could no longer remember even if they had the desire to. However, from different corners of the globe, letters and emails began to trickle in.

From Alik and Hanka Kremer in Toronto came a remarkable document. It was testimony given by a man named Dr. Moses Feigenberg in 1946 at the Landsberg DP (Displaced Persons) camp in Germany. The language of the deposition was Yiddish, but it was recorded in transliterated Latin script. Fortunately, my mother was able to translate it for us. Here are some excerpts:

Historical commission in Landsberg
Wilne under Nazi Oppression
as told by Moses Feigenberg
recorded by Moshe Waisberg
Landsberg November 1946

The HKP camp was established on September 17th, 1943, and had employed up to 1,500 workers (families included). At the beginning of September 1943, the chief of HKP, Major Plagge, found out that the ghetto of Wilno would be soon liquidated. He was a cultured and benevolent man who wanted to rescue his Jewish workers. Thus he then organized a work camp for his workers, named Jewish Work Camp HKP. He established the camp in the two big Jewish buildings on Subocz 37 . . .

The month of July was arriving. Up to 1,500 Jews who were still in the HKP camp were entirely cut off; they were not let out for any work and received no provisions. The guard around the camp was much strengthened. One could not even think of getting out. Everybody was looking for a hiding place inside the camp. The word "Maline" was passing from mouth to mouth. Everyone could only be sitting, waiting for a miracle . . .

On one of those horrible days Major Plagge, the Chief of HKP, appeared in the yard of the camp. In the presence of (SS) Oberscharfuehrer Richter, Plagge made a speech to the Jews. He explained that these were difficult times for the German Army. It was not out of the question that the camp might not have to evacuate. He comforted the Jews that he might possibly go with them. But his speech brought no assurance, to the contrary, it made them sure that their end was near.

From this testimony by Moses Feigenberg it is clear that in 1946 Major Plagge's prisoners clearly remembered him as being benevolent and doing what he could to try to save them. What was added to the story in this document was the fact that, according to Feigenberg, Plagge made his warning to the Jewish prisoners in the presence of Oberscharfuehrer Richter, the SS man overseeing the HKP camp. Surely this was a risky undertaking. The only problem was that none of the other survivors I knew could remember Richter being there. My grandfather made no mention of him, and neither my mother nor Bill Begell could remember any members of the SS as having been present at all. At my urging, Bill wrote to me about his recollections:

Dear Michael:

My recollection of Plagge's speech is as follows:
Toward the early evening—about seven o'clock—on July 1, 1944, it was still light and Major Plagge gathered a group of the HKP inmates and proceeded to speak. It was not an official speech, people just gathered around him. Plagge said that we all must have heard that the front line is moving west and that HKP's assignment is to always be a certain number of kilometers behind the front line. Therefore, HKP is being moved away

from the front. As a result, you the Jews and workers will also be moved. It is natural to think that since all of you are highly specialized and experienced workers in an area of great importance to the German Army, you will be reassigned to a HKP unit. I cannot assure you that it will again be my unit, but it will be a HKP unit. You will be escorted during this evacuation by the SS which, as you know, is an organization devoted to the protection of refugees. Thus, there's nothing to worry about . . .

This is my recollection of the speech. I have repeated it to myself hundreds of times over the years. I also remember thinking that this overt warning to us that we were about to be killed (by mentioning the SS as an organization for the protection of refugees) was made with a human stroke of the pen, so to say, because—and I repeat—because he didn't have to say it at all, since there was nobody from the SS present and he did not have to protect himself by making such remarks. These thoughts have been in my mind since that time and I stand by them. There was no SS-man present. Michael, please keep me in the loop. I will contribute whatever I can.

Best regards,
Bill

These conflicting testimonies brought out a flurry of emails among Salomon Klaczko, Joerg Fiebelkorn, Bill Begell, my mother, and myself as we debated who exactly was present at Plagge's warning and what this meant in terms of the risks he took and his motivations for taking them. Salomon Klaczko felt that during such times, when all involved were living in the midst of a police state, people were forced to speak in code, hiding the true meaning of their message from some while having it clearly understood by the intended recipients:

Karl Plagge was surely aware about the fact that among the Jewish people in the Vilna Ghetto there were Jewish policemen who cooperated officially with the SS and the Gestapo, and people who did it unofficially. Plagge was forced to speak to the Jews in the "Heeres Kraftfarzeug Park" in such a hidden manner, that no denunciator would have been able to prove formally that he, Plagge, really alarmed the Jews. But evidently he was clearly understood. Hence, at least Samuel Esterowicz was clever enough to decipher the hidden message formulated by Karl Plagge . . .

The fact of presence or absence of an official member of the SS is relatively irrelevant. Plagge certainly knew that among the Jews there were some confidential reporters to the SS. Hence, the direct or the indirect presence of the SS and the Gestapo was necessarily taken for granted by Major Karl Plagge as soon as he spoke publicly. It would be very naïve to assume some other hypothesis.

Bill Begell gave the following response:

We are now engaged in a real historical debate about the events surrounding Plagge's speech. There are psychological aspects and aspects of recollection as well as of chronological points of view. I agree that it really does not matter whether there was indeed an SS man present on July, 1944. Salomon is right, there must have been spies there, Jewish, Lithuanian, German or Polish. What is important now, I believe, is whether Plagge tried to communicate the impending danger to the HKP Jews during his speech. That, again in my opinion, is a proven fact. The rest, behavioral or philosophical, is irrelevant. Plagge had warned us in no uncertain terms. I know that the group of us (about 3 dozen) who escaped through the window in the machine shop knew exactly what we are escaping from and we were totally aware of Plagge's role in warning us.

As we debated these points[3] and prepared our application to Yad Vashem, other interested parties were being drawn into our research group. There was Mira Van Doren, my mother's childhood friend from Vilna whose family had escaped to New York before the war. In addition, Salomon Klaczko had contacted a sociologist he knew, Dr. Helmut Dahmer at the Technical University at Darmstadt, where Plagge had earned his engineering degree in 1924, to let him know about their unusual alumnus. Word gradually traveled within the Technical University until the Plagge story reached the attention of a woman named Dr. Marianne Viefhaus. Marianne was a retired archivist at the university who had special interest in the historical contacts between the Technical University and students from Lithuania. There had been many

3. I later obtained further information about the presence of an SS man at Plagge's speech from interviews and correspondance with HKP survivors over the following year. Some distinctly recall seeing "Golosheyka" ("Gooseneck," i.e., SS Obersharfuerer Richter) standing next to Plagge as he spoke. I have finally concluded that there was indeed an SS man standing next to Plagge during his speech.

Lithuanian exchange students in Darmstadt over the years dating back to the early 1900s. She had many contacts in both Poland and Lithuania and was well versed in the history of the Holocaust in Vilna. She and some of the other archivists were fascinated to hear news of a formerly unknown graduate of their school who had played a role in rescuing Jews in Vilna during the Holocaust. She began to search the archives for clues to his background.

On February 20, 2001, members of the Plagge research group were suddenly jolted away from their debates over the HKP testimonies they had collected. News came from Salomon Klaczko in Germany that Marianne Viefhaus had made an amazing discovery of documents pertaining to Karl Plagge. These new discoveries disclosed details about Karl Plagge's conduct during the war that went far beyond anything that the HKP prisoners had known about. Suddenly a door opened that would carry us to revelations that we could scarcely have imagined possible.

6

THE DISCOVERIES

When I became head of the Kraftfahrpark (HKP) in Poland and Russia, I saw the civil population there in a very poor condition, without any rights or legal protection. There existed "soldier's letters" that informed the members of the German army that the Polish people were inferior and that the German soldier had to act as a "Herrenmensch," a superior human being. I never understood this kind of behavior and never acted in the manner as specified in our orders. I took the decision to always act against the Nazi rules and to also give my subordinates the order to act in a very humane manner towards the civilian population . . . I did that because I thought it was my duty. There needed to be German people who could be seen by foreign countries as doing good. I was ashamed.[1]
—Testimony of Karl Plagge at his denazification trial, Darmstadt, Germany, 1947

In Darmstadt, Germany, Dr. Marianne Viefhaus was in earnest pursuit of Karl Plagge. In the university archives, she found his school records with a graduation date in 1924 with a degree in mechanical and chemical engineering. She also found records that he had been employed by an engineering firm called "Hessenwerke" in Darmstadt during the 1930s. Hessenwerke was no longer in business, but by looking in the Darmstadt Chamber of Commerce archives she found that the company had been owned and run by a family named Hesse. Checking the modern Darmstadt phone book, she saw that there was still a family named Hesse living at the same address that was listed for the owners of Hessenwerke in the archives. She gave the number a call and was able to talk to an elderly woman named

1. Plagge denazification file: Hessisches Hauptstaatsarchiv Wiesbaden 4.1.3. / 520 / Spruchkammern / Dl / Plagge, Karl. English translation can be found in Appendix A, 201, 212.

Irma Freese who was the daughter of the now deceased head of Hessenw-erke, Kurt Hesse. Mrs. Freese remembered Karl Plagge well as he and her father had been good friends. She said that after the war, German families did not discuss their wartime experiences. Whether it was due to guilt for unspeakable deeds or the general horror of the war experience for all Germans, talking about the war was not an acceptable topic of conversation in postwar German society. However, before finishing her conversation with Marianne, she did say that after the war, "Karl Plagge became cleared from incrimination because he saved many Jews."

This last comment loomed large in Marianne's mind. First of all, it would appear that some of his friends knew of his actions on behalf of Jews during the war. Secondly, this statement implied that Plagge may have had to defend himself against the common postwar accusation by the Allies that he had participated in war crimes. If this were the case, he may have had a denazification trial. Denazification in Germany was a process in which the victorious Allies attempted to identify and purge all Nazi war criminals from positions of power in postwar Germany. First, all Nazi Party members were required to fill out a lengthy questionnaire about their activities in the Nazi party and conduct during the war. If anything about their history implied a possible role in war crimes, they had to undergo a trial in a "Spruchkammer" or Denazification Court. Looking in the State of Hesse archives in Wiesbaden, Marianne found that Karl Plagge had indeed had a denazification trial. Most importantly, she found the trial transcript.

As Marianne read the court's file, she discovered that Karl Plagge had been a member of the Nazi Party. He had joined the party before most Germans—in 1931, two years before Hitler came to power. This implied that he did not join due to social pressures or career aspirations. People who joined the party at such an early date generally did so out of conviction. Because of this early date of party membership, as well as the fact that he had commanded a German labor camp where many Jews were killed, Karl Plagge was ordered to undergo a trial and had to defend himself from the charge of being a war criminal. He hired a lawyer and then proceeded to enlist friends and colleagues who had not been members of the Nazi Party to speak on his behalf. This dusty old file, having been stored unread since 1947, contained testimonies by Plagge's subordinates from HKP, his employer Kurt Hesse, and from Karl Plagge himself. Additionally, there was testimony from a representative of Jewish survivors of the HKP camp who were living in the Ludwigsburg DP camp near Stuttgart, Germany, at the time. They too testified at Karl Plagge's trial. Marianne Viefhaus had discovered an archival treasure that would cast a revealing beacon of light into the past.

On a snowy morning in Connecticut in February 2001, I sat down at my computer to check my email. Upon logging on I saw that my mailbox contained multiple excited messages, all in German, sent between Salomon, Joerg, and Marianne. Due to my inability to speak German I was confused as to what the email messages could possibly mean. I turned to my mother and Bill Begell, who speak some German, which they both had learned during the war. They told me that these emails started with an exclamation from Salomon which declared to Marianne, "You are an angel!" After our initial puzzled inquiries, Salomon, Marianne, and Joerg explained what had been found and its significance. Within a few days, I received a large airmail package from Marianne, which contained a copy of the original denazification trial transcript. I quickly asked Marcus Schneider, the high school exchange student from Germany, to take on the task of translating this find, which he immediately agreed to do. For the next several weeks he worked steadily at translating the file, sending me his completed work in weekly ten-page increments. The file told an amazing story.

In the denazification trial transcript, Karl Plagge presents his biography, his history of activity within the Nazi Party, and an explanation of his conduct during the war. This is followed by a series of witnesses who testify about their observations of Plagge both before and during the war. As one moves through the forty pages of single-spaced typed transcript, a clear and compelling story unfolds. It is a tale that sweeps through the history of Germany in the first half of the twentieth century. The trial shows how Karl Plagge started as a naïve activist who supported of the Nazi Party because of its promises to return order and prosperity to Germany. The trial testimony then tells how over time he was transformed into a hard-nosed, clear thinking opponent of the Nazis and their policies. Here, in summary, is the story found within the denazification file of Karl Plagge, former major of the German Wehrmacht.

Karl Plagge was born on July 10, 1897, in Darmstadt, Germany. His family was a well-established, noble minded family, proud of their Prussian heritage. There was a family tradition of combining military service with medical science—several generations of Plagge men had served as military physicians over the years. Plagge's father was also a military physician but died in 1904 at the age of 42, leaving his wife to care for six-year-old Karl and his older sister.

Immediately after graduating from high school in 1916, Karl was inducted into the German army to serve in World War I. He was sent to the Western Front, where he fought in the battles of the Somme, Verdun, and Flanders. In 1917, he was captured and spent three years in a British prisoner-of-war camp. While a POW, he contracted polio and was left with a permanent disability of his left leg. Upon returning home to Darmstadt, he enrolled in the Darmstadt University of Technology. He had always dreamed of becoming a physician like his father, but due to his family's poor finances, was forced to take a shorter course of study in mechanical and chemical engineering. He completed his studies in 1924 and married a woman named Anke Madsen. Due to the economic distress in Germany after the war, Plagge and his wife were unable to set up their own household and continued to live with Karl's mother at Hoffmannstrasse 22 in Darmstadt.

Economic conditions became markedly worse in 1930 as the Great Depression swept the globe. Karl became unemployed. In an attempt to earn a living he took additional course work in medical chemistry at the University of Frankfurt-am-Main and then opened a small pharmaceutical-medical laboratory in his mother's house, with Anke working with him as a medical technician. They struggled to eke out a living as the economic conditions in Germany became increasingly desperate. Along with economic problems came increasing social unrest, with clashes breaking out between conservative forces and socialists. For proud German families like the Plagges, a Germany afflicted by street riots, mass unemployment, and hunger was shocking. When this was combined with their own precarious economic situation, they found themselves feeling increasingly insecure.

During these difficult times, Adolf Hitler's National Socialist German Workers Party (Nazi Party) began to increase in popularity. Hitler promised the reestablishment of order and a return to economic prosperity. Karl Plagge testified that he was attracted to the message given by the Nazis: they promised to end unemployment, stimulate the economy with government projects, and place limits on the wages of the richest members of society. Hitler's words made Plagge hope that things could get better, that Germany could return to a time of unity, pride, and prosperity. He joined the Nazi Party in December 1931, wanting to help them get the country back on its feet.

Plagge began to work with the local party organization in Darmstadt as a minor local supporter, lending his hand in their organizing efforts. During the next two years the Nazis swept into power as Hitler was made chancellor of Germany and seized the reins of government. After Hitler came into power in 1933, the Nazis began to rapidly purge all opponents from the government and then throughout society. They also began to showcase their racial theories and enact anti-Semitic laws. Beginning in 1933, Plagge began to realize that there were an increasing number of Nazi policies that he disagreed with and felt uneasy about:

> Soon after Hitler came to power I realized that I couldn't always agree with some of the party's measures. I couldn't understand their personal policies against their defeated political opponents because I was a man who believed in compromises between political interests and not in the inconsiderate removal of all opponents. Also the loud-mouthed habits and the general show-off behavior of many of the party administrators and members wasn't very appealing to me. I also disliked the unscientific doctrines about the racial question. But I believed during that time that those disagreeable aspects were only transitional and were going to disappear, leaving a fair and humane political administration.[2]

After ruminating about these concerns, Plagge decided that he should become more active in the party in order to intervene and mediate those aspects of party policies that he found objectionable. First, at his town group leader's recommendation, he became a "house block leader" (neighborhood organizer). However, he soon found that because of his polio-related disabilities, he was not able to do the walking and stair climbing required by the job, and had to step down from the position. Next, he offered his services with the party's speakers' bureau as a scientific lecturer, giving talks on his areas of scientific and technical knowledge. However, he refused to attend any of the party's ideological classes, which propagated the Nazi racial theories, as he found their scientific theories and ideologies to be bizarre and unscientific. Due to his scientific and technical skills he was asked to head the party Educational Institute in Darmstadt. He hesitated before taking this position, wanting to make sure that the classes at the institute could be taught free of ideology. After convincing himself that the institute would be

---

2. Plagge denazification file, Appendix A, 199.

teaching courses on science, foreign languages, and other topics without party ideological interference, he accepted the post.

However, while he was very motivated to teach scientific and linguistic classes to the general population, the party had other ideas. It began to infiltrate the faculty with party ideologues who in Plagge's mind were poisoning the institute with their unscientific ideas. He came into increasing conflict with the local party administrators because he resisted the dissemination of party ideology within his educational institute. He came under pressure from the party hierarchy to acquiesce and conform. In what could be the first indication of his future conduct during the war, he refused to comply with the directives of party administrators. At about this time he refused to buy and wear the Nazi uniform, even though it was a party requirement to do so. He began to have constant friction with his superiors within the Nazi Party as he insisted on running his institute in a way that he thought was proper. Eventually, in 1935, the superintendent of education for the party in Darmstadt denounced him for trying to dilute the ideals of the party. When Plagge continued to refuse to comply with party orders, the superintendent fired him from his position as head of the educational institute. The superintendent made several accusations against Plagge. First he accused him of being friendly with Jews and Freemasons. He also charged that in opposition to party policies excluding Jews from German businesses, Plagge treated non-Aryans in his medical laboratory. The superindendent threatened to bring Plagge before the party court for these transgressions. Fortunately for Karl Plagge, the superintendent never followed through on his threats. After this falling out, Plagge, who had worked for the party out of idealism, became completely disillusioned with the Nazis. He refused to take part in party functions, and gradually began, over time, to work against the party and its increasing control of German society.

In an attempt to augment his income, Plagge applied for a part-time job at an engineering firm called Hessenworks in 1934. In doing so he became acquainted with its owner, a man named Kurt Hesse, and over time, they became good friends. It turned out that Kurt Hesse was married to a half-Jewish woman, Erika Hesse. Because of his wife's "non-Aryan" status, Kurt was under pressure by the Nazis to divorce her. He refused to do so but worried that his firm might come under attack because of his wife's heritage. Between 1933, when they came to power, and 1935, the Nazis began passing an increasing number of anti-Jewish edicts now referred to as the Nurem-

berg Laws, which they used to discriminate against Jews and their businesses. Jews were stripped of their German citizenship and the general
population was not allowed to marry or do business with Jews. If a business
were labeled as "Jewish," it would be boycotted, and only allowed to do
business with other Jews. Many Jewish businesses that relied on commerce
from all corners of German society went bankrupt because of these rules.

At the denazification trial Kurt Hesse testified that he hired Plagge initially
because of his party membership, hoping that having a National Socialist in
a high position within his company would give him some measure of protection against the anti-Jewish measures that threatened both his family and his
business. When hiring Plagge, Hesse sensed that even though he belonged
to the party, Plagge was not an ideologue who would spread Nazi propaganda throughout the business. Even as he was attacked by the authorities
and shunned by his neighbors, in Karl Plagge, Kurt Hesse felt instinctively
he had met someone whom he could trust:

> I am Aryan but my wife is Jewish. I stood under increasing pressure
> due to this. Plagge was always good to me and gave me advice. He sup-
> ported me mentally and was honest to my family. He never tried to excuse
> the crimes committed by the Nazis. He believed those were only phenom-
> ena at the beginning that would disappear after a while. In 1938 I needed
> to hire a full time engineer. I needed someone in a high position who
> was a member of the party . . . I needed to have someone for "outside,"
> someone who could help make it seem as if the business was national-
> socialistic. But I didn't want someone who would make propaganda to
> come into my business. I knew that he wouldn't make propaganda and
> that I could trust him. I never regretted having hired him.[3]

As the anti-Jewish policies of the Nazis increased in intensity through the
1930s, Plagge experienced increasing guilt and "inner mental conflict" about
what was happening. He did whatever he could to shield his friends, the
Hesses, from the threats of the Nazis and their racial policies. On November
9, 1938, the Nazis organized a nationwide attack on Jews and their businesses. Synagogues were burned, shops looted, Jews were beaten up, murdered, arrested. This event became known as Kristallnacht, "the Night of the
Broken Glass," and was meant to signal that the Jews were total outcasts

3. Plagge denazification file, Appendix A, 218.

from society and that they should leave Germany. While many Jews did try to leave, others soon found that the nations of the world did not want them—they could not get entrance visas even if they wanted to emigrate. Many of Germany's Jews, including Kurt Hesse and his wife Erica, were thus trapped in the midst of a nation that had become virulently anti-Semitic, with nowhere to go. As the anti-Jewish brutality of the Nazis worsened, Plagge tried to help and support his suffering friends. Shortly after Kristallnacht, in the midst of a wave of anti-Jewish terror, Erika Hesse gave birth to a son, whom she and Kurt named Konrad. Hoping that his status as a party member would help protect the family, Karl Plagge became the baby boy's godfather.

In early 1939, Plagge realized that the Nazis were pushing the country into another world war. Here Kurt Hesse describes the moment, at an engineering conference, when Plagge suddenly understood what lay ahead:

> The event that shocked him fundamentally was the meeting of German engineers in Stuttgart. He went there as a representative of my business because many technical and scientific speeches were being made. I also went there. We spoke a short time after the convention. He was totally shocked, I had problems recognizing him. He couldn't get over the fact that Dr Ley [a high-ranking Nazi Party official] said in the most uninhibited manner that in three years the German flag would wave over Warsaw. By then, he [Plagge] had mentally left his former party. And his anti-Nazi opinion was still growing.[4]

Within a few short months, war did break out when Germany invaded Poland in September 1939. Plagge was immediately drafted into the Wehrmacht, where he was initially given the rank of captain, along with the command of a vehicle repair unit in Darmstadt. By the outbreak of war, Plagge was decidedly anti-Nazi and took the opportunity to quit the Nazi Party. Plagge wrote:

> I used the possibility as a soldier to break off my party membership and from the beginning of the war, I didn't pay any party contribution, all the more considering that now I had come into clear opposition to the National Socialist methods of violence.[5]

4. Plagge denazification file, Appendix A, 218.
5. Plagge denazification file, Appendix A, 201.

Karl Plagge, age 20, seen when he served as a lieutenant during World War I.

Karl Plagge (L) seen with a comrade during his internment as a British prisoner of war in 1918.

Anke Plagge working in her husband's medical laboratory in the mid-1930s. During these economically difficult times the couple lived with Karl's mother, and he worked two jobs, one in his medical lab, seen above, and a second as an employee of Hessenwerke.

Karl Plagge (seated far left) sitting next to his bride Anke Madsen on his wedding day in 1933. Note that both Plagge and his father-in-law wear the "Brownshirt" uniforms of the Nazi Party military wing, the SA. Wearing the party uniform was the custom of many middle-class supporters of the National Socialists during the party's rise to power.

Karl Plagge, center, seen with his fellow HKP officers and unit NCOs following a military parade in Vilna in 1942.

Major Karl Plagge in 1944. In this wartime photo, probably taken while he was home on leave, Plagge seems tired and pensive, looking as if the weight of the war was on his shoulders.

A relaxed Karl Plagge photographed at his godson Konrad Hesse's confirmation celebration in 1952.

Businessman Saloman Klaczko was intrigued by my "Plagge search letter" and shared it with his business partner, Joerg Fiebelkorn.

Retired German Army Colonel Joerg Fiebelkorn gained access to the Bundesarchive files that finally revealed the identity of Karl Plagge.

HKP survivor Bill Begell now runs a scientific publishing company in New York City.

HKP survivor Simon Malkes is a retired engineer living in Paris, France.

Dr. Marianne Viefhaus, the amazing archivist who discovered Plagge's denazification trial transcript as well as a myriad of other documents that slowly revealed Karl Plagge's secret heroism.

JUDEN GAB ER ARBEIT,
HILFE UND SCHUTZ
ALS WEHRMACHT OFFIZIER
IN WILNA BEWAHRTE ER
VIELE JUDEN
VOR DEM HOLOCAUST

KARL PLAGGE
1897–1957

1924 ABSOLVENT DER
TECHNISCHEN HOCHSCHULE
DARMSTADT

Memorial Plaque honoring Karl Plagge, unveiled in 2003 at the Technical
University of Darmstadt. The stone at the bottom symbolizes the Jewish
tradition of laying a stone or pebble on a cemetery memorial as a sign of respect
to the deceased and to show that someone had come to visit their grave.
The plaque reads: To Jews he gave work, help and shelter. As a Wehrmacht
officer in Vilna he protected many Jews from the Holocaust.
Karl Plagge 1897-1957
In 1924 he finished his studies at the Technical School in Darmstadt

When Germany attacked Russia in June of 1941 and occupied Vilna, Plagge was transferred to take command of the HKP 562 unit. Upon arriving in Vilna, he began to see the genocide that was being carried out against the Jews as well as the oppressive treatment of the Poles. He later said:

> When I came to Poland . . . I saw unbelievable things that I could not support . . . I decided then to work against the Nazis.[6]

Plagge began by ordering his soldiers to treat all civilians humanely and properly. He made it clear that violence or abuse toward unarmed civilians, whether they be Jews or Poles, would not be tolerated in his unit. One of Plagge's Lieutenants, Alfred Stumpff, describes the tone that Plagge set within the HKP unit:

> Karl Plagge . . . was my direct superior in the motor vehicle repair park in Vilna from June 16th 1942 until October 2nd 1942 where I served as a high lieutenant. During that time, I found that Major Plagge had an honorable and human mentality and strongly rejected the German policy of full extermination of the whole Jewish population in the occupied Eastern territories. He openly explained this to me in our discussions. Major Plagge demonstrated his opinions by really helping the endangered people; this not only took great courage but was also very dangerous for his position and himself.
>
> Mr. Plagge himself always treated the Jews in a very proper and humane way and wanted his subordinates to do so as well. A good example is the following incident that represented a rare violation of Plagge's rules towards a Jewish worker.
>
> One day I saw by chance how a sergeant from Wiesbaden, who was very proud to be a member of the civil SS, assaulted a Jewish worker, hitting and kicking him. When I confronted the sergeant with the incorrectness of his behavior he excused himself by saying the Jew lied to him. He then used the common national-socialistic phrases that the Jews are our enemies and aren't worthy of protection from a German. I told him that it was disgraceful for a soldier to threaten and to kick a defenseless person and that if he really wanted to fight Germany's enemies he should serve on the front. He declared that he was a member of the SS and made

---

6. Plagge denazification file, Appendix A, 212.

veiled threats to tell the local administration about this incident. I reported the incident to Plagge and he had an even more serious discussion
with the sergeant and ordered him to report to the front. Normally Plagge
didn't have the right to do that, but afterwards the sergeant himself filed
an application for going to the front and so he disappeared from the park
very quickly after the incident.[7]

Plagge had learned from his experience in Darmstadt before the war that
to be openly antagonistic toward the Nazis would cause him to be demoted
or even arrested, which would not allow him to accomplish any of his goals.
Five years later, in Vilna, he moved more subtly, encouraging those who
secretly disagreed with the party, and transferring party stalwarts and "big
Nazis" out of the unit. While Plagge was not publicly vocal about his political
views, his men understood his inner leanings. The following is testimony
given by Friedrich Asmus, one of Plagge's subordinates in Vilna:

> The former major of the Wehrmacht Plagge was my direct superior
> during the war for about three and a half years. During this time he never
> . . . made any kind of provocative speech. It was known in our unit that
> comrades who were opponents of National-Socialism were never disad-
> vantaged but found a like-minded man in Major Plagge. "Big Nazis, Jew-
> eaters, and harassing people" were neutralized, displaced, or removed
> from the unit. I know about people, of higher rank than I, who acted in
> a too National-Socialistic way and were forced to leave the unit. Slave-
> driving methods were not tolerated.[8]

Plagge's main method of resistance against the genocide was to give work
permits to Jewish workers, allowing them to save themselves and their family
members from the *aktions* that swept the Vilna ghetto. To the outside authorities, he kept up the guise that he needed these skilled Jewish workers to
carry out his duty of running an efficient vehicle repair operation. However,
in reality, many of the Jews were unskilled and owed their jobs to Plagge's
benevolence. Here again is Lieutenant Stumpff:

> The large Jewish population of Vilna was herded into a ghetto. There
> the German administration distinguished between the "usable Jews" with

7. Plagge denazification file, Appendix A, 196, 216.
8. Plagge denazification file, Appendix A, 207.

their wives and children who could work for the Deutsche Wehrmacht or the war economy and who lived in a special part (after my memory it was called Ghetto A). The rest of the "unusable Jews" became victims of extermination aktions and lived for a while in another part (Ghetto B). The employment in a factory of the Wehrmacht meant longer survival for the Jews during that time. Mr. Plagge employed in his factory Jewish workers in great numbers. There were many Jews who weren't really useful or necessary for the work that had to be done.

The park employed, for example, Jews as barbers, shoemakers, tailors, and cooks. Jewish women and girls worked as cleaning workers and garden workers. Additionally, there was a Jewish doctor for the observation of the civil workers' health. Naturally, the park wasn't allowed to employ such people and Mr. Plagge could have gotten in serious trouble by doing so. These people were camouflaged to the outside as professional workers of the motor vehicle repair park. I knew from personal discussions with Mr. Plagge that he employed the majority of these Jews only to save them from extermination.[9]

Plagge did not worry too much about the real efficiency of his unit; his main goal was to protect as many workers as possible. At his trial, he stated:

> I did not volunteer for this war and did not want to prolong the conflict by spurring on my labor to produce the needed resources with even greater efficiency.[10]

Plagge was also quite concerned with the nutritional status of his workers and their families. The German authorities had provided rations for their soldiers and Lithuanian civilians, but rations for the Poles and Jews were below subsistence levels. While the Polish population was malnourished, they at least were able to buy food on the black market. For Jews locked into ghettos across Europe, there was an active danger of starving to death. Plagge took several measures to try to ameliorate the hunger among both his Jewish and Polish workers. His quartermaster, Heinz Zeuner, testified about Plagge's concerns at his denazification trial:

> I was the sub-superior of food administration in the motor vehicle repair park that he commanded when we came first to Russia . . . He was

---

9. Plagge denazification file, Appendix A, 195–196.
10. Plagge denazification file, Appendix A, 202.

especially concerned about the civilian workers in the park and I had to get extra rations for them (potatoes, flour, vegetables, . . .). For example, he ordered weekly observations about his workers' weight to convince himself that they got enough food.[11]

Lieutenant Stumpff also recalled the efforts that Plagge made to feed his workers:

> The Jews got their food rations in the ghetto and didn't have any right to get them from our park administration. Even so, they got an extra lunch during the time I served there just like the Polish workers; it was mostly a warm soup or another warm meal. Because the park didn't have any right to obtain extra food, the whole administration and particularly Major Plagge was always worried about how to get food like potatoes, vegetables and horse meat . . . Because the German administration placed Wilna under Lithuanian sovereignty the Polish population was discriminated against by the Lithuanians in order to get enough food rations and other life amenities. So, Mr. Plagge organized a special food supply for the Polish civil workers and their families. This turned out to be very difficult and he had to put a great effort into overcoming the resistance of the Territorial Commissioner (who can be compared in his duties to a district administrator) at the beginning. That's how it was guaranteed that the employed Poles really got their whole food rations. As an extra, the park provided them also with a warm meal every day.[12]

During the war a variety of factors were at play, threatening the survival of both Poles and Jews in Lithuania. While the SS was actively murdering Jews in the forest of Ponary, the rest of both the Jewish and Polish population was threatened by the lack of basic social institutions needed for a population's survival. In addition to three million Polish Jews who died during the war, three million Polish Gentiles died as well. Many died from hunger, cold, and lack of medical care.

Plagge carefully analyzed the living situation of the civilians in Vilna and, with the precision of an engineer, carefully laid plans to provide them with life saving necessities. Here Staff Sergeant George Raab enumerates Plagge's efforts:

11. Plagge denazification file, Appendix A, 193.
12. Plagge denazification file, Appendix A, 197.

During my service at the motor vehicle repair park I was in the rank of a staff sergeant and my duty was to work on personal affairs. I frequently talked with Major Plagge about the discriminating treatment the civilians had to endure by the German civil offices, the SD [Secret Police] and the military police. I always knew that he hated the Nazi methods of handling civilian affairs, and he did everything in his power to help, defend and protect these miserable people.

Major Plagge created the following social institutions for the well being of his civil workers:

a) A park kitchen that served a wholesome lunch for the park workers and also to the workers who worked in faraway workshops belonging to the park

b) Creation of park-owned stores that supplied the workers and their families with food and meat

c) Creation of a park-owned hospital for the workers and their families (about 40 beds) supplied by army supplied medications

d) Creation of a "Unterstuetzungskasse" (cash) that supported civil workers who were in debt

e) Workers' supply of shoes, underwear and working clothing, accomplished through a lot of negotiation with the Lithuanian offices

f) Workers' supply of winter potatoes and wood accomplished through a lot of negotiations with offices and distribution centers, but also through his own wood-cutting program.[13]

In addition to creating a basic infrastructure that sheltered both Jews and Poles from the life threatening hardships they encountered during the war, Plagge was frequently called on to rescue workers and their families who were caught in the *aktions* that swept through the ghetto. During the summer of 1941 the Lithuanian police or *Khapuny* (grabbers) would snatch Jews off the streets of Vilna and take them to Lukishki prison. They would be kept there for a day or two and then taken to Ponary for execution. Later, a similar pattern continued when the SS and Gestapo carried out *aktions* within the ghetto: first arrest and imprisonment in the Lukishki prison followed by transport to Ponary and execution. Survivors recall that while German soldiers usually scrutinized a worker's papers and respected the protection

13. Plagge denazification file, Appendix A, 203–205.

given by a valid work permit in a Wehrmacht workshop, the Lithuanian *Khapuny* would often arrest any Jew they encountered, ignoring their papers altogether. Once taken to Lukishki and placed in the hands of the Gestapo, an arrested Jew was doomed unless a German authority from their workshop came to claim him as an essential worker. Even the intervention of the Wehrmacht on their behalf was no guarantee, as the SD (Secret Police) was always inclined to kill Jews rather that spare them. During the denazification trial, Plagge's men described how he struggled to keep ahead of the killing machine. Here again is Sergeant Raab:

> Mr. Plagge freed a large number of Jews (about 70) from the Lukishki prison. These Jews were to be deported to extermination camps, but were saved because of his protest at the SD office. He knew those workers personally and told the SD officials that they were indispensable for his park, but in reality they weren't and he knew that. He was allowed to enter the prison and he not only freed the workers but also their family members. All those people really loved him from then on for that action . . . I also knew that he allowed, during the persecutions, a number of Jews to hide, with his knowledge, on park territory until the end of the SD *aktions*.[14]

Plagge's men also described numerous individuals that Plagge personally saved from execution. There was the physician Dr. Baluk, who was arrested during the "provocation *aktion*" in 1941 but freed at the last moment before execution due to Plagge's intervention. Another physician, Dr. Wolfsohn, and his elderly father were arrested during an *aktion* carried out by the SS in the ghetto. Dr. Wolfsohn sent word to Plagge of his arrest and Plagge provided HKP work permits for both him and his father, even though neither of them were qualified workers. Here Lieutenant Stumpff describes a similar episode:

> The wife and children of one of our Jewish workers visited relatives in the so-called Ghetto B ("unusable Jews"), where they were arrested during a military police raid and brought to an extermination camp. In his despair the Jewish worker beseeched Major Plagge to save his family. He immediately went to the camp and after a long discussion with the commandant freed the worker's wife and children.[15]

14. Plagge denazification file, Appendix A, 205.
15. Plagge denazification file, Appendix A, 197.

HKP survivor Marek Swirski, who now lives in Israel, tells a dramatic story of how Plagge used deception to save his father David from the SS.

> I will describe here one significant episode, among others, which happened to my father.
>
> When leaving the kitchen after work one day, an SS officer searched a few Jews and found on my father and one other, some food hidden in their trousers. The SS man became furious and started screaming. He took out his pistol either to kill them or only to frighten them when suddenly Plagge saw the scene and came together with his driver and asked the SS to hand the Jews over to him. He said he intended to give them a proper lesson. The SS man accepted Plagge's offer. Plagge and his driver took the two Jews into a nearby barracks. He struck his whip on a table and asked the Jews to cry loudly and then had them cut their faces with a razor to draw blood. The two Jews, one of them my father, were then presented to the SS who allowed them to leave and return to the Ghetto.
>
> This episode really traumatized my father. He was very grateful to Karl Plagge, who again enabled him to escape the SS murderers with his life.[16]

During the two years of the Vilna ghetto from fall 1941 until September 1943, Plagge continued to engage in these life-and-death struggles with the SS and Gestapo over his workers and their families. He manipulated the rules established by the German bureaucracy to protect his workers. He gave them work permits, he freed them from prison and he fed them, all under the guise of trying to run an efficient vehicle repair operation. To the outside world he presented himself as a stern, earnest Prussian, intent on fulfilling his orders. Neither the SS nor many of his workers understood his true feelings and intentions; the latter seemed to sense that he was different, but unless they were among those who Plagge personally saved, they did not know for sure what he was up to. Plagge usually tried to act according to the regulations set up by the German occupying administration to protect himself from any potentially fatal accusations that he was working against the authorities. An example of these methods can be seen in an episode de-

16. Marek Swirski, who was an eight-year-old boy in the HKP camp, was discovered in Israel in 2003; upon the urging of the Plagge research group, he submitted this testimony to Yad Vashem.

scribed by Plagge where he successfully protected one of his officers from the charge of treason:

> At the beginning of 1944 one of my officers reported to me, as the disciplinary superior officer, that captain Plisch had said the following words during the previous evening: "One should shoot Adolf Hitler, the sooner the better." A witness of this statement was a certain paymaster named Mueller who was also a member of my unit. So, I found myself in a very difficult situation. On the one hand, I liked captain Plisch because he was an honest and decent character, but on the other hand, the accusation was quite serious. I feared that some officers would report it to a higher and more influential officer if I were to acquit him of that "crime." All soldiers of the German army knew the kinds of inhuman decisions and judgments that were given by the military courts to those who committed similar "crimes."
>
> Despite the danger, I decided to defend the captain and to protect him from his unhappy destiny, which would result in the death penalty because he openly expressed an opinion that many of us had thought about. First, I ordered paymaster Mueller to my office. I had a little discussion with him about what the consequences for captain Plisch would be—that he would have to go to the military court because his action promoted the "disintegration of the Wehrmacht." I discovered that paymaster Mueller was a like-minded man, which allowed me to put down the incident. But because the officer who reported the case wanted a better examination of the incident, we decided together what words to use as we drew up the protocol papers.
>
> The result of our discussion was a deposition that contained only diverse, unimportant expressions but not the incriminating ones as reported. I showed this protocol to the informing officer and told him that the incident was cleared up. But I also said to him that I was wondering how he could denounce a comrade who was careless. He hesitated and was angry, but in the end agreed with the document and declined further examination of the case. The incident was thus filed away and none of the three involved people spoke about it again.
>
> As the superior officer, this decision was very risky because the denouncing officer could always accuse me of high treason and tampering with witnesses. It had happened on occasion in similar incidents which

became known to other people by accident and that the superior office sent all involved people to the military court where they often faced severe sentences. Also, there was a high risk because the character of the denouncing officer was unfathomable. He himself was a heavy drinker who often said irresponsible words under the influence of alcohol and whose action then could never be predicted. But I took that risk because a breach of duty seemed to me quite less serious than to send a man to the military court where he would have to face the final decision.[17]

Through the years of the Vilna Ghetto, Plagge's manipulations were quite successful. He was able to establish a series of vehicle repair shops throughout Vilna as well as support services to keep his workers fed, clothed, and cared for medically. However, in the fall of 1943, the rules changed and Plagge's plans began to unravel when the SS decided to liquidate all the Jews in the Vilna Ghetto. They began with the Estonian *aktion* on September 1. Suddenly, no Jewish work permits were honored. Plagge discovered that not even he could safeguard his workers. Here is Sergeant Raab's description of that day:

> The military administration planned to deport about 100 people (men, women and children) to the slate mines in Estonia. They were already in a transport train when a friend of theirs informed Mr. Plagge. He immediately went to the train station and ordered them to leave the train, even giving them military protection. The highest SD officer of Vilna then arrived after Plagge left and ordered the military escort to bring them back in the train. They left for Estonia. Subsequently, there was a serious clash between Plagge and the SD officer. Plagge was very furious and desperate.[18]

Plagge could see that his methods of the previous two years were no longer sufficient. It was during this perilous time, just before the SS swept into the ghetto to deport the remaining Jews of Vilna, that Plagge achieved his biggest triumph on behalf of the HKP workers and their families: he formed a separate HKP labor camp on Subocz Street outside of the ghetto at the outskirts of town.

17. Plagge denazification file, Appendix A, 206–207.
18. Plagge denazification file, Appendix A, 204.

For years, HKP survivors have wondered how Plagge managed this miracle. Some HKP survivors thought that he traveled to the Lithuanian capital of Kovno to argue his case, others said that he went all the way to Berlin to lobby on behalf of his workers. The stories all agreed that Plagge spoke to his superiors to protest the planned killing of his skilled Jewish workers by the SS and proposed that he be allowed to form a special labor camp outside of the ghetto.

It was not until 2003, sixty years after the liquidation of the Vilna Ghetto, that Marianne Viefhaus found testimony by Plagge that illuminates his methods:

> When I learned that the Ghetto should be liquidated . . . I immediately consulted the SD and argued that the Jewish workers must be preserved for HKP. After consultation with the SD in Riga, this [HKP camp] was approved. I was obliged to accommodate them [the Jewish HKP workers] safely . . . I heard that the Ghetto was already surrounded. I therefore drove at night with trucks to the Ghetto entrance and, with the help of the Judenrat, succeeded in bringing out a large number of Jews from the Ghetto. A selection was not possible. About 800 Jews—men, women and children—were taken to HKP.[19]

This testimony confirms that the HKP camp was formed on Subocz Street due to Plagge's personal intervention. Through his actions the HKP Jews and their families were given a safe haven where they were to stay, relatively protected, for the next ten months. A week later the rest of Vilna's Jews were deported to Ponary and death camps throughout Poland, where almost all of them died before the end of the war.

During the ensuing nine months that the HKP camp on Subocz Street was operating under his command, Plagge managed to keep the majority of his inmates relatively safe from the SS. There were notable exceptions, namely when the runaway prisoners David Zalkind, his wife, and his child were killed in November 1943, followed by the killing of thirty-six Jewish

19. Bundesarchiv—Ludwigsburg, 204 AR 332/71. Plagge's testimony regarding this crucial period was found buried in the 1956 trial transcript of Nazi war criminal Karl Jaeger. Jaeger was the commander of Einsatzkommando 3 and head of the Security Police in Lithuania. His forces carried out most of the killing of Lithuania's Jews during the war.

women by Bruno Kittel and his SS troops. Most significantly, he was unable to prevent the "children's *aktion*" that occurred on March 27, 1944, while Plagge was on leave in Germany. Upon returning to his post in Vilna, he reportedly told the head Jewish representative in the camp, Nyona Kolysh, that if he had been present he may have been able to prevent this terrible *aktion* from occurring. This may have been wishful thinking on his part, as the children's *aktion* was carried out simultaneously throughout Lithuania. It is clear that, as the fortunes of war turned against the German Wehrmacht, their relative strength in their power struggles with the SS declined. Indeed, after the September 1943 formation of the HKP camp, there is no evidence that Plagge was able to prevent the SS from carrying out any of their deadly activities against his workers once they chose to act. Plagge commented on this in the following passage:

> I took upon myself a great deal of risk because I hindered the SD and the party in their actions. There were some serious clashes between the SD leadership and me. My superior office also reproached me for being too emotional and sentimental in my behavior towards the civil population. Because of my social actions, toward the end, they forbade all new measures I wanted to take.[20]

By fall and winter of 1943–44, it appears that Plagge had pushed the SS as far as he could without crossing the line into obvious treason. Looking back on those days, one wonders how he was able to continue to shield his workers without tipping off the authorities as to his true motivations. At his trial many of his former officers wondered aloud how he managed to avoid accusations from the Gestapo. Here Sergeant Raab comments:

> His actions in favor of Jews and foreign workers (Poles, Lithuanians) carried a high risk for him, because he often had serious conflicts with the dangerous SD. There was also the risk that different people were aware that he was helping and supporting enemies of the state.[21]

Plagge himself said only this:

> I myself was not in contact with the SD but had many difficulties with it. I wasn't liked very well there. But they didn't persecute me. When I

20. Plagge denazification file, Appendix A, 201–202.
21. Plagge denazification file, Appendix A, 205.

spoke with some of them personally they admitted the cruel things they were doing . . . all of them said they had orders to follow and they wouldn't act against orders.[22]

Regardless of whether he could have been prosecuted, as time passed and the fortunes of the Wehrmacht declined, Plagge's ability to act on behalf of his workers waned. By the time the Red army approached Vilna in July 1944, Plagge was unable to maneuver any longer within the Nazi hierarchy. He describes his situation:

> Due to the collapse of the front, the military administration dissolved the park and I was transferred to a military workshop which I took as a personal slight. I think the reason for the closing of the motor vehicle repair park had to do with the fact that my regiment commander accused me of being too soft in the treatment of my workers.[23]

In the end, all he could do was warn his workers about the dissolution of the HKP camp and the danger they faced from the SS once his unit was evacuated from Vilna. In a characteristic manner, he made his warning in broad daylight, in the very presence of *Oberscharfuehrer* Richter, the SS representative in the HKP camp. For approximately 250 of his prisoners, this warning would be lifesaving. Plagge's frustration at being unable to intervene to save his prisoners at the final hour is evident in the following testimony, given in 1956:

> When, in the summer of 1944, HKP was ordered to relocate to Eastern Prussia, we wanted to take the Jews with us . . . In the middle of the chaotic retreat I learned that there was a clearance gang of SD in the camp and that there was shooting . . . When I drove there, they refused me admission.[24]

After leaving Vilna in July 1944, Plagge felt totally alienated from the German war effort. He felt he had been betrayed by the Nazi Party and he felt guilty that he had not been able to save the majority of his workers from the

22. Plagge denazification file, Appendix A, 212.
23. Plagge denazification file, Appendix A, 202.
24. Bundesarchiv—Ludwigsburg, Besuch vom 23.07.–25.07.2003, 204 AR 332/71.

SS. He concentrated on trying to protect the men in his unit from harm during the last year of the war.

> The war and the sad development of the national-socialist system destroyed my ideals and even before the end of this terrible war I was deeply embittered towards all the people who deceived and tricked me, those who were responsible for the whole misery and hardship of the war. That was the reason why in 1945 I tried to prevent all bloodshed and destruction and led my whole division into American captivity.[25]

This last goal he was able to accomplish. Avoiding any and all fighting, he led his unit toward the American lines and surrendered to American forces on May 2, 1945, without the loss of a single man from his unit.

Two years later, at his denazification trial, he was surrounded by his men, who testified as to his exemplary conduct toward them and his prisoners. His men talked of their personal gratitude to Plagge, how he had protected them during the war. Then, unexpectedly, a woman arrived at the courthouse wanting to testify on behalf of some Jewish residents of the Displaced Persons camp at Ludwigsberg who were survivors of the HKP camp. The witness's name was Maria Eichamueller:

> I have to say the following words: Last Christmas I was in the DP camp at Ludwigsburg near Stuttgart. My girlfriend, whom I visited, knows the Jewish lawyer Dr Paula Zanker who is in charge of the Jews in the camp. Through the help of my girlfriend, Dr. Zanker asked me to look for a Mr. Plagge here in Darmstadt with the reason that there are different Jews in her camp who want to thank Mr. Plagge. They told her that Plagge had always cared about them and that he helped them in a difficult time. They want to support him with their food and money if he lived in misery. There is also a Jewish father in Stuttgart who says that Plagge saved his son's life. I immediately went to the police in Darmstadt to find Mr. Plagge when I came home. I found different Plagges but not the one I looked for. On Saturday I accidentally read in the newspaper that there is a trial with a Mr. Plagge going on. I immediately came here.[26]

According to witnesses of the trial who were later interviewed by Marianne Viefhaus, the court was initially quite skeptical of the testimony of

25. Plagge denazification file, Appendix A, 202–203.
26. Plagge denazification file, Appendix A, 217–218.

Plagge and his men. The witnesses said that the unexpected entrance of Mrs. Eichamueller to testify on behalf of Jewish HKP survivors was "like in a film" and had a dramatic effect on the judges and those present in the court-room.[27]

This news, that some of his former prisoners had sought Plagge out, expressing thanks and offering any assistance they give could to him, was a great relief for my mother. Since I first began my quest to find Plagge, she had been asking herself why she and her parents had not tried to find and honor him immediately after the war. She felt guilty and ungrateful for not acknowledging Plagge's lifesaving deeds decades before. I tried to reassure her that these feelings were entirely misplaced. In the years immediately following the Holocaust, survivors still had to concentrate on survival and starting new lives. In my mother's case, she and her parents escaped from Soviet-controlled Eastern Europe and became displaced persons in Italy after the war. After going to the University of Rome and meeting my father, she emigrated to the United States and started a new life in a new land. There was not the time nor the means to begin a search for a man whose full name she did not know, a man who may not have even been alive. Even so, after reading the denazification file, my mother was especially gratified to hear that Plagge himself might have gained some solace from the words and actions of those whom he saved.

Following the testimony of Plagge, his men, his friends from Darmstadt, and the representative of the Jewish prisoners in the Ludwigsburg DP camp, the court had to decide how to rule in the Plagge case. During denazification proceedings, the court could give one of five designations to the accused. Each designation had a corresponding level of punishment:

1. Main war criminals
2. Activists
3. Less burdened by guilt
4. Fellow travelers (hangers-on)
5. Not guilty

Looking back on this dramatic trial, I wondered whether Plagge had been acknowledged for being a true hero of anti-Nazi resistance during the war.

27. Marianne Viefhaus interview with Dr. Hans Madsen, Plagge's brother in-law, 2004.

After all, it was clear to me that if more Germans had acted like Plagge, the Holocaust would never have occurred. In postwar Germany many returning soldiers were claiming that there was nothing they could have done to prevent the slaughter, that they had to follow orders or possibly face fatal consequences. Joerg Fiebelkorn, who joined the new German army in the 1960s, says that his superiors all used this line to excuse their conduct during the war. In Karl Plagge we had a dramatic example of one who chose a different path. How would this be judged so soon after the war by Germans, many of whom had actively or passively helped the Nazis?

Before sentence was passed, we find in the trial transcript the prosecution and defense recommendations to the court. The prosecutor made no recommendation as to how the court should find the defendant, leaving it up to the court to decide. This implies that the prosecutor (whose job was to pursue and press charges against those responsible for the Nazi war crimes) felt that this defendant was innocent of any guilt. However, in a most puzzling turn of events, Plagge himself, through his lawyer, asks for a designation of group 4, "Fellow Traveler, Hangers-On."[28]

Following the prosecution and defense requests, the court gave the following opinion and verdict:

> Spruchkammer (denazification court) Darmstadt County, State of Hesse

> The leader of the court declared on February 9th, 1948 after sequestered consultation of the Spruchkammer laws . . . announce the following decision:

> The person in question, Karl Plagge, born 07–10–1897, living in Neunkirchen/Odenwald is classified in accordance with paragraph 12/I as hanger-on (fellow traveler).

> After paragraph 18/I he has to pay a unique extra payment of RM (Reichsmark, currency) 100.

The court judges give the following explanation for their ruling:

> During his military service there were many actions that could relieve the person in question from his burden. The incidents he described were

28. Plagge denazification file, Appendix A, 219.

not only confirmed by the former members of the Wehrmacht but also by the appearance of the witness Maria Eichamueller. His actions in favor of Poles and Jews would show resistance described in paragraph 13, if it could have proven that it was of anti-national-socialist nature. The help offered by the deported Jews in Ludwigsburg shows that the person in question participated in an uncommon manner in the saving of lives of persecuted people. The court observed that the person in question was not a persecutor nor a militarist nor a beneficiary of the Nazi regime in the sense of the law. He proved that despite his early participation in the Nazi movement that he later rejected its methods and ideals and that additionally, he fought against them. In the end, the court had to answer the question if the person in question would best fit in designation 5 or in designation 4. Resulting from the belief that the anti-national-socialistic motive of his actions is not proven, that most likely that his humanism was more important, the court finishes the trial with the categorization of the person in question into designation 4: fellow travelers or hanger-on. The reason is that he has to be seen through his attitude as a nominal member of the NS movement.[29]

In this opinion, we see the judges following a convoluted path trying to explain their verdict through legalistic hair splitting. The Spruchkammer law stated that a Nazi party member could be found "innocent" if his actions proved "anti-Nazi" beliefs. The judges, while acknowledging Plagge's unusual and exemplary conduct, justify their verdict of "Fellow Traveler" by asserting that his actions were made due to humanistic rather than the required anti-Nazi motivations!

In Germany, Salomon Klaczko and Joerg Fiebelkorn were furious with this outcome. Having studied the conduct of Wehrmacht soldiers for years, Joerg felt that it was clear that Plagge was unlike any other case he had ever encountered. One of the aberrations of the denazification process was the fact that the Allies used the German judicial system to conduct the trials. This was the same system, with the same judges presiding, as during the Nazi years. In impassioned emails, Joerg explained this paradox:

Unfortunately, the Allies believed that the German judiciary had been completely uncorrupted by Nazi ideology, with the result that all the Nazi

29. Plagge denazification file, Appendix A, 222.

judges, who had sentenced thousands to the death penalty for just being a Jew or having shown any resistance to the Nazi ideology, carried on as judges after the war. Not one German judge was put to trial—not one German judge was dismissed! As late as in the 70's the "governor" of the State of Baden-Wuerttemberg, Karl Filbinger, had to retire, because it became public that he had sentenced to death two young soldiers for "desertion" in a prisoners of war camp in August '45—three months after the surrender, not to speak about the many others, who were killed due to his judgments before May '45! These were the people who had to run the denazification trials.

Joerg felt that these same judges could see in Plagge a man whose actions put the rest of Germany to shame. To proclaim him innocent would have highlighted their own shortcomings during the war:

> It is a fact that many Nazis were rated "not guilty," while Karl Plagge was rated a "fellow traveler." He was the witness for the moral failing of so many others, particularly among the lawyers and judges.

Still, we have to puzzle about why Plagge himself asked to be declared a "fellow traveler." From the denazification file, we could see that he was not fond of "loud mouths and braggarts," as he described the Nazi officials he interacted with before the war in Darmstadt. Was it possible that he was just being humble? Those of us reviewing the file suspected that it was something more than mere modesty that prompted him to request this sentence. The designation of "fellow traveler" carried with it fines and court costs, not a trivial matter in the impoverished days after the war. In order for us to understand Plagge, his conduct during the war and his actions during the trial, we needed to learn more about Plagge's own thoughts, his motivations and feelings regarding what happened during the war.

Fortunately for our research group, Marianne Viefhaus was still hard at work at the Technical University of Darmstadt. On March 16, 2001, she announced another important find:

> Another piece of good news: I discovered the godson of Karl Plagge who is mentioned in the denazification file as born just after the pogrom of 1938, son of the friend and witness Kurt Hesse and his wife. Yesterday I called him . . .

Reading over the denazification file Marianne had remembered that in 1938, shortly after Kristallnacht, Plagge had become godfather to Kurt and Erika Hesse's newborn son Konrad in an effort to protect him and his family from anti-Jewish measures. Marianne had noted the name of this child and, following his archival records, traced him to a small town in southwestern Germany. From there it was a simple matter of looking up his name in the phone book and calling him. Konrad Hesse immediately agreed to help us with our research. He started by sharing something that had eluded us before: a picture of Karl Plagge. Konrad found a photo taken of Plagge at his own church confirmation celebration in 1952. Marianne quickly scanned the photo, attached it to an email, and sent it across the world to my mother and me. Finally, I was able to see the human face that went along with the name of a man I had been chasing all these months. Gazing into the eyes of the man appearing on my computer monitor, I was struck by how warm and friendly he seemed. I had always imagined him as a stern officer who carried himself with Prussian formality. Instead, I saw an almost shy looking man with an eager smile and caring eyes.

Konrad Hesse remembered Plagge very well. He was 19 years old in 1957 when his godfather had suddenly died of a heart attack, old enough to have personal recollections about Plagge's personality. It seemed to me that Konrad Hesse was as close as I was going to get to my dream of speaking with Plagge's family. I wrote him a letter, telling him of our search for Plagge and the many grateful people who owed their lives to his godfather:

Dear Mr. Hesse,

My name is Michael Good, I am the son of a Jewish woman from Vilna who during the Second World War was protected from genocide by your godfather, Karl Plagge. Since returning from a trip to Vilna that I made with my parents during the summer of 1999, I have been doing research trying to find out more about "Major Plagge," the man who my mother and her parents, as well as other survivors of the HKP work camp, credit with saving their lives. I have wanted to understand why he acted so differently from most of the other Germans that my family encountered during the war and to thank any relatives he might have for his bravery. While it does not appear that he has any direct descendants, you would appear to be, as his godson, the closest thing to a child that Karl Plagge had. It is thus to you that I would like to send words of acknowledgment and thanks for his good deeds . . .

Marianne told me that Konrad was very moved by my letter and the story of HKP survivors searching for Major Plagge and his descendants. He wrote back, speaking of his memories of Plagge and the lasting impression that his godfather made on him while he was growing up. Here are some excerpts of his letter:

Dear Mr. Good

My name is Konrad Otto Karl Hesse. I was born on 19th December 1938 in Darmstadt . . .

My third given name "Karl" refers to my godfather, Karl Plagge. The photograph, which you received via Mrs. Viefhaus, was made at the celebration of my confirmation in 1952.

Mr. Karl Plagge was, apart from Dr. Bruno Guenther, one of the two real friends of my parents. Before the war, my parents had a large circle of friends and acquaintances. However, in 1936, my father was confronted with the question as to whether he should separate himself from his non-Aryan wife or whether he would accept being excluded from all public offices, associations and clubs. My father decided for his wife.

This caused the loss of his "friends" and "acquaintances" with the exception of the two friends mentioned above, i.e. Plagge and Guenther.

My mother later explained to me what she had recognized in the following way, "People usually act cowardly, one like all, all like one. They only pretend to stand for the ideal of life, one for all, all for one . . ."

Mr. Karl Plagge personified the man who was carrying a heavy burden in respect of his subjectively felt, assumed guilt. During the initial years of the National-Socialist movement he had joined the party in good faith. The slogans of a romantic and idealistic character were tempting. In the misery of the German Reich the NSDAP seemed the only positive force for a new beginning. The reality, i.e. that criminals were acting for their own benefit and for criminal goals, became visible only at a later point in time. Even though Mr. Karl Plagge did everything in his power to limit damages by a human attitude once he had recognized this fraud and the reality, he was tortured by his conscience. In his view, it was not enough! He suffered because of this until his death.

And yet, my godfather remained true to himself. The crimes and murderous goals and deeds of this time did not constitute a proof and reason for him that everything German and Prussian was bad. Not all people of the bourgeoisie had been bad during that time, nor that only bad things had been done. My godfather lived for me in an exemplary fashion . . . [after living] under the most pronounced personal distress, [he wished] to orient all of one's strength towards the future and not to waste the power of life in lamentation and self-pity. The *future* of the people had to be *secured* . . .

According to the words of Luther, "My God, here I stand and can do no different" or "If my last day were tomorrow, I would still plant my tree today." [Karl Plagge] represented a humanity of noble chivalry and learned purity for the future of his beloved fatherland . . . [He stood for] the responsibility of the stronger in the sense of "only by the deed will the word become valuable," modesty, being prepared to follow one's conscience, the courage of one's convictions, reverence of women, families and the moral demands of the Ten Commandments.

Konrad then describes an episode when he was twelve years old and he attacked an older girl who had bullied and tormented him for years. Plagge reprimanded him severely, saying:

"A man has to be chivalrous, particularly towards ladies and those who cannot defend themselves. Otherwise he will remain a servant all of his life." Mr. Karl Plagge unfortunately died in 1957, long before I faced the challenges of life. But looking back to these years of my childhood and youth I remember; Mr. Karl Plagge personalized the stature and depth of a man who was committed to his own internal values . . .

I am grateful to my uncle that he showed me a way for my later life, which gave me the ability to live by following his ideals. This attitude geared to people, I have always endeavored to pass on to many, many people.

In this sense, Karl Plagge is still living among us today!
My very best wishes,

Yours
Konrad Hesse

Konrad's letter added flesh to the sketchy image I had of Karl Plagge. He was born in the nineteenth century and, having flirted with modern fascist thinking in the 1930s, returned to traditional values such as duty, honor, and protecting the defenseless. During his trial he said ". . . I did that because I thought it was my duty . . . I was ashamed." Here was a man who listened to his inner conscience. Plagge, along with the rest of Germany, had been seduced by Hitler and his promises. However he, unlike most Germans, was able to see his own folly and, in spite of the social pressures surrounding him, returned to his basic instincts, which told him what was right and what was wrong. Konrad tells us that, in spite of his efforts on behalf of his Jewish workers, Plagge was always filled with guilt over his role in helping bring the Nazis to power. Whatever good he did during the war, Konrad recalls that "in his view it was not enough!" Now we could understand his actions at the denazification trial. Plagge asked for the designation of "fellow traveler" because of his deep sense of guilt for having helped create the genocidal monster that he later struggled against. Thus we see that in the years after the war, in spite of all the testimony of his subordinates and friends, Plagge did not consider himself "innocent."

By spring of 2001, the German press began to discover the story of Karl Plagge thanks to an article Marianne Viefhaus had written for the Technical University of Darmstadt's newspaper. Several newspapers ran articles, and Marianne was interviewed by local TV affiliates, which aired stories during the evening news in Darmstadt and Frankfurt. Then *Der Spiegel*, the largest weekly newsmagazine of Germany, interviewed Marianne and me for a story about Plagge. He was called "the Schindler of Darmstadt." These stories were widely read throughout Germany, and in turn were then run in newspapers throughout Europe and North America. Marianne and I began to get calls from reporters around the world wanting to know more about this unusual high-ranking German officer who worked to save Jewish lives in the midst of the Holocaust. A question that was repeatedly posed was why no one had known of this story before; how could such a figure who had saved so many people have disappeared into obscurity?

A cousin of Karl Plagge's named Erika Vogel read some of the newspaper articles about him in Darmstadt and contacted Marianne. She told Marianne that she was twenty-three years younger than her cousin and had lived just down the street from Karl Plagge during the 1920s, when Karl and his wife Anke were living with his mother at 22 Hoffmanstasse. She and her children had not seen Karl since before World War II and were surprised to learn of his activities in Vilna during the war. The family had not known anything about his role in saving Jews. She said that the Plagges had once been a large and influential family in Darmstadt, but had gone into a sudden decline after World War II. Some sons were killed during the war, some family members were killed in the Allied bombing of Darmstadt and others either never married or, like Karl, did not have children. The result was that there were no other living relatives from the Plagge family other than Erika and another aging cousin living near Bonn. Mrs. Vogel had a picture of Karl Plagge which she agreed to send to Marianne. Soon a photo arrived of Karl Plagge, in his uniform with the rank of major. It appears to have been taken while he was on a leave from Vilna, probably during 1944. Unlike the smiling postwar photo supplied by Konrad Hesse, this photo shows an exhausted, almost haunted man. Gazing at this picture I thought I could see the pain and sorrow of the events in Lithuania deep in his eyes.

A Professor Wette from the University of Freiburg, who had been studying case histories of German soldiers who had resisted Nazi policies of genocide during World War II, contacted Marianne. He told her that in the course of his research he had come across two brothers from Vilna named Joseph and Isaac Reches. They were both physicians and had come to Germany in 1992 looking for a "Major Plagge." They said that this Major Plagge had saved their whole family in Vilna during the war. While Professor Wette was not able to help them to find Plagge or his family, he was interested in their story, which they wrote down for him in German. After realizing that Marianne and our group were investigating this same Plagge, Professor Wette sent the Reches brothers' story to Marianne. She emailed it to me and I asked Marcus Schneider to translate the document for me. I read it with great interest. The Reches told a familiar story—a family saved from the liquidation of the Vilna ghetto by a mysterious but benevolent Wehrmacht major. They told of being protected in the HKP camp and then of Plagge's warning that the SS was coming. This warning prompted the Reches family to hide from the SS. Like other survivors, they experienced days of hardship and terror while concealing themselves from the SS as the camp was liquidated. As to their current journey, Joseph Reches said:

> After the war my father tried intensively to find out what happened to this man who saved the lives of about 300 Jews. This search was impossible during the Soviet times. Now we try to execute our father's last will

and testament and we want to invite the children or relatives of Major Plagge to Vilna. He was a German Wallenberg . . .[30]

From this testimony, I could see that I was not the only one searching for Plagge. I began to wonder how many of Plagge's workers and their families had been trying to find him after the war. I knew that in 1947, Dr. Moses Feigenberg had corresponded with Plagge, but lost track of him upon immigrating to Israel. The HKP survivors from the Ludwigsburg DP camp who had testified for Plagge had lost contact with Plagge after they left the DP camp in the late 1940s. Now I could see that the Reches family had been looking for Plagge as well. It gave me some measure of comfort that I was not alone in my obsession to find this man, that other HKP survivors and their children had felt compelled to find him too. I could also see that what had made my search more successful than those carried out by the Reches brothers and others was the new power of the Internet, which allowed my query letters to be passed to hundreds of recipients around the globe. I feel certain that many of Plagge's prisoners had been looking for him and would have made contact with him if not for their dislocation as refugees and the barriers that were quickly erected between east and west by the cold war.

After hearing about the Reches brothers, I decided to try to personally interview as many HKP survivors as I could find. I wanted to hear their recollections of HKP and of Karl Plagge and collect as much testimony as possible in order to document what had happened in Vilna and the HKP camp. I expected to hear stories similar to those told by my mother, grandfather and Bill Begell, who seemed to view their time at HKP as relatively benign, especially when compared to what had happened to Jews in the ghetto. The three of them certainly felt that they owed their lives to Plagge. Both Bill and my mother had rebuilt their lives and were able to look at the world and their subsequent lives in a positive way. However, as I called other HKP survivors in Montreal, Toronto, and New Jersey, I found that each one had coped in their own way and many could not look back with any semblance of composure. Many of the HKP survivors I talked to were deeply scarred by their wartime experiences, including their time at HKP. Some were hesitant to discuss the war years; talking about the war was too painful

30. Testimony of the Reches brothers, http://www.hometown.aol.com/michaeldg/plagge-reches.doc.

for them. Many had lost their mothers, fathers, or siblings. Some were the only survivors of their family. As I interviewed them, some had trouble holding back their tears. I could tell that even sixty years later they were fragile, that these memories were very difficult for them to unearth. My mother and grandfather had told of some of the violent events that occurred during their time at HKP: the execution of the Zalkinds and their daughter, the children's *aktion* and the final days before liberation. But they told of these events in a calm voice, speaking to posterity. As I interviewed other HKP survivors, I began to feel the raw terror that was present at these violent episodes; the emotions they evoked could still be felt in these former prisoners as they told their stories today. I began to realize that the portrayal of HKP and Plagge that I had heard from my parents and grandparents represented one perspective, but after talking to other HKP survivors, I could see that other, darker points of view existed as well.

Harold T[31] from New Jersey was particularly traumatized by two events. He vividly remembers how the prisoners were forced to watch the execution of David Zalkind and his wife along with their child after their runaway attempt in November 1943. He recalled that another prisoner named Schneider was chosen and forced to perform the hanging. The victims forgave Schneider, saying that they knew he had no choice. The first two times that Zalkind was hung, the rope broke. Zalkind begged for his life, saying it was the law that if a hangman's rope broke that the condemned man should be spared. Ignoring his pleas, Bruno Kittel of the Gestapo shot him in the back of the head. Forced to watch the executions all the prisoners were told that if they shed tears, they would be killed as well. Harold had to help dig the graves and cover the bodies with lime. Harold, along with all of the HKP inmates, was also very traumatized by the children's *aktion*. He told me his recollections of how the Lithuanian guards came into the camp and captured the children. He still remembers them grabbing the children by the feet and swinging them into the trucks. He became choked up as he described how the children often hit their heads when they landed in the truck beds. He says he has carried the memories of the Zalkind executions and the Children's *aktion* with him all of his life. They remain painful to him to this day. When a local rabbi asked him to tell his story to a class, he declined because the memories were too difficult to revisit. Still, he said that compared to

---

31. Here and going forward, I have changed the names of HKP survivors who are not part of the Plagge Research Group in order to protect their privacy.

places like Auschwitz, HKP was "a picnic." As we spoke, he seemed almost embarrassed that he was so scarred by his memories when there were so many other Holocaust survivors who had gone through experiences that were far worse.

Sarah K, who also lives in New Jersey, says that she was fourteen years old when the Children's *Aktion* occurred. She was initially taken by the Lithuanian guards and was being led to the truck that was taking the children to their deaths when an SS man grabbed her out of line and threw her aside. When she tried to get up she was clubbed in the head with a rifle butt. In the end she was spared, she thinks, because she looked old enough to work.

Aaron P from New York recalls that the day after Plagge's speech he gave his place in a carefully constructed maline to his sister, brother-in-law, and their two children. Tragically, this maline was betrayed to the SS by a Jewish collaborator, Nika Dreyzen, and all the Jews hiding there were killed. He also carries traumatic memories of several of his friends and family members being shot and killed after they, like Bill Begell, jumped out of the blacksmith's window and ran from the camp. Aaron recalls how his mortally wounded sister-in-law begged them to leave her so they could save themselves. Several days later after liberation he came back to look for her, but to his sorrow found only her body decomposing in the summer heat.

Nathan S from Montreal recalled a day when he and his work detail from the carpentry shop were a few minutes late for work. He says that the sergeant in charge of the carpentry shop, a vicious man, beat all twenty-five prisoners with a nightstick, one at a time. Mr. Fein, one of the best carpentry workers, was badly beaten and took more than a week to recover. Nathan was at the end of the line and thus was one of the last to be assaulted. The sergeant was tired after beating so many others so his blows lost their power, and thus Nathan was not badly hurt.

After talking with these survivors, I began to see that living in HKP was no picnic. Regardless of whether one thought that Major Plagge was trying to protect them, he obviously did not have control over the actions of the SS. Living under the constant threat of the SS coming into the camp was terrifying in and of itself. Anyone who witnessed cold-blooded executions and the killing of children must have been severely traumatized by what they saw. Through my talks with the HKP survivors I could see that many carry the memory of HKP as a terror-filled, grim place that haunts them to this day.

With regard to Plagge and his intentions, the opinions of the HKP survivors were quite varied. While they all agreed that the formation of the HKP camp on Subocz Street had saved their lives, some thought that Plagge had engineered its formation, while others thought that it would be impossible for a captain (his rank in 1943) to have pulled off such a feat. This latter group felt that the Wehrmacht must have had its own reasons for saving HKP, but doubted that Plagge had done it on his own. Others agreed with my mother and grandfather that it was Plagge who thought up and arranged their transfer before the liquidation of the ghetto.

When asked whether they thought Plagge was trying to save his Jewish prisoners, there was again a wide range of opinions. One group found it unbelievable that any German would consciously try to save a Jew. Based on their experiences in the Vilna ghetto and in HKP, they felt that all Germans were vicious killers. Plagge seemed less bad, but being a German, they could not imagine that he was fundamentally different, just less bad than the rest.

To illustrate how perspectives differed among HKP survivors, one can look at the stories of how Plagge freed prisoners from Lukishki prison after they had been captured in the ghetto. At his denazification trial Plagge's men described this as having been an act of bravery. The Jews from the Ludwigsburg DP camp whose representative testified at Plagge's denazification trial also made reference to how Plagge saved lives in such a manner. Nathan S had another perspective. He said freeing prisoners from Lukishki was not an uncommon practice, even outside of HKP. He said that the Lithuanian police frequently arrested Jews they came upon, often ignoring their papers. If the Jew worked for a Wehrmacht workshop, and his German supervisors heard that one of "their Jews" had been grabbed, they frequently would go to the prison and free them if they came in time. If they came too late, the Jew would have already been sent to Ponary and killed. Nathan likened it to dogcatchers catching stray dogs and taking them to the pound. If the owners claimed them in time, they could be set free, if the owner was late, the dog was killed. As Nathan described things, in the Vilna Ghetto, the Jews played the roles of stray dogs, the Lithuanians were dogcatchers, and the German soldiers acted as dog owners. It was not only Plagge who sent his men to fetch Jews from prison; this was also done by many of the German workshops who did not want to lose a skilled worker. In Nathan's mind the stories told at the denazification trial did not necessarily indicate that Plagge was extraordinary in his desire to save his Jewish workers, but rather that he, like other Wehrmacht officers, did not want to lose a skilled worker.

Others felt that Plagge was indeed trying to save his workers. Vera T from New Jersey typified this group. Vera said that Plagge was distinctly different from the other Germans. First, he was not SS or Gestapo, but Wehrmacht, which was different. Vera says that all the Gestapo and SS men were killers. Vera thought that Plagge actually wanted to save his workers. She and other HKP workers thought he was doing what he could to save them. "He did what he could . . . if he could have done more, he would have."

Aaron P felt strongly that Plagge was actively trying to save his workers. He said, "Plagge was a very good man, a 100% friend of the Jews. He gave work not only to mechanics but to any Jew who applied at HKP without any questions." He had heard stories that after the liquidation of the Vilna Ghetto, Plagge was approached by some of the HKP Jews asking that he try to save 110 Jewish men who had been captured by the SS. Aaron reported that Plagge arranged to have these doomed men brought into the camp[32]. Aaron told me that in his mind, Plagge was a real gentleman, "like a father to the Jews" who did everything he was able to save his workers. Unfortunately "in the end, it was not enough" and most of the workers were killed by the SS. However, he feels that Plagge "did what he could." When asked whether he thought Plagge took risks in helping his workers, Aaron replied, "any German who tried to help Jews was taking a risk."

Nathan S also thought that Plagge was trying to save his workers, but he observed that Plagge did so only by working within the rules. He explained that high-ranking German officers had a fair amount of leeway in what they did and said. They were safe as long as they did not disobey orders. Nathan was unsure if Plagge took any risks to protect his workers. He thinks that the Gestapo may have known that Plagge was protecting his Jewish workers, but tolerated this as long as he did not go too far. Nathan thought that Plagge did indeed argue with the Gestapo command to form the HKP camp

32. Nathan P's testimony is corroborated in recently discovered documents found by Marianne Viefhaus in Ludwigsburg, Germany. These documents reveal testimony from the trials of Nazi war criminals in which Jews describe how, after the liquidation of the Vilna ghetto, 110 Jews were discovered in hiding and were slated for execution by the SS. After Kolysh, the Jewish head of the HKP work camp, appealed to him for help to save these 110 Jews, Plagge made up what is clearly a fabricated "emergency" repair job which he claimed would require 200 workers. Through this act he succeeded in bringing these 110 Jewish prisoners into the HKP camp, saving them from imminent death. See also testimony of Elias Gurewitz Bundesarchiv—Außenstelle Ludwigsburg -Postfach 114471611 Ludwigsburg, 204 AR 332/71 p 1471–97. This same incident is also described by Yitzhak Arad in *Ghetto in Flames* (Holocaust Library, 1982), 443.

before the liquidation of the ghetto. He thinks that the SS agreed because after the liquidation of the ghetto they needed a few Jews around to justify their own existence. He explained that if there were some residual Jews in the area for them to watch, they would be allowed to stay in Vilna, keeping their cushy jobs well behind the front lines.

Of all the HKP survivors I talked to, Nathan S had the most contact with Plagge. Harry was 16 when the Germans came to Vilna; he and his family were taken to the ghetto along with the rest of Vilna's Jews. He got a job at HKP and was put to work in an animal barn set up by Plagge outside of the ghetto. At the barn, he helped raise and care for Angora rabbits (about 200) whose fur was shaved, baled, and then sent back to Germany by Plagge. Additionally, there were cows, pigs, and other animals raised to supplement the food rations of the Wehrmacht soldiers. He recalled that Plagge often came by to check on the barn to see how the operation was running. He didn't think that any of the food used in this barn went to feed the prisoners, but was for the German Wehrmacht personnel only. He said the prisoners were very hungry, even malnourished, but were able to buy some extra food from the guards or from Poles whom they met coming back from the HKP workshop. Prisoners were fed a lunch at the HKP workshop consisting of rehydrated peas and chunks of bread, about half a bowl full. In contradiction to the claims of Plagge's quartermaster at the denazification trial, Nathan says there was no meat. However, unlike in the Vilna ghetto, where those caught smuggling food were severely punished, in HKP the black market was openly allowed. He says that the only truly well-fed prisoners were the kitchen workers, who diverted food for themselves and also to sell. He said the kitchen workers were "fat like horses."

Initially, there was not a lot of work for the prisoners, as Plagge had given permits to as many Jews as possible without regard to HKP's actual manpower requirements. Some of the prisoners were woodworkers and cabinetmakers, so Plagge set up a woodworking shop and had them make furniture, which Nathan says was very nice and which he thinks Plagge shipped home to his family. Nathan thought that both the rabbit fur and the furniture were for Plagge's personal benefit. He recalls that Plagge had a temper as well. In one episode, Plagge had one of the prisoners, a shoemaker named Mr. Zachs, make him a pair of leather boots. However, when he tried the boots on they did not fit. This may have been because of the difficulties fitting his polio-crippled foot. Plagge became angry with the shoemaker and began yelling at him for wasting good leather.

These interviews with HKP survivors painted a different, more complicated picture of Plagge and the HKP camp than the one that I had been formulating during the previous two years. Why was there such a wide variation in the perceptions of the HKP prisoners? Some, like my grandfather, Bill Begell, the Reches family, and Aaron P viewed Plagge as a hero who actively tried to save Jewish lives, while others had no awareness of such a motivation and found this thought to be a new and startling one. My grandfather as well as Plagge's men described a HKP camp where Plagge prohibited cruelty against the prisoners and tried to furnish more food for them. Yet some of the prisoners described savage beatings by their guards and said that they were always hungry, on the edge of starvation. Plagge's men testified that their commander took extraordinary measures to free prisoners destined for execution. Some of the survivors reported that this was a widespread practice and had to do more with maintaining workshop efficiency than any humanitarian motives. Whose description of HKP was correct? The relatively idyllic one provided by my mother, my grandfather, and Bill Begell as well as Plagge and his men during the denazification trial, or the grim visage of HKP described by some of the other survivors of the camp?

Several months and hundreds of emails passed between the members of the Plagge research group and me as we discussed these issues. Given the differences in perception and memory that one faces when interviewing any set of witnesses, it is difficult to reconcile the varying versions of events that people carry with them into the future. When dealing with 60-year-old memories of the Holocaust, being certain is all but impossible. However, after sifting through the HKP survivor's personal accounts and comparing them to what historical documents we have, I have formed my own thoughts on the divergent opinions revealed by my HKP survivor interviews.

Let us look first at the issue of food distribution. In the denazification trial transcript, Plagge and his men spent considerable time discussing how they tried to procure extra food for the HKP workers, both before and after the liquidation of the ghetto. Plagge's quartermaster emphasized how worried Plagge was about the nutrition of his workers and recounted how Plagge worked to supply extra food to both his Jewish and Polish workers. Nathan S scoffs at the quartermaster's claim that the meat from the pigs, cows, and horses he cared for were used to help feed the prisoners, saying that the prisoners were given no meat, that it all went to the Wehrmacht troops. Joerg Fiebelkorn supports this view, saying that it was Wehrmacht policy that units in the occupied territories were fed using local resources, usually at the expense of the local population. Obviously, Plagge's first duty was to feed his men. However, it is clear that Plagge provided food supplies in addition to the rations allowed to civilians by the German occupying administration. Rations for Poles were at near starvation levels, and those for Jews were below subsistence levels. In most of the camps and ghettos throughout Europe, great efforts were made to prevent food smuggling. As a result, there was widespread starvation. However, in HKP there was a flourishing black market for extra foodstuffs; Plagge even allowed a "store" for black market provisions to exist within the HKP camp from which prisoners could buy extra food. Virtually all of the HKP survivors recall that there was an active black market in HKP and that both the prisoners and their guards profited from it. Thus, a prisoner's level of hunger depended on how much money he had; those with money were able to buy what food they needed, while the poorer workers had to get by on the basic starvation rations plus what extra calories Plagge was able to supply through his food supplement system. My family also testified to the fact that money was an important factor in the hunger equation within the camp. I recall the story of my grandmother's concern, as she and my mother were being driven toward the black van by Kittel and his men after the execution of the Zalkins, for getting the gold cigarette case hidden in her girdle to my grandfather. She worried that without these valuables he might be destitute and hungry. In the end, unlike most Nazi-run camps and ghettos, no one starved to death at HKP. Plagge did succeed in providing food for his own troops and enough extra calories for his workers to protect them from death by starvation. Thus the Jews of HKP avoided a fate so many others succumbed to in Nazi-occupied Europe, even if they were not able to afford to buy food supplements from the camp's black market.

Then there is the issue of how the prisoners were treated. Plagge testified that he explicitly instructed his men to treat the HKP prisoners with civility and respect. His men in their depositions and trial testimony corroborated this as well. My grandfather specifically commented on the fact that Plagge influenced the atmosphere within the camp in a benevolent way.

Lieutenant Stumpff testified about the disciplining and transfer of the abusive sergeant from Wiesbaden after he was caught beating a Jewish prisoner. Given all this, what are we to make of Nathan S's account of the beating that was given to 25 prisoners in his workshop for being a few minutes late for work? The answer is, in my opinion, that all of the testimonies, that of my grandfather, Lieutenant Stumpff, and Nathan S, are true. HKP was, after all, like a small town, with 1,250 Jews and 250 soldiers. Plagge had contact primarily with his officers and made it clear to them how he wanted things to be done in the HKP camp and workshops. He made efforts to gather a group of officers into his unit who would be sympathetic to his views and would try to carry out his instructions. However, just because the officers of HKP wanted things done in a certain way does not mean that in actuality that was how it always turned out. While violent episodes by Plagge's Wehrmacht troops did occur, it appears to me that they were relatively rare. The two instances described by Lieutenant Stumpff and Nathan S are the only two episodes of violent brutality being committed by Plagge's own men that I have encountered. It is even possible that the sergeant mentioned in both stories is in fact the same man. Within the 250 soldiers in the HKP unit there were undoubtedly some with sadistic tendencies, and in a prisoner/guard setting the sadists are at a distinct advantage. However, in HKP the sadistic guards could not be too overt; their activities had to be hidden from the officers and Plagge. As a result, most of the violence and brutality that occurred within the camp was committed by the SS and Lithuanian guards, not by Plagge's Wehrmacht troops.

Next we turn to the question of personal gain. Nathan S describes how he worked raising angora rabbits, shearing their wool and bundling it up. He thinks that Plagge sent this wool home to his wife. Similarly, in the carpentry shop some of the workers were ordered to make furniture, whose destination was unclear. Nathan personally saw that Plagge ordered a pair of custom-made leather boots to be made and then became angry when they didn't fit. Rabbits, furniture, boots—was Plagge engaged in the exploitation of slave laborers for his own personal gain? Some could postulate that Plagge's supposed benevolence in saving his Jewish workers actually served the purpose of lining his own pockets. When I first interviewed Nathan S and heard these stories, I had difficulty reconciling these seemingly self-serving actions with my image of Plagge as the righteous officer defending his prisoners from the bloody excesses of the SS. However, over time I began to understand these stories from a different perspective. Looking at the big picture, Plagge's various work projects can be seen in a context other than greed. In fact recent documents reveal that these projects were part of an ingenious scheme devised by Plagge to keep his Jewish workers employed and out of the hands of the SS.

Plagge and his men testified that he gave work permits to large numbers of Jews who had no skills applicable to the vehicle repair work that HKP was supposed to perform. Having given all these people work permits, he could not very well have had them loitering about looking idle. Plagge and his men were under the jurisdiction of the SS, who oversaw the upkeep and care of slave workers in their vast network of slave labor camps across Europe. SS officers often came into the HKP workshops to inspect operations there. Unemployed Jews were earmarked for extermination by the SS, they certainly were not going to spend resources on the hungry mouths of prisoners who did not even contribute labor to the Third Reich. So, Plagge put these Jews to work in barns, carpentry shops, kitchens, and gardens. During the winter of 1944 Plagge set up clothing repair workshops for the women and older children. Their labor was "rented out" to private German contractors who were paid by the Wehrmacht to repair clothing for the army. The end result was that everyone in the HKP workshops and camp was busy doing things. Any visiting observer making a casual inspection would see that all of Plagge's prisoners were diligently working for the benefit of the Wehrmacht. The fact that their efforts had nothing to do with vehicle repair would be difficult to discern from a superficial tour. Fortunately for Plagge, the administration and accounting for all the slave workers in the camp was extremely complex. There were overlapping jurisdictions and layers of control between the SS, the Wehrmacht, and private companies that were contracted to oversee some of the work. As long as he was able to keep his workers employed in some capacity, and as long as the SS profited from that labor, they would turn a somewhat blind eye to the fact that each HKP worker was not really vital to the war effort. Rather than being motivated by self-gain, it seems clear that many of the products such as cabinets and rabbit fur were a necessary by-product of having given many more work permits to Jewish workers than HKP actually could legitimately use for car repair work alone.

In the spring of 2003 more documents emerged from Vilnius that support the hypothesis that Plagge tried to manipulate the vast Nazi bureaucracy to make room in the camp for the many workers who really had no skills. Researchers at the Vilna Gaon Jewish State Museum, while searching through a box of documents marked only as "1943–1944" at the Lithuanian

State Archives, found a series of three letters between Plagge, the Commander of the Kaunas concentration camp, and the Vilna quartermaster's office. The letters were apparently written following orders to all Jewish labor camps in Vilna that nonessential workers be transferred to the Kaunas concentration camps under the jurisdiction of the SS Economic Services. Plagge undoubtedly was aware that a trainload of 4,000 Jews from Belarus, who were supposedly being sent by the SS to work in Kaunas, were actually taken to Ponary and shot. Thus, when orders arrived that the women and children at the HKP camp should be transferred to Kaunas, he understood the implications of such an order and began to look for ways to keep them in his camp. In general, the SS had two competing sets of motivations when dealing with Jewish prisoners. First was their ideological bent to destroy the Jewish race, sending all Jews to their deaths at Ponary. However, there was also a competing profit motive for SS commanders, as the SS "rented" out the services of Jews under their jurisdiction to the Wehrmacht and private German firms who used slave labor. This resulted in the possibility of large sums of money being funneled into the coffers of the SS and its leaders. Both of these competing motivations played into Plagge's approach to bargaining with the SS.

In studying the letters, it appears that Plagge had a verbal discussion with the commander of the Kaunas concentration camp, SS-Obersturmbanfurher Goeke, about his desire to keep the women working for two clothing repair firms (named Reitz and Herbert Meier) within his own HKP camp. Plagge proposed to Goeke that all prisoners at the HKP labor camp at 34 Subocz Street be made available to the Wehrmacht for any work that arose in Vilna, be it in the vehicle repair shops, or in clothing repair work. Interestingly, Plagge posited a system whereby the control and allocation of workers for different jobs would be controlled by the Wehrmacht, but the "rent" for the workers would continue to flow to the SS. The money to pay for the workers would come either from the Wehrmacht or the private firms that worked for it. He emphasized that keeping the women in Vilna would also greatly enhance the moral and productivity of the essential skilled work of the men employed by HKP in the vehicle repair works. Plagge's proposal would put control of the women prisoners in the hands of the Wehrmacht bureaucracy, rather than that of the SS. In this first letter, maneuvering to counter Plagge's proposal, Goeke writes to Plagge, first pointing out the problem of having unproductive prisoners who are a burden to the local quartermaster's headquarters and then making a counterproposal that would protect his "turf" and keep the women firmly under SS control:

Copy
Kaunas Concentration Camp's Commandant's Office
File No.: Arb.Eins. 16/2. 44-Au February 8, 1944

Concerning Employment of Jewish Workers
Based on Jan. 13, 1944 verbal discussions
Enclosed: 3 requests[33]
To whom: K.P./Ost/562
Vilna

Resuming the discussion during the inspection of work places with Major Plagge, referring to Jewish workers employed for the Reitz firm, Please bear in mind that:

It is impossible to deny that the prisoners for Reitz and Herbert Meier are a burden for the local headquarters. As previously, it is plausible that K.P./Ost/ has been trying successfully to find a productive occupation for the prisoners who cannot be employed in the vehicle workshops. Since it cannot be otherwise, when you pay for the work power to K.P./Ost and to the firms, please present urgently new requests written on enclosed forms to the local Commandant's office, to bring new work power to the K.P./Ost vehicle workshops.

In the request the only persons to be mentioned are the prisoners who really work there. The K.P./Ost must make a list for the Reitz and Herbert Meier firms, stating how many and what kind of workers are working in these firms' repair and knitting workshops, because the firms present separate applications. The remaining work power is distributed in percentage to the three employers, for those are prisoners who are not useful for the functioning and maintenance of the camp. Therefore, all three employers should share their maintenance expenses.

On this occasion, we ask to send SS-Unterscharführer Richter to the firms with the requests to enable final examination of the requests upon their reception.

33. The appendix has not been found in the archives.

Please settle the above mentioned situation urgently.

Signature: SS-Obersturmbanfuhrer and Camp Commandant Goeke
Signature: F.d.R.d.A. Captain and Adjuvant[34]

In the second letter, Plagge writes to the quartermaster's unit (Army
Lodging Services HUV 190), who must allocate funds to pay for the women's
upkeep while they work in his camp. In the letter he argues against the SS
proposal that the HKP women be put under the direct control of the SS-run
Kaunas concentration camp (which might or might not leave them in Vilna,
depending on the murderous whims of the SS). He warns that transferring
the women away from HKP would devastate the productivity of the essential
vehicle repair work done at HKP, as his workers' "willingness to work and
enthusiasm" depended on their wives and children being protected with
them in the HKP camp:

Car Park (Ost) 562
File No.: 12069/44

O.U., February 14, 1944

Received February 18 1944
Concerning: Employment of Jewish work power
Based on: doc. Issued by the Commandent of the Kaunas concentration
camp
File No. arb. Eins. 16/2 44-Au. For K.P./Ost/562

Addressed to: Army 190 Lodging Services
Vilna

The Vilna Jewish ghettos, having been liquidated, the Car park/Ost/562
protested urgently to the superior SD leadership in Riga (Oberfuhrer
Piffrader) and therefore achieved that approximately 500 Jewish skilled
workers be left for K.P.O. 562 park's vehicle repair works on the
condition that they work in a closed concentration camp.

The Jewish workers' willingness to work and enthusiasm depended
primarily on leaving in Vilna not only the men, but also their wives and

34. "The HKP Jewish Labor Camp, 1943–1944," publication of the Vilna Gaon
Jewish State Museum, 2002, document no. 15, 80.

children. Therefore, upon consulting the SD services and receiving their explicit approval, it was decided that the wives and children would be left in Vilna and transferred to the labor camp on Subotch street. Presently, there are 1243 Jewish persons in the labor camp: 499 men, 554 women and 190 children.

With the aim of finding urgently jobs for the women who are not occupied at work, we found employment for them. We consequently consulted upon coordinating the question with the Military Economy Services Vilna Branch (Captain Klipfl). 311 women are working on army and air force's orders for clothing, for the Reitz Uniform-Sewing factory and Herbert Meier's at the labor camp, where the firms have placed their machines and equipment for sewing blankets, coats, stockings and other housewares.

In November, the concentration camp K.P./Ost/562 was transferred to a different administration, according to the regulations for all Eastern concentration camps. It was taken over by the main office of SS Economy Services D2 in Oraniewnburg- Berlin, and came to be submitted to the Kaunas Concentration Camp. From that time on, all workers have been allocated upon demands of the corresponding headquarters. In this case, the workers have been allocated for K.P.O. 562, presenting the account for 4 Reichsmark for one worker specialist, 3 RM for an auxiliary worker, 3 RM for a female worker specialist, and 2.5 RM for a female auxiliary worker. All the money orders which are received are being handed over to H.U.V. 190. The latter transfers the money and/or verifies the bill accounts.

The Kaunas concentration camp, in its letter from Feb. 8, 1944 (the copy of which is enclosed), has been asking up to this date for separate requests for the workers employed at the car workshops and those working for the firms. The firms now have to present the requests personally.

The Park sees a danger in the fulfillment of these official regulations, since now the SS can freely dispose of the female workers and use them for works outside their place of residence, for instance at the Kaunas concentration camp. This may happen for lack of material for the camps firms, which need little work power. Therefore, having certain supplies or for other reasons, the SS may regard the work in Vilna less urgent than work elsewhere.

This contradicts the idea of maintaining the male K.P.O. 562 workshops workers' interests and willingness to work, keeping them together with their wives. Additionally, the Vilna military unit is deprived of the best and most valuable work power. The Park suggests the following:

The H.U.V. 190 in Vilna requests all labor camp's male and female Jewish workers from the main SS Economy Office, and regulates the distribution of these workers according to Office's needs in Vilnius, i.e., for the army and air force clothing enterprises, in which case the firms Reitz-Uniformwerke and Herbert Meier will not be forgotten. The K.P./Ost/562 also orders the specialists from H.U.V. 190 and then pays compensation to H.U.V. We would like to ask you for an essential solution, to verify whether the suggestion of K.P.O. 562 will be accepted.

Major and Park Chief
Signature Plagge[35]

Unfortunately, the local Wehrmacht quartermaster's office (H.U.V. 190) rejected Plagge's proposal, saying that their office did not have the manpower to administer the arrangement proposed by Plagge.

Project!
Army Lodging Services 190
Vilna, February 21, 1944
File No. 27d
Concerning: Using Jewish workers
Based on local letter from Feb. 17, 1944, Br.B. No.12069/44
To: Car Park Ost 562
Vilna

The Administration does not agree with the suggestion made in the aforementioned letter, for lack of the necessary workers.
Therefore, we ask you to contact the Military Economy Vilna Branch, for it has a better orientation in finding employment for Jewish workers by interested entities, such as the army and anti-aircraft defense, as well as private firms. On certain conditions, this organization would be able to establish the contacts to take the labor camp over.

35. "The HKP Jewish Labor Camp, 1943–1944," publication of the Vilna Gaon Jewish State Museum, 2002, document no. 16, 86.

Joerg Fiebelkorn explains the meaning of this exchange between Plagge and Goeke and the Wehrmacht bureaucracy:

> It goes without saying (to me) that Plagge knew that the SS would take any chance to get hold of anyone whom they saw "unemployed"—even against the interest of the Wehrmacht. Therefore Plagge tried to convince the Wehrmacht administration that it would be preferable to have the women of the HKP-workers available for any kind of work at any time and without administrational troubles like setting up daily lists for the request for labor force at the SS. Plagge proposed a new system, which would have given him the power to employ and save all at the HKP camp on Subocz street . . . Plagge's proposal is simply aimed at a complete hand over—or kind of "rent-out" of all inmates of Subocz Street to the pertinent local administrational body of the Wehrmacht. This would have drawn Subocz Street away from SS-supervision. Unfortunately HUV did not accept the proposal. Their statement "we do not have the manpower . . ." not only included the need for additional administrational work by the Plagge proposal, but also for the guards for Subocz Street, which in this case would have become the duty of HUV and Wehrmacht men. . . . To my impression SS officer Goeke somehow mistrusted all the beautiful arguments of Plagge, supposing some deals between Plagge and the uniform manufacturers out of his direct control and against his never ending zeal to get hold of any "unuseful" worker for Ponary. And although disguised by the bureaucratic language, the mistrust of SS-officer Goeke is seen in the threatening undertone in his letter to Plagge. It was a clear "affront" to Major Plagge and therefore the proof for the mistrust, to send a low ranking sergeant, Richter, to control the handling of the name-lists at HKP and the uniform works.

In the end, Plagge's complex attempts to gain full control of his Jewish workforce failed. The Jewish HKP workers, their wives and children stayed under SS Control. While the wives and children of the HKP workers did remain at his camp through the winter of 1944, he was not able to protect the children who were taken by the SS during the Children's *Aktion* on March 27, 1944. However, Plagge did succeed in keeping over 500 relatively nonessential women (as well as a few "illegal children" who remained in hiding) in the protection of his camp until the Russian Army approached Vilna in July 1944. Through these letters we have documentary evidence of Plagge's

heroism at work. Obviously he took great care not to show his true intentions to the murderous SS; thus his steps are quite difficult to follow. Indeed,
even with a team of historians, translators, and former army officers to help,
it is difficult when first looking at these letters to figure out what is going
on. However, with careful study, Plagge's methods emerge. These letters
speak to the complex political and bureaucratic waters that Plagge navigated
as he tried to keep his workers and their families away from the fate designated by the SS for Vilna's Jews: execution at Ponary.

While historical perspective and access to letters and documents discovered in archives has allowed us to understand what Plagge was trying to
accomplish in his work camp, one question that my interviews with HKP
survivors raised was the riddle of why there was such a difference in perception among the HKP survivors regarding Plagge's motivations and the extent
of his efforts on their behalf. While my grandfather, mother, Moses Feigenberg, the Reches family, the refugees at the Ludwigsburg DP camp, Bill Begell,
and Aaron P all strongly believed that Plagge was actively trying to protect
his Jewish workers from the SS, some of the other prisoners were less certain, almost surprised at the thought of such a notion. Harold T, Anna T,
and Sarah K had no awareness that Plagge might be actively trying to save his
workers, only that he seemed less vicious than the other Germans. Nathan S
thought that Plagge was indeed trying to save his workers, saying that this
made him, "better than the other Germans," which was not exactly a glow-
ing compliment given what he thought of Germans in general. How are we
to reconcile this wide variation of perception?

To begin with, after speaking with the HKP survivors, I have come to see
that the trauma of the Holocaust has had a lasting emotional effect on the
former prisoners and that each one has dealt with their scars differently. The
trauma of the Holocaust has colored the perceptions of HKP survivors not
only toward Plagge, but toward all Germans. One survivor told me a story
that illustrates this point. L.G. was a young boy during the war and one of
the few children to survive the children's *aktion* at HKP. After the war, L.G.
and his family lived for several years in a DP camp and then moved to Canada, where they struggled to make ends meet. They decided to rent out an
attic room in their apartment. Responding to an ad for the apartment, a
German woman came to look at the rental, and L.G.'s mother began to
speak to her in German. When L.G., now a teenager, heard German being
spoken in his home, he became so distressed that he had to run out of the

room and lock himself in the bathroom. He then began to vomit violently. This story speaks to the magnitude of the aversive feelings that many survivors had to all things German after their horrible wartime experiences. For people who have deep, terrible associations between Germans and their experiences during the Holocaust, it would be very difficult to think of any German in a positive way, let alone the commander of a concentration camp. For many survivors, German soldiers were all lumped in one category: killers.

Simon Malkes, is an HKP survivor who feels strongly that Plagge saved his life. Simon, who now lives in France, says it is difficult for those of us looking back to understand the dynamics between Germans, even benevolent Germans, and their Jewish prisoners. In a letter to me, he recalled his impression of Plagge, as well as the distance between him and his workers:

> Plagge, I see him like he would be facing me now: a straight, tall, handsome & noble looking man wearing thin glasses. We saw him rarely as he was passing by, never talking with anybody. No Jew would have dared to talk to him, or even look at him. Remember, we were forced into a slavery-like behaviour "untermentschen." We were afraid to say something to a German. This made us invisible—like rats. I know, it is hard to understand now for normal people like you; one had to go through it.

Beyond the perceptions of the HKP survivors, it must also be remembered that Plagge could in no way be open about his thoughts regarding the Nazis or his attitudes toward Jews. Salomon Klaczko explains the environment that he had to contend with:

> I have tried to understand why many of the HKP inmates did not recognize the humanistic drives of Karl Plagge as a German officer. In the Autobiography of Samuel Esterowicz a list of names of Jewish collaborators is given, who belonged to the Jewish Ghetto Police or were Gestapo agents in the Ghetto. Some of them were paid—as an incentive for their collaboration—by allowing them either to live in the HKP or to have their families there.
>
> Karl Plagge was therefore forced to be permanently in a defensive attitude, in order to avoid any rumor to go around qualifying him as a "Judenfreund," one of the most offensive insults a Nazi could express to another German. A German woman who had a pure friendly relationship to a Jew was qualified as a "Judenhure" = "Prostitute of Jews" and sent

to a concentration camp. Plagge was forced to avoid any suspicion as a "Judenfreund," which the Jewish collaborators could have transmitted to the Gestapo. The SS and the SD would have used with pleasure such a denunciation of a Jewish collaborator in order to destitute Plagge. As a consequence, he was forced to behave with a poker-face, in order to hide his real sympathies. No doubt, a normal HKP inmate would have never had an opportunity to discover the real feelings of Plagge.

After puzzling over the different attitudes toward Plagge found among the HKP survivors that I interviewed, I have finally concluded that as in most things human, HKP survivor's attitudes and perceptions were shaped by their own personal experiences and contacts. If someone was a skilled worker and did useful work in the vehicle repair workshops, it could seem that one's survival was due to technical skills and ability to do useful work. This was after all why the HKP camp was formed and Plagge did his best to convince all around him that the camp and the work done within it were essential for the Wehrmacht's war efforts. During our interviews, several of the workers emphasized how skilled the Jewish workers were when describing their time at HKP. They felt that they were able to survive because they were capable, hard working artisans that the Germans were unwilling to lose until late in the war. As for the motivation of a particular German, some workers dismissed this as a naive notion. In their view, the Germans they encountered in Vilna were like a rabid pack of wolves—vicious, deadly, and within whom any semblance of compassion or reason was not to be imagined. They viewed the Germans as killers. For some, trying to understand the inner workings of their minds was like trying to understand the thinking of a wild animal. Trying to understand the inner psychology of an authority figure like the commander of their camp was something that had never occurred to some of the workers, at least not until I asked them about it. During our interviews, some of them seemed mystified at the thought. The survival plan of these Jews was to stick to being indispensable to the German war effort and, when that no longer was enough, of going into hiding when the end drew near.

In contrast to those workers who did real useful work at HKP, there were many Jews who, like my grandfather, had no technical skills. They found themselves at HKP and had to wonder how in the world they and their families were still alive. To this group, many of whom were intellectuals whose survival depended on learning who was in charge and who benefited from the goings on in the camp, understanding what Plagge and his officers were thinking was of central importance. So they observed him and pondered over his enigmatic visage, trying to figure him out. The more they studied Plagge, the more they had to conclude that he was different. He was not looking for bribes or personal favors. Some who had personal contact with him (Gershon Reches and Nyona Kolysh, the head Jewish representative at the camp) reported that Plagge was actually motivated to protect his workers. Why this was so, no one knew. Many concluded his attitudes and the conditions he created in the camp (including their own presence) could only be explained by the theory that he was a good man who disagreed with the horrors around him. The unskilled Jews and their descendants carry this image of Plagge with them to this day.

After the many discoveries the members of the Plagge group had made, there were still some mysteries left, mainly the question of Karl Plagge's motivations. The denazification file and interviews with HKP survivors gave us a much clearer picture of what had happened to the people who were in Plagge's camp. We could see that conditions in Plagge's workshops and camp were much better there than for Jews elsewhere in Vilna and Nazi occupied Europe in general. Almost a quarter of Plagge's Jews survived the war compared to less than 2 percent of Vilna's Jewish population overall. However, the question of what Plagge himself thought of his actions remained mysterious. Neither Plagge's men nor his prisoners had spoken directly to him about his inner thoughts. We had some hints when in the denazification trial he said he acted out of shame for what was being done in the name of Germany, and his godson Konrad Hesse recalled that after the war he was filled with guilt, thinking that he had not done enough. But, even after all we had found, most of what we knew about Karl Plagge's inner thoughts was speculation and conjecture.

A year passed after Marianne's unveiling of the denazification file, the discovery of Konrad Hesse and the interviewing of the HKP survivors. The members of the Plagge research group and I digested the material we had and reflected on our findings. Over time I began to think that we had found all there was to uncover about Plagge. All known archives had been searched, it seemed all of Plagge's living relatives had been identified, most of the HKP survivors that my parents and Bill Begell knew had been interviewed. I thought our research was largely complete, and began to write the first draft

of "The Search for Major Plagge." However, unexpectedly, yet another discovery was made that would allow us to see deeper into the mind of Karl
Plagge. This new breakthrough was made possible by a man in Canada who,
as a young boy in the HKP camp, had spent four months following the
Children's *Aktion* hiding in a trunk.

Eliezer Greisdorf was eight years old when he, along with his older
brother, parents, and uncle went to the HKP camp on Subocz Street. He was
hidden during the Children's *Aktion* by his Uncle, Leibl Greisdorf, and then
was kept concealed each work day in a trunk so that, being an illegal child,
he would not be discovered. He was able to leave his confinement only in
the evening when the grownups returned from the HKP workshops and allowed him to move about under careful supervision. He was hidden so well
that neither my mother nor Bill Begell knew of his existence in the camp.
Eliezer recalls that after they had been at HKP for a time, his family began
to see that in many ways, Major Plagge seemed different:

> It was during our incarceration in HKP that my family became aware
> of Major Plagge as an unusually decent soldier. On several occasions, he
> came to inspect the camp and to speak to us. Why he took an interest in
> us, only he knew. During those visits, it became known that he always
> instructed the camp administrator that he wanted no cruelties or punish-
> ments to take place while he was there.[36]

Eliezer also tells the story of Plagge's warning, a deed that prompted his
family to immediately enter a hiding place:

> On his last visit he came to say good bye, some days before HKP was
> closed. During his speech he emphasized several times that the evacua-
> tion would be carried out by the SS. Consequently, anyone who was still
> able to think clearly knew that this was the end.[37]

After emerging from several terrible days in a *maline* in the HKP cellar,
young Eliezer saw hellish scenes in the camp courtyard, including a pit that
was filled with dead Jewish neighbors who had been executed by the SS

36. From cover letter accompanying the "Plagge Letters" written by Eliezer
Greisdorf to Fanie Brancovskaja.

37. From cover letter accompanying the "Plagge Letters" written by Eliezer
Greisdorf to Fanie Brancovskaja.

during the previous days. Eliezer and his family ended up in a DP camp near Stuttgart, Germany, after the war. One day in 1946, his father and uncle learned that the American authorities were looking for witnesses to testify for or against a list of Germans who were being tried for possible war crimes. They saw Karl Plagge's name on this list and immediately volunteered to testify on his behalf. As we now know, it was because of testimony like theirs that Karl Plagge was not convicted of being a war criminal. After his trial, Karl Plagge apparently made contact with some of his former prisoners, many of whom were living in DP camps in the years immediately after the war. Because of the continued hostility and anti-Semitism in Eastern Europe, as well as the terrible memories that their homelands carried, most Jewish survivors in DP camps were trying to find a way to emigrate to the West. Using an intermediary named Dr. Paula Zanker, who was the lawyer for the inmates of the DP Camp in Ludwigsburg, Germany, Plagge wrote letters to Eliezer's father and uncle, David and Leibl Greisdorf. He then arranged a visit with the family while he was on a business trip for Hessenwerke in Stuttgart in March of 1948. He spent a day visiting the Greisdorfs, and later wrote a deeply emotional note to the Greisdorfs thanking them for their hospitality and reflecting on their conversations about the war during their day together. David Greisdorf kept Plagge's letters for the rest of his life, bringing them to Canada where he eventually brought his family, including his youngest son, Eliezer.

After his father died, Eliezer found among his belongings three letters written in 1948, all in German, from Karl Plagge to his father. He kept these letters for over 15 years, unsure of their content or their significance. Finally, in 2002, he sent them to the Association of Former Ghetto Prisoners in Lithuania for safekeeping. Some of the members of this historical society had been in contact with Marianne Viefhaus and knew of our group's interest in Karl Plagge. They therefore sent copies of these letters to Marianne. She transcribed the handwritten letters into her computer, and emailed them to us. For the benefit of those group members who did not understand German, she told us that they gave a distinct impression of Plagge's humanity and thoughts on the disastrous world that had motivated his life saving activities. One of the German-speaking members of our Plagge group, Mimi Sherwin of the Vilna Project in New York, was deeply moved as she read the letters in their original German. She wrote to me, saying:

After reading these extraordinary letters from Major Plagge . . . I feel absolutely impelled to write you. I am not only astonished by the discovery and preservation of these letters, but their contents had me absolutely in tears. I was literally crying. These letters could only have been written by a good person. They were written simply and from the heart.

After an initial translation by my mother, I asked two professors at Wesleyan University, Dr. Peter Frenzel, a professor of German studies, and Dr. David Morgan, a professor of German history, to help with the work of bringing Plagge's complex, classically styled German prose to life in English. At long last, the thoughts and feelings of the man we had searched for were laid bare as he talked to the people whose lives he had saved.

Here are two of Plagge's letters to the Greisdorfs, the first written before their visit, the second after:

Diploma Engineer Karl Plagge
Neunkirchen im Odenwald
Via Darmstadt-Land

Neunkirchen i.O.
Feb. 20, 1948

Dear Herr Greisdorf:

How strange and puzzling are the ways we are led in life! Always and ever-more my dreams and thoughts are engaged by the thought, where could those people be now who grew into my heart while close to me during that dreadful time. Who among all those friends might have survived the cruelty and the hell of this war and got out of it alive? Who could escape the demons of those tormented, cruel years we were forced to witness? With deep inner distress I read the book: Passover Book 5706 (1946),"The Confessions of a Survivor" by Dr. Mark Dworzecki, who also came from Vilna and was finally rescued by some miracle from many extermination camps. How much bravery and greatness of heart was responsible for the fact that in those days they did not despair and give up on life. How often back then I admired them and almost envied them for their courage and their mutual trust.

You yourself, my dear Herr Greisdorf, are known to me by name but no longer by your physical appearance. How miraculous it is that we will now once again be brought in contact with one another! And it would for me be a profound and heartfelt joy to meet with you once again, that is if you are not all too sorely reminded of what surely must have been the most terrifying time of your life. Since I discovered through Dr. Zanker and Frau Eichamueller, that you had been searching for me to thank me for the regrettably inadequate help I was able to give you, then let me say this to you:

What I was able and permitted to do for you and your friends was only the obvious duty of any feeling person towards his fellow human beings in distress. It was also at the same time much too little when measured against the horrific situation in which all of you found yourselves at the time. It needs no thanks. But there exists—I am convinced—an inner bond between people suffering distress whose destinies have crossed with one another. Though you and yours suffered a fate a thousand times worse than mine, I also was subjected to much suffering during the war and in the postwar time. I believe that people tested by suffering can really understand each other. In this sense, dear Mr Greisdorf, our getting together could bring us both a great inner joy.

I wrote to Dr Zanker about the possibility of our meeting in Stuttgart or in Darmstadt and she will kindly let you know about it. Until then I remain with kindest regards,

Yours very truly,
Karl Plagge

March 7, 1948

My dear, honored Herr Greisdorf,

Permit me to express my heartfelt thanks again to you and yours for the extremely hospitable reception that I found at your house. Today I'm sending you an electronics text with the request that you give it to your brother, who delighted me so with the book on physical chemistry. My wife, too, sends her warmest thanks for the fine things that I brought back to her.

I still reflect quite a lot on the afternoon we spent together as "house philosophers" and "house politicians." How few people there are nowadays with whom one can hold a calm and rational conversation, in these times that have so confused the thinking of people of all nations. I believe that we achieved a deep understanding in these hours together, and I regard it as a double gift of fate that in you I have found, not just in general one of the few survivors from the hell of those days, but also such a shrewd, level-headed man of great goodness of heart. Just the fact that you remember with gratitude the (alas!) much too slight, inadequate help that I could give, shows me your noble character. Gratitude is a much rarer flower on this desolate earth than, for instance, the doing of so-called "good deeds," for which one can impute a great variety of motives. There is only one motive for gratitude, namely a good heart.

I sincerely hope, dear Herr Greisdorf, that your wishes for your future may soon come about. Somewhere in this world there must be a place where people still live peacefully together, without hating and fighting each other. To be sure, in general the wise men of all ages have always said one thing, and the fools, that is, the immeasurable majority in all ages, have always done something else, namely the opposite. And that's the way it will continue to be, and when we leave this world it will be just as bad and imperfect as when we entered it, in spite of all the political parties that mean to make it a better place. And we shouldn't let it bother us, for in the world of the intellect there is no pain and everything is knowledge. Humanity wades through a red sea of blood and wars toward the promised land, the wilderness is long, and a man scales the cliff of his fate with torn and bleeding hands. What is an individual to do in the midst of this madness and confusion? I know only one thing: During this brief existence I mean to love and protect all people carried to my heart by a wave of this sea, just as far a human being can do this. I must do it in order to fulfill at least something of the greatness my heart drives me to. I will often be disappointed, but I will give love, even when I don't believe in love; I will do it not from weakness, but from duty. Harboring hatred and rancor and reciprocating them is weakness—overlooking them and restraining them through love is strength. I believe, dear Herr Greisdorf, that you understand what I mean. And if I ask you to retain not only the memory of me but also some friendship, I do this in remembrance of that afternoon when we spoke together as like-minded human beings about human things. I believe that the time has come for all right-minded, well-disposed people to extend their hands to each other across national boundaries to form a community of "the solitary among the nations." For whoever seeks truth and justice nowadays remains solitary in the midst of a blind multitude crying for power and violence.

Please give my cordial greetings to your lady wife, likewise your dear children and your brother and his family. Don't lose hope. It's always wise to hope, and your plans may be realized more quickly than you think, during your current lengthy wait.

In friendly remembrance and with heartfelt greetings,
Yours,
Karl Plagge[38]

After reading these letters, I could see that Mimi Sherwin was right; they could only have been written by a good man. Plagge's efforts to overcome the evil he saw around him had been successful, and, just as my father had been able to reunite with the Niemenczyn peasants who saved him, Plagge had seen the fruition of his efforts in this meeting with his former prisoners. He was not a perfect man. He may have joined the Nazi Party and helped bring them to power. He may or may not have risked his life, being careful to always play by the rules. He did not save the majority of his workers. But following his heart, he did what he thought he was able to do. He did not take the suicidal path of a martyr; neither did he follow the less difficult path of conformity taken by so many other Germans. He carefully stepped onto a new path that rang true to his sense of duty, of right and wrong. It was a path that would keep him, his men, and a large number of his prisoners alive through the war. His words rang clear to me: "What I was able and permitted to do for you and your friends was only the obvious duty of any feeling person toward his fellow human beings in distress." Characteristically humble, he downplayed his acts of heroism, calling them "inadequate" in comparison to the horrors endured by the Jews of Vilna. But those of us looking back on those years are not misled; he saved hundreds of lives by his actions, and there are hundreds, perhaps thousands, of people alive today

---

38. The Plagge-Greisdorf letters are written in a very formal, emotional, and classic German. Initially they were translated by my mother and then on separate occasions by Professors Peter Frenzel and David Morgan from Wesleyan University. The first letter presented here in English was translated by Pearl Good and Peter Frenzel. The second letter is David Morgan's translation. All translations and the original German version can be found at http://www.hometown.aol.com/michaeldg, in the Plagge Document Depository.

due to his courage. The Talmud teaches us that to save one life is to save a world. Karl Plagge teaches us that our actions do matter, that following one's conscience can cause ripples of goodness and life to flow through the years and across the generations.

It is a testament to his own humility that after visiting with the Greisdorfs, Plagge quietly went back home. Without fanfare, he lived the final ten years of his life in Darmstadt, slipping into obscurity and almost vanishing from history's view.

WHO IS A HERO?

Dr. Paldiel, I urge you to listen to the voices of these Jewish survivors of the Vilna Holocaust. They were there, they understand better than anyone what dangers they faced and just how they survived. They tell us that they lived because of a man named Karl Plagge. They instructed their children to seek him out and to give thanks for his moral acts, taken at considerable risk. Even after sixty years we continue to pursue this imperative to honor his name in anyway we can. Because we know in our hearts what our diligent research has shown with documentary evidence: that we are alive today because of the courage and bravery of this unusual German soldier. A man named Karl Plagge.
—Letter from Michael Good to Dr. Mordechai Paldiel, Chairman of Yad Vashem's Righteous Commision

When I was a young boy, I used to engage in childhood fantasies, imagining myself as a hero. Early on, I imagined that I was a fighter pilot, flying missions against the Luftwaffe, shooting down their fighter planes and bombers. As I grew older, my daydreams grew more detailed and elaborate, and I imagined myself as a superhero who could alter the course of history. I dreamed that I was a secret agent in Germany just before the war, setting out to assassinate Adolf Hitler, thus changing history and preventing the Holocaust from ever happening. However, in these fantasies, I always had a hard time coming up with a scenario in which I didn't end up being caught and killed by the Nazis. This was a problem for me; even as a daydreaming young boy, it was hard for me to imagine that I would have to die in order to save the world. I used to wonder, did I really have to die in order to be a hero? Couldn't I make a real difference without having to make the "ultimate sacrifice?" Couldn't I be one of those "small heroes" whose lesser acts tip the balance between good and evil upon which the world and humanity depend on?

In January of 2002, I received a letter from Yad Vashem in Israel, informing me that the Righteous Among Nations Review Committee had declined our application to have Karl Plagge recognized as a "Righteous Among Nations" rescuer. As is their policy, they would not elaborate on the reasons for their decision.

After an initial period of consternation, the HKP survivors, my friends in the Plagge Group, and I appealed Yad Vashem's initial rejection, enclosing some new materials gathered since our first application. I urged them to consider the risks that an ordinary German military man took when trying to counteract the terrible crimes being carried out by his countrymen:

> Plagge was different from non-German rescuers, who were primarily civilians and usually members of an occupied population. As an officer in the Wehrmacht, Plagge was expected to further the war through his actions and support the war mentally as well. To do less would be considered treason. As a German officer who opposed the war and the Nazi regime, he thus had a difficult task—to appear to support the war and its goals while actually undermining them secretly through his actions. It was the need to hide his true feelings from the authorities during the war, as well as the unpopularity of such rare actions within Germany after the war that has made it so difficult to objectively document Plagge's true intentions. One must look at what Plagge said during the war to his prisoners, and of course to his actions themselves to uncover his intent. I recently met with Isaac Reches, who was a 9 year old boy in HKP during the war. Isaac's father, Gershon Reches, was a work leader in the HKP camp and had considerable personal contact with Karl Plagge during the war. Most significant to the questions that are being raised about Plagge's intent was his statements to Gershon Reches that he preferentially gave work permits to Jews rather than to Poles as they were the most endangered group in Vilna at the time. This, coupled with the ample evidence that he gave jobs to unskilled workers testifies to the fact that his intentions were to save Jews.

After another year of waiting, the HKP survivors and members of the Plagge research group received a reply from the review committee at Yad Vashem. They rejected our application once again, saying that they could not see what Karl Plagge was risking through his efforts to employ Jewish workers in his unit:

> In the Karl Plagge case, we fail to understand what possible risks he had to fear from his superiors. He was not involved in hiding Jews, or

arranging their illegal flight and escape. He simply put them to work in a workshop that was serving the German military. The fact that he treated his Jewish, as well as non-Jewish, workers in a decent manner can only with great difficulty be construed as acting contrary to the interest of the Wehrmacht. On the contrary, he could probably claim, and perhaps he indeed did so, that his good treatment of his workers was for the interest of the war effort, that is, that they were producing more efficiently.

This second rejection of our application to honor Karl Plagge at Yad Vashem was both upsetting and infuriating to many of the HKP survivors and the members of the Plagge research group who had supported Plagge's application. It became clear that what had seemed obvious to us, namely that Plagge was trying to save Jewish lives and took considerable risks in doing so, was not so obvious to others who had not immersed themselves in studying this unusual man. The rejection forced us to examine the risks that Plagge took on during the course of the war and also to look at the broader philosophical question of who exactly is a hero.

We first looked at the risks that Plagge faced by befriending and then protecting Jews. There is clear documentary evidence that shows that a German officer who had any friendly associations with Jews was putting himself at both professional and personal risk by such an association. Joerg Fiebelkorn has found orders in the archives from the chief of the Wehrmacht's Personal Affairs branch, General Rudolf Schmundt, who gave the following order, which demanded absolute anti-Semitic behavior on the part of Wehrmacht officers:

> Not even the most casual connection between an officer and a member of the Jewish race is acceptable. The actual hard fight against the Jewish-bolshevist world-enemy demonstrates with particular clearness the true face of Judaism. The officer therefore has to reject from his inner conviction any connection to him. Whoever violates this intransigent bearing, is not acceptable as officer. The subordinate officers are to be instructed in an appropriate manner."[1]

In Vilna the archives show the following directive given to local Wehrmacht troops on April 7, 1942:

1. From a general order given in October 1942 by General Schmundt to "clarify the attitude of an officer to Judaism again and beyond doubt." Supplied by Joerg Fiebelkorn in personal email on June 10, 2003.

The Jew is our enemy and the sole guilty person for the war. Therefore there is no difference between Jew and Jew, they are all equal. The employment for work is forced labor, therefore social communication with Jews as well as any private conversation is most strongly forbidden. Who will associate privately with Jews has to be treated as a Jew.[2]

There was a clear line drawn by the Nazis, forbidding Wehrmacht officers from having any friendly or social contact with Jews as well as prohibiting any actions on behalf of any Jew. The Vilna directive's threat that "those who associate privately with Jews will be treated as a Jew" is especially ominous as this was a period when Jews were being actively exterminated by the Nazis. In fact, in Vilna there was a German soldier named Anton Schmid, who was caught crossing the line by helping Jews hide from the SS and was executed in April 1942 for his actions. It is clear that Plagge also crossed these forbidden lines on many occasions both before and during the war. We see this first when he became a godfather to a Jewish baby (Konrad Hesse) during the height of anti-Semitic fervor in Germany after Kristallnacht in 1938. Later on, during the war, he acted continuously on behalf of his Jewish workers. Through such actions as staging a beating to free two workers captured by the SS, by sending troops to the railyards to take Jewish workers off of the transports to Estonia, by making extraordinary efforts to form a separate HKP work camp which he then filled with unskilled Jewish workers, by arguing with Commander Goeke to retain control of the female workers, and by warning his workers that the SS was coming to kill them, he left a dangerous trail of deeds that could expose his inner motivations. He was always under the threat that each maneuver would be the one that exposed his true intentions to the SS. In my mind there is no doubt that if the SS or the Gestapo understood the true motivations behind his actions, Plagge would have been court-martialed and executed. If we recall the story that Plagge related during his trial about the drunken officer who made a derogatory remark about Hitler and could have faced the "ultimate" penalty, one understands the ease with which the Nazis invoked the death penalty. During the war the Nazis executed over 40,000 German soldiers for any act

2. From the Vilnius State Archive," Guidelines and instructions for the employment of Jewish workers," April 7th, 1942. Found by Kim Prievel, graduate student at the University of Freiberg, for his masters thesis, supplied to the author by Kim Prievel and translated by Joerg Fiebelkorn and Marianne Viefhaus.

of disloyalty, big or small. From this story it does not take much imagination to see that someone who was actively working against the Nazi party on behalf of Jewish "enemies of the state" would have been in grave danger if his true aims had been discovered.

The second question that the disappointing rejection from Yad Vashem caused us to ponder was the issue of just who is a hero and why we label someone as a hero. Given the differing reactions to the story of Karl Plagge, be it among the HKP survivors or institutions such as Yad Vashem or the Technical University at Darmstadt, it would seem that deciding who merits this designation is anything but clear. Literally, a hero is defined as "one who shows great courage." In common usage, I think we label as heroes those who act as we would hope to act in situations where there is moral, social, and/or physical danger. All of us can think of situations about which we wonder, "What would I do if I were in that situation?" Most people act instinctively in a way that is safest, taking the most expedient path. We admire those who put their own self-interest aside and take risks for the benefit of others. Most commonly, society labels as heroes those who put their physical safety at risk for the good of the community. We erect war memorials for those who risked or gave their lives in the cause of freedom; we praise emergency workers such as firefighters and policemen who jeopardize their safety while serving the public. But what about those who do not hold jobs that put them in physical danger? Are there actions that they might contemplate that society would consider heroic? In fact, society does admire and encourage actions that uphold our centrally held values and protects the well being of the community. The citizen who thwarts those who would harm others, or a whistle-blower who points out corruption or dishonesty within an organization, both put their own positions at risk in order to prevent wrong-doing. We generally praise these kinds of actions as heroic.

As I have thought about who is deemed to be a hero, I have come to realize that this designation is very dependent on the society in which one lives and the values that it holds. In Nazi Germany, I have no doubt that members of the SS were considered heroes for carrying out their difficult job of eliminating the Jews from the face of the earth, a task that was highly valued by Nazi society. Today, in Islamic fundamentalist circles, suicide bombers are held in high regard as martyrs, dying while fighting against the Israelis or the American infidels. For Americans and Israelis, both these groups are considered criminals working for causes that we find repugnant.

So, it is quite possible for one society's hero to be another society's villain. Heroism is very dependent on social context. Those who risk themselves to further goals or values deeply held by their society are labeled as heroes; those who resist those values are considered traitors or criminals. Thus, for the Jews that he saved and their children in the modern Western world, Karl Plagge is a hero. However, if his own countrymen had known of his efforts during the war, he undoubtedly would have been arrested and possibly executed as a treasonous criminal.

In the Jewish tradition, someone is heroic if he puts his own well-being aside in order to protect the oppressed and, while acting in a moral manner, performs good deeds. So, I find myself asking, how does Karl Plagge measure up when looking at whether he acted morally, protected the oppressed, and performed good deeds? He certainly performed good deeds, and, in my mind, he also put his well-being aside when acting on behalf of his Jewish workers. Beginning with his decision to become Konrad Hesse's godfather, he stuck his neck out on behalf of the oppressed. Joerg Fiebelkorn explained to me what a daring move this was in 1938:

> A strong and convincing indicator for Plagge's opposition to the Nazis was his readiness to become godfather of Konrad Hesse as late as 1938. According to the notorious Nuremberg Laws, passed in 1935, Konrad was a "Half-Jew" as his mother was rated "Jew." As the godfather was officially noted in the "family book"—the document containing all births, baptisms, marriages and deaths of a family—this was an official act documented by the local authority. Please remember: Plagge, a Nazi party member, becomes godfather of a non-Aryan child—this was without a doubt a violation of the Nuremberg law, which forbade by threat of severe punishment any personal contacts between Jews and "Aryans." Plagge's behaviour was a demonstration against the declared Nazi law, open and visible to at least all the neighbours and relatives—a number of people large enough to contain at least one denunciator. Even the clerk, who noted Karl Plagge in the family-book as godfather, could have been an informant. To my eyes, here already Plagge decided to act against the Nazis: he could not gain anything (except the thankfulness of his friend Hesse), but underwent the risk of being relegated and socially discriminated by the Nazis.

Once in Vilna, Plagge continued to act in a manner dictated by his moral values in support of those endangered by the Nazi genocide. At his denazification trial in Darmstadt, Plagge spoke of how he was ashamed for Germany and that he acted out of a sense of duty to help the oppressed Jews and Poles around him. From this testimony we can see that for Karl Plagge, values such as duty and how one's actions were seen by others weighed heavily on his mind. Due to his own inner moral sense, it was important for him to do good. Unlike the majority of Germans who lacked empathy for the people they conquered, Plagge valued the perspective of others, including those of the subjugated peoples in conquered Eastern Europe. He could put himself in their position and was ashamed of how he and his countrymen appeared in their eyes. In his letter to David Greisdorf, Plagge later said:

> What I was able and allowed to do for you and your friends was only the obvious duty of any feeling person towards his fellow human beings in distress.

This line, "what I was able and allowed to do," is central to what makes the story of Karl Plagge so compelling to those of us looking back and contemplating his conduct during the war. We have seen that Plagge was cautious in his actions, always trying to mask his activities under the legitimacy of his orders as a Wehrmacht officer. He tried whenever possible to play within the rules, manipulating the system against itself. Under the guise of the earnest Wehrmacht commander committed to supporting the war effort, he was able to use the German wartime bureaucracy's own rules to save lives. By taking this approach, he was able to avoid the threat of immediate execution that awaited anyone found to be helping "enemies of the state." He did his work indirectly, using the slave labor machine to protect people earmarked for death. His ultimate aim, to save lives, was unwavering throughout the war. But his methods were subtle, not the methods of a swashbuckler who, along with his protectees, would have all too easily been discovered and killed.

In October 2004, Marianne Viefhaus discovered a previously unknown relative of Karl Plagge's wife, Anke Madsen, a man named Dr. Hans Madsen. From Dr. Madsen she received family photographs of Karl and Anke on their wedding day and also a photo of Karl Plagge standing with fellow officers at a military parade in 1942. Most significantly, Madsen also gave Marianne a letter written by Karl Plagge to a Jewish attorney named Strauss, whom he had met in 1956 in Stuttgart, Germany. Strauss had apparently urged Plagge to write down his thoughts and recollections about the war. After initially declining this suggestion, Plagge changed his mind and wrote Strauss a deep and philosophical letter. In the five-page letter, he discusses some of his recollections of his time in Vilna during the war and his thoughts on his conduct as well as that of those around him. This letter, written a year before his death, speaks of a deeply moral man who struggled with the insanity and violence that surrounded him as he tried to find a virtuous path through the hell that threatened to engulf him during the war.[3]

Plagge spoke of how his experiences affected his views of God and religion:

> One had to be a witness of this outrage, in the course of which the only choice that remained, was to hate or love the God who permitted all these things. This was the cause for me to revise my religious views and I resisted loving a creation that martyred people and would even gas children and would let people be guilty as happened here. If the order of the world was determined through death, then it was perhaps better for God not to believe in Him and, instead, to struggle against death with all one's strength, without lifting one's eyes to heaven, where God was silent.

Regarding his fellow Germans who were perpetrating a "disgraceful outrage," he had the following observations:

> I have spoken with many of these "Scourges" who were responsible for the horror and have long reflected upon their words. I have perceived these men as blind tools of a hallucination and I must tell you that these people have also moved me to pity, because I saw what a dreadful schism dwelt in their souls. They weren't in a position to resist against the outbreak of that stupidity, inertia and bestiality that is imparted to people on the way as the unfortunate heirs of their heritage.
>
> In my canteen . . . I once met a drunken SD man, who was breaking down crying because his terrible conscience oppressed him to his very foundation. He belonged to an execution squad which for months had committed horrible abuses. He sought to drown his despair in alcohol. I sat next to him and tried to look into his soul. What I found was a man with deadly psychic wounds, a human wreck, who was held together only through the power of military discipline. He was not, or only quite dimly,

3. The letter can be found in its entirety in Appendix B

aware of what he had perpetrated and his attempts at justification resulted in a terrifying ignorance.

Finally, after discussing how he managed to bring his workers to the camp on Subocz Street and protect them from the SS, Plagge laments his inability to prevent the death of the camp's children:

> However, I was unable to prevent the murder of the children. I was on leave during these days. Whether it would have been dared in my presence and succeeded I do not know. Those children who remained hid in prepared known hiding places and they survived until the final evacuation of the park.

This remarkable letter confirmed to me that our previously fashioned portrait of Plagge, created from a mosaic of fragments scattered across the globe, was surprisingly close to the self-portrait that Plagge himself painted a short time before his death. He was indeed a deeply thoughtful, virtuous man who struggled to find a way to protect his Jewish workers and his troops while avoiding the moral crevasse that so many of his fellow Germans plunged into while following Hitler and the Nazis.

In his letter to Strauss, Plagge downplays any notion that he was an exceptional hero and comments on what might have occurred had other Germans chosen the path that he took:

> Perhaps other places lacked only a little determination to similarly act to prevent and reduce the horror. I have never felt that this took special courage. It required only a certain strength that anyone can derive from the depths of moral feelings which exist in all human beings. Beyond that perhaps, in addition, a little good will, an occasional good idea and devotion to the task at hand is necessary. I didn't have the feeling that I was exposing myself to special danger because my arguments were always reasonable, honorable and indisputable on the humane as well as the technical level.

In spite of his humble attempts to minimize the danger of his actions, Plagge's words compel us to question what an average, well-intentioned person could have done, short of risking his or her life to stop the genocide machine as it rolled across Europe. We must not forget that the Nazis put up formidable barriers to anyone who would consider helping Jews.

In October of 1941, the Nazis passed laws requiring the death penalty for any Christian who hid a Jew, or even knew of Jews in hiding but did not report them to the authorities. These laws were widely publicized, and the initial executions were made quite public. If anyone in a household were caught hiding Jews, everyone in the home, including children, would be executed. Even smuggling a loaf of bread to some hungry prisoners could be punished by summary execution or imprisonment in a concentration camp if one was caught by the Germans. In cities and towns across Nazi-occupied Europe, citizens learned quickly what happened to those who resisted the Nazis in the slightest way. A neighbor who threw a loaf of bread over the ghetto walls to the hungry Jews inside was deported to a concentration camp. Even if the sentence was relatively short, one might never return from such an exile. As the war went on, the Nazis murdered civilians for even minor offenses. In Torun, Poland, the Germans executed twelve young boys aged eleven and twelve for having broken a window at the local police station. Such vicious killings had the intended effect; normal people were terrorized from breaking any of the Nazis' rules for fear of overwhelming retribution.

We can see that Plagge himself was well aware of the dangers of life under the Hitler's rule when he said in his letter to Strauss, "We lived in a time when one who stated that two times two is four could be sentenced to death." However, looking back on the war years, we see that in spite of the Nazi terror, many, like Plagge, did resist.

Some joined resistance movements; others risked death to hide Jewish friends, neighbors, or even perfect strangers. As of January 2004, Yad Vashem had recognized 20,205 rescuers who risked death to save Jews. Most of these rescuers were simple people helping a Jewish friend or a Jew that they encountered in desperate need. For the most part they were not like Oskar Schindler, the famous German rescuer immortalized in Steven Spielberg's film Schindler's List, who saved over 1,000 Jewish lives in Poland. Usually their heroism consisted of saving one or two lives through daily sacrifice and courage stretching over years of German occupation. Through their individual good deeds, these righteous rescuers saved thousands of Jewish lives during the Holocaust. They may not have cinematic memorials, but at Yad Vashem and in the hearts of those they saved and their descendents, they are remembered.

This brings us again to the question once again of who is a hero. Is it the superheroes of my boyhood dreams that change the world for the better, or the more limited actions of smaller, more common "heroes" that make a difference? In my mind, if humanity is to advance in a direction that leaves genocide in the past, it is the average person that will be the deciding factor. It will be millions of average people and how they act that will ultimately decide whether hate and genocide will continue to plague the future of mankind. Plagge himself was very humble, calling his efforts "inadequate" in the face of the horrors of the Holocaust. He felt guilty that he did only what he was "allowed to do." Yet, as Joerg Fiebelkorn points out, if more Germans had acted in the "inadequate" manner exemplified by Plagge, history would have progressed in a very different way:

> Plagge writes that he did only what he was "allowed" to do. Therefore, he was deeply convinced that he did not have the right to call himself an "anti-Nazi." Here again we come to the point that if everyone in Germany had done "what he was allowed to do" in the sense of true citizenship and good neighborliness, the Holocaust would have been impossible. All those who did not resist the small and big atrocities against their Jewish neighbors, all those who killed women and children under the excuse that they had to obey orders, all those judges who sentenced a slave laborer to death for having stolen a tiny piece of bread; they all claimed that it needed heroism and the readiness to be killed if one dared to resist the Nazi government. Plagge is the document that shows that they were all cowards and liars, guilty for standing aside and neglecting the cries of their own neighbors.

Thus, in Plagge we have a different kind of hero, one who "does what he can" to follow a moral path and help those in need. This kind of heroism may not be one that immediately garners accolades from a review committee at Yad Vashem or shames the judges at a denazification trial away from their self-serving postures, but in my mind this kind of heroism sets an example for the type of action that we can all aspire to.

In early 2004, after uncovering the HKP letters between Plagge and SS *Obersturmbannführer* Goeke (arguing over the fate of the HKP women) and learning of Plagge's dramatic rescue of David Swirski (where he pretended to beat David and his companion in order to satisfy the SS man who threatened to kill them), we asked that Plagge's case be reviewed by Yad Vashem for a third time. This time around we left nothing to chance. I wrote an annotated summary of all the evidence we had gathered over the previous five years and sent it to the Righteous Commission at Yad Vashem. We asked several HKP survivors, including David Swirski's son Marek, to send notarized copies of their testimony to the commission, giving additional first hand accounts by those whose lives were saved by Karl Plagge. Simon Malkes (the HKP survivor from France) traveled to Jerusalem and personally lobbied on behalf of Plagge's application with members of the commission. In the end, our persistence and tenacity paid off. On July 22, 2004, Yad Vashem's Righteous Commission met in plenary session and voted unanimously to bestow the Righteous Among Nations award to Karl Plagge.

Our final success at Yad Vashem was both a relief and a source of satisfaction. Not only had the feelings of my mother, grandfather and other HKP survivors who wanted to give thanks to Plagge been validated, but I could now be sure that in the years to come, even after the HKP survivors and their children have died, that the story of Karl Plagge's bravery and moral fortitude will be preserved for future generations at Yad Vashem. Plagge's award was also great a source of joy for my mother. After hearing of the news from Jerusalem she wrote to the members of the Plagge group:

> I am so grateful to you all—you all had crucial roles in this accomplishment . . . My debt of gratitude, unpaid for almost 60 years, is at last paid in full—or can one ever pay for one's life?

Even before our eventual success at Yad Vashem, the HKP survivors and the Plagge research group had succeeded in commemorating the good deeds of Karl Plagge in other venues. In October of 2002, my mother and father, Bill Begell, Susan, and I were invited to Darmstadt, Germany, to attend a ceremony at the Technical University of Darmstadt (TUD) in honor of Karl Plagge. Marianne Viefhaus had raised awareness at the university about the story of their unusual graduate, and the TUD decided to commission a physical memorial to Plagge on campus. In addition, the Darmstadt city council promised to name a street in his honor.

For my mother and Bill Begell this trip caused mixed emotions. They were obviously anxious about going to Germany, a place filled with the descendents of those who had killed their families, but they also derived great pleasure in finally being able to travel to Plagge's hometown and publicly pay respect to the man who saved their lives. We were all also very gratified to finally be able to meet Marianne, Solomon, and Joerg, the friends whom we had met in cyberspace and who had made all our discoveries possible. After having exchanged thousands of emails over the previous three years, it was with great pleasure that we came to find that they were as warm, gracious and insightful in person as they had seemed over the internet. Together we toured Frankfurt, visited Karl Plagge's grave in Darmstadt, and attended a ceremony at the Technical University of Darmstadt to honor Karl Plagge and announce the memorials that were being dedicated to him. At the ceremony, the chancellor of the University, Hans Seidler, Marianne Viefhaus, Bill Begell, and I all made comments in front of the Darmstadt press corps. In my remarks, I tried to speak of the significance of Jewish Holocaust survivors and present-day Germans bridging the enormous cultural divides that the war had created between us:

> It has been the friendship of Salomon, Joerg and Marianne which has spanned a great gulf of time, distance and painful memories. They have given us the opportunity to grasp the hands which they offer in friendship, and come to Germany today. I hope that people around the world, many of whom face seemingly unbridgeable ethnic and religious divides can look at this gathering as a sign of hope, that even the worst strife between groups of human beings can, over time, be overcome.
>
> I am a man who has lived his entire life in America. The events of the Holocaust occurred in a far away time and place from my busy life in the United States. Yet, I, as well as my children, owe our existence to the deeds of a man from Darmstadt, Germany. It was his moral fortitude and righteous actions which spared the life of my mother and in turn, the lives of the generations that follow her. For those of us who look back on this man and those times, there is much to ponder and learn. His example shows us what one moral man can accomplish, even in a sea of seemingly infinite darkness and despair. The good that he accomplished stretches across the decades, through generations and into a new century. For the hundreds of us alive and enjoying life today, I would like to extend our thanks and gratitude to his memory.

A year after our trip to Germany, Marianne Viefhaus traveled to the United States to visit Susan and me in Connecticut. We enjoyed several days of touring the local countryside, viewing the fall colors and treating her to a New England Thanksgiving feast in our home. During the weekend we took a short train ride down to New York City where we met Bill Begell. During a day filled with happy greetings and warm feelings, I thought about how far I had traveled during the previous four years since we left on our trip to Vilna. For so many years I had been afraid to confront the horrible images and memories associated with the Holocaust. I wouldn't read books or watch movies about it and avoided all conversations about those terrible times. Even though my parents had always told me that the children of the Nazis were not responsible for the crimes of their fathers, I unconsciously found it hard to be with anyone from Germany. If I met a German, I always immediately calculated how old they or their parents were during the war, wondering whether they or their family members were responsible for the destruction of my family. Just meeting a German caused a near anxiety attack. Obviously such thoughts did not make it easy to start an open and meaningful dialogue. As far as I know, no one in my family had ever considered actually visiting Germany or welcoming German visitors into our homes. Yet as I sat with Marianne, Bill, and Sue in a quaint Italian restaurant in Greenwich Village, I marveled at the wonders that had transpired during the previous four years. I had traveled to Vilna to experience the telling of my parents' stories in the very places where their historical hardships had occurred. Since beginning my search I had plunged into reading about the Holocaust, trying to understand how it transpired. My bookshelves now sag with volumes about this once forbidden subject, volumes which, while still painful, have been read from beginning to end. Through my discoveries about Major Plagge, my interviews with HKP survivors, and dialogues with Germans such as Marianne Viefhaus, Joerg Fiebelkorn, Salomon Klaczko, and Konrad Hesse, I have gained a very unusual perspective for a child of Holocaust survivors. Certainly, like many of the children of survivors of my generation, I have heard and absorbed the stories of the Holocaust as experienced by the victims themselves. However, unlike most children of survivors, I have also had the opportunity to think about what those years were like for ordinary Germans who had no burning hate or desire to commit genocide.

When I had walked through the deserted streets of the Vilna Ghetto, I had felt haunted by the empty apartments that seemed filled with the ghosts of Vilna's dead Jews, who seemed to ask, "Why are you alive?" Thus, when I first set out to find Major Plagge, I wanted to not only thank his descendants, but also to answer the question of why he acted as he did to protect his prisoners from the genocide. I needed to answer the question that had burned inside me; why were my children and I alive? The answer that I found was that our family was saved by a man who had empathy for those around him and who felt responsible for the unintended consequences that his early acts as a Nazi Party member had resulted in. Karl Plagge looked at the world through the eyes of the oppressed Jews of occupied Poland and was ashamed of what he saw. Now, sixty years later, I have found myself trying to see the war through the eyes of ordinary Germans who lived through its horrors, trying to understand how difficult the decisions they faced were. From this perspective I can truly see how exemplary men like Karl Plagge were. Similarly, my search has introduced me to present-day Germans who, out of their generosity of spirit, have spent countless hours helping me and my family pursue our quest, and, in doing so, have healed wounds that have been open for more than half a century. It is the work of decent human beings named Plagge, Viefhaus, Klaczko, Fiebelkorn, and Hesse, who made it possible for our family to bridge what had once seemed like an impossible chasm. They made it possible for us to arrive in Germany to give thanks for the deeds of a moral German man whose acts had saved our lives. It was this same process that brought Marianne, Bill, Susan, and I together in New York as we shared a happy meal, recounting all our mutual accomplishments together.

It is my hope that the healing that has occurred through the search for Major Plagge and our subsequent discoveries will affect not only my mother and me, but perhaps generations still to come. In many families, stories are told about ancestors that emphasize what each particular family sees as the best example of what they are about. In many ways this book itself is an extension of such a tradition of family story telling, I hope that it will carry my parents' stories of survival and lessons about the generous people who made our survival possible to my children and grandchildren. When I think of my family's wartime stories, I see some common themes involving its central characters that demonstrate the importance of the core values that we hope to pass on to succeeding generations. These themes consist of acting morally in general (e.g., do unto others . . .) and then acting specifically to aid those in need. My maternal grandfather, Samuel Esterowicz, won the respect of his customer Mr. Poddany through his honesty. Due to this respect, Mr. Poddany made sure that his friend Samuel was among those employed within the HKP workshop, saving Samuel and his family by placing them under the auspices of Major Plagge's unit. Later, Samuel was willing to risk sharing the knowledge of the HKP maline with my mother's cousin, Gary Gerstein, and his talkative mother Nina in spite of the danger that this use might cause the discovery of this precious resource that the whole family was to depend on. My paternal grandfather, Dov Gdud, was honest and well loved by those who knew him. Before the war, he helped neighbors in need with loans or by giving them jobs. As a result of his previous generosity, his neighbors later risked their lives to hide both my grandfather and father after they escaped German executions. During the war he shared his resources with others in hiding, even though it may have put him at risk of running out of funds for himself and his son. Karl Plagge was a thoughtful, moral man who tried to do what was right. Before the war he tried to protect Kurt Hesse's infant son by becoming his godfather. When confronted with the genocide occurring in Vilna, Plagge tried to do what he could to protect his Jewish workers from death. After the war these same Jewish workers tried to help him during his denazification trial. In the stories of these three men, one can see a reoccurring pattern of moral thought and conduct later being rewarded by those who were helped. As the Bible teaches, "Cast out your bread upon the water, after a time it will return."[4]

These three men, Samuel Esterowicz, Dov Gdud, and Karl Plagge, were all brought together in the crucible of the Holocaust in Vilna. They were in many ways quite different. Dov Gdud was a devoutly religious man, a rabbi who followed a way of life dictated by traditional Jewish religious precepts that had been passed down for generations. Samuel Esterowicz was a thoroughly modern man, an atheist in fact. He lived a secular life while following the guidance of the great Western philosophers. Karl Plagge was a staff officer in Hitler's Wehrmacht who had a Prussian upbringing in a middle-class German family. These men all had very different backgrounds, which externally make them seem quite different. However, at their cores we see striking similarities. They all had deeply held moral beliefs, and these same beliefs later shaped their wartime conduct and survival. When all the cultural trappings are pared away, what these three men shared was their desire to do what they believed was right, and when confronted with people in need they did what they could to help them.

This in fact is the main lesson that I take from my family's experience: Do what you think is right and when confronted with people in need, do what you can to help. It seems too simple, almost trite, yet this is what I carry with me from my family's stories as I go about my day-to-day life. My

4. Ecclesiastes 11:1–2.

children and I are alive today because sixty years ago these three men tried to conduct themselves as their consciences dictated. When they saw their fellow man in need, they tried to help. What I find most encouraging about their actions is that, unlike the life-risking feats performed by traditional heroes, these men saved lives by taking smaller, less terrifying risks. When listening to stories about traditional heroes who risk their lives for a cause, I must confess that I doubt that I would ever have the courage to duplicate their conduct. My father says that one never really knows until one is presented with a situation and forced to act, but I suspect that I am like most—not unusually brave. In contrast, when I look at the risks and deeds of my grandfathers and Major Plagge, I am able to say to myself, "I think I could do that." If this is the response of the average person, then this is a path that many could aspire to follow, not just the rare, unusually brave hero.

Is it possible to encourage humanity's capacity for altruism, so that more follow the path that leads away from hate and genocide? While the answer to this question currently seems clouded in doubt, I think that those of us who do feel it is possible must try to teach our children a very simple lesson: try to do what is right and, when confronting people in need, do what you can to help.

In order for one to be empathetic toward those in need, one should be able to appreciate one's own good fortune. It is this appreciation of how fortunate we are that has compelled many of the HKP camp survivors and their descendants to explore how this came to be. I have found it to be most heartening that my family was not alone among Plagge's former prisoners in searching for him, wanting to thank him for his help in bringing about their survival. For his former HKP prisoners and their descendants who were to search through the obscuring mists of time to look for him and thank him for saving their lives, Plagge left us with the following words:

> Gratitude is a much rarer flower on this barren and desolate earth than the performance of so-called "good deeds," for which one can ascribe the most varied kinds of motives. For gratitude there is only one motive: and that is a good heart.

These words, characteristically humble and generous, reveal the kind heart of a man who saved so many with his efforts. That we should have found such a heart through the horrors of the Holocaust is an irony that certainly gives one pause for thought. While the Holocaust shows us the worst that humanity is capable of, Plagge's story shows us the power of one man to choose the path of goodness and how his actions can have positive effects for generations to follow. How one decides to take that path is one that all of us must ponder as we try to understand how to bring out the best in mankind and protect against the worst. Within the story of the Holocaust, with its infinite horrors, I find a few rays of hope for the future of humanity. For me that hope lies in the example of Karl Plagge.

ACKNOWLEDGMENTS

My journey of the past five years, first traveling to Vilna, then searching for Major Plagge, researching documents, interviewing survivors, and finally writing this book, has depended on the kindness and generosity of many, many people. Looking back, I am humbled at how little I would have accomplished without their helping hands.

First, I am grateful to both of my parents, William and Pearl Good. Their willingness to share their stories and then embark on emotionally and physically draining journeys sparked the seeds of curiosity that led to life changing work and discoveries. Their own example of remembering without bitterness and their appreciation of their own good fortune has been a great example for all their children and grandchildren who live in a time when it is sometimes hard to understand what is trivial versus what is important.

Of course, I never would have made any of my discoveries were it not for my friends in Germany: Soloman Klaczko, Joerg Fiebelkorn, and Marianne Viefhaus. Their generous spirits and keen intellects have enriched my family's life. I hope that our mutual research will enlighten a wide circle of readers trying to understand good and evil and the choices that lie between them. These three friends also extended us warm welcomes and were unbelievably generous with their time during our visits to Germany. I am also indebted to Konrad Hesse for helping in illuminating his godfather's thinking and personality as well as for providing me with the first photograph of Karl Plagge. Similarly, I am very grateful to Mrs. Erika Vogel and Dr. Hans Madson for giving us information about Plagge's family and providing photos of him in uniform. Dr. Madsen also helped us immensely by sharing the Plagge-Strauss letters, which proved to be so enlightening in regards to Karl Plagge's own views on the war.

Three HKP survivors, Bill Begell, Simon Malkes, and Lazar Greisdorf, joined Marianne, Joerg, Salomon, my mother, and I in the Plagge Research Group and gave invaluable advice to a "young American kid" who needed so much guidance. In addition to helping with research, Bill Begell, an engineer who now works in publishing, introduced me to my agent, Alan Wittman, and also gave me beginner-level lessons on the world of publishing.

I owe a great debt of thanks to the other HKP survivors that I talked to: Nathan S, Harold and Anna T, Vera T, Sarah K, Aaron P, and Isaac Reches, all of whom allowed a stranger calling from afar to open and explore painful chapters in their lives. Their willingness to speak with me helped me greatly to understand views and opinions about HKP and the war that I could not have appreciated from my family's perspective alone.

Sharon Maloney, an accountant by profession, was the first "normal, non-Holocaust-obsessed person" to read the manuscript and pointed out the myriad of terms that she was unfamiliar with. I can never thank my birding buddy David Titus enough. A professor of history at Wesleyan University, he spied the Plagge manuscript on my desk one day, snatched it up, and returned it full of pencil marks for revision. After I did a rewrite he went through it a second time. My work benefited greatly from his experienced eye, and I am very grateful for the highly professional advice and encouragement he gave out of the goodness of his heart. David Titus introduced my manuscript to his department mate, Professor David Morgan. David helped both with the translation of the Plagge-Greisdorf letters as well as with the historical chapter on the destruction of Jewish Vilna. Both David Titus and David Morgan displayed professional generosity that was quite breathtaking in its abundance. Their love of learning, knowledge, and superb teaching abilities were clearly demonstrated by their willingness to freely help an amateur who landed on their doorstep. I would also like to acknowledge the help of Wesleyan University professor Peter Frenzel, who kindly took the time to provide me with the first professional translation of the Plagge-Greisdorf letters. I was also helped by a retired high school teacher from Middletown, Connecticutt, John Niemczyk who not only was generous with his red pencil in pointing out flaws in the early manuscripts, but also gave me much encouragement after my first rejections from publishers. My thanks also to Leslie Bulion, a friend and children's author who also offered much encouragement and good advice.

I want to express my deepest thanks to Marcus Schneider, who in the midst of his stint as a high-school exchange student devoted considerable time and energy to translating the denazification file and other documents. His efforts helped display the treasures that Marianne Viefhaus had discovered to my English-reading eyes. Additionally, I would like to extend many thanks to Mimi Sherwin, who volunteered her free time after work at the

Vilna Project to help translate Plagge's letters. Her previously unknown linguistic talents were much appreciated. In fact, her translation of the Plagge-Strauss letters finally captured the elegance of Karl Plagge's prose, which had so impressed all our friends in Germany but was difficult for those of us in America to actually see. I would also like to thank Rose Newnham, a graduate student at Columbia University, who helped me through the painful process of pruning my somewhat rotund manuscript down to trimmer, more readable dimensions.

My warmest thanks also go out to my mother's lifelong friend, Mira Van Doren, who has a vast knowledge of all things pertaining to Vilna, and has helped me over the years as I struggled to bring myself up to speed on the world of Jewish culture and heritage that existed in Vilna before the war. It was Mira's son Adam Van Doren, a documentary filmmaker, who first encouraged me to write a book about Karl Plagge.

Many thanks to my agent, Allan Wittman, who agreed to take on the task of helping a novice author to publish a first book. His guidance and patient explanations were an indispensable guide as I took my first steps in this new world. Also in the area of publishing, I must extend my deepest thanks to my in-laws, Angie and Bernie Possidente, and their neighbor, Professor Benjamin Harshav, who led me to my big break with Fordham University Press. In the spring of 2003 they had read about their neighbor, Yale Professor Benjamin Harshav, who had just edited and published *The Last Days of the Jerusalem of Lithuania*, a new English translation of Herman Kruk's diary from the Vilna Ghetto. They sent me the newspaper clippings about Professor Harshav, which soon led to correspondence with him. His generous offers of help led to an introduction to Helen Tartar at the Fordham University Press, and the rest is history. What can one say but thanks to family, in-laws, neighbors, and generous spirits!

Many thanks to editorial director Helen Tartar at Fordham University Press, as well as Robert Oppedisano, Kate O'Brien, Chris Mohney, and the rest of the crew at Fordham Press. Their support and enthusiasm for this project guided me each step of the way along my maiden voyage into the world of publishing. They made what could have been a painful, difficult process into an exciting adventure.

My deepest gratitude is reserved for my loving wife Susan and our children Jonathan and Rebecca. They journeyed halfway around the world to explore our family history together and gave me enough love, support, and encouragement to sustain me during these five years of work. I hope they will look back on these years as a time of discovery that has enriched our family both now and for the future.

Finally, I hope would like to express my profound gratitude to the Gasperowicz and Paszkowski families as well as to Karl Plagge himself. Without their brave efforts my parents would not have survived the war and neither my children nor I would be alive. I hope that this book will help many people to remember their humanity, moral fortitude, and bravery in the years and generations to come.

GLOSSARY

aktion German term describing a military action (mission/operation) carried out by Nazi forces to capture Jews for deportation or execution.

Aryan Nordic racial background glorified by the Nazis.

Bundesarchive Federal archives of Germany.

denazification Postwar process used by Allies to rid German society of former Nazi war criminals.

Einsatzgruppe Mobile "task forces" (regiment size) or killing squads that committed mass murder of the Jewish populations of Eastern Europe and Russia during the Holocaust.

Einsatzkommando Unit under the command of the Einsatzgruppe.

Gele Shain ("Yellow Life Certificates") Yellow-colored work permit that protected the life of a worker, his wife, and two children in the Vilna Ghetto.

Gestapo Secret state/political police of the Nazi Party.

ghetto Small, sealed area of a city where Jews were forcibly moved to and confined by the Germans.

Heeres Kraftfahr Park (HKP) Military vehicle repair park (depot).

Judenfreund "Friend of the Jews," an insulting, derogatory description by the Nazis.

Judenhure "Whore of the Jews," a derogatory description of a woman showing any kindness or friendship toward a Jew.

Judenrat Jewish leadership council set up by Nazis to help them rule Jewish populations trapped in ghettos.

khapuny (grabbers) Lithuanian paramilitary policemen who roamed the ghetto arbitrarily arresting Jewish men for execution.

Kristallnacht (Night of the Broken Glass) Night of November 9th, 1938, when Nazis organized nationwide anti-Jewish riots in which Jews were attacked, synagogues burned, and Jewish shops looted.

maline Hiding place.

pogrom Anti-Jewish race riot.

Ponary   Execution grounds in a forest outside of Vilna where 70,000 Jewish men, women, and children were executed by the Nazis and their Lithuanian collaborators.

Schirrmeister   Master sergeant in the German army in charge of equipment.

SD   Military secret police or security department; the Nazi Party security service.

Spruchkammer   Denazification court.

SS   Nazi military force that oversaw and carried out genocide during the Holocaust.

Standartenfuehrer   rank of colonel in the SS.

Strashuna   Name of the street in the Vilna ghetto where the Esterowicz family lived, 1941–1943.

Der Stuermer ("The Stormer")   A vehemently anti-Semitic weekly newspaper published by the Nazi Party.

Untermentschen ("subhumans)   Racial description given by Nazis to Jews and other "lesser races."

Vilna   English translation of Wilne, the Yiddish name for Vilnius, Lithuania.

Wehrmacht   German army.

Wilna   German name for Vilnius.

Wilne   Yiddish name for Vilnius.

Wilno   Polish name for Vilnius.

APPENDIX A
Transcript of the Denazification Trial of Karl Plagge

These copies originate from the Main Archive of the State of Hesse in Wiesbaden (4.1.3 Abt. 520 Spruchkammer (Denazification Court)/D1/Plagge, Karl), translated in 2001 from original German by Marcus Schneider, with English editing by Michael Good.

Karl Plagge's denazification trial took place on February 9, 1948. The first fifteen pages of Plagge's denazification file are made up of pretrial depositions and court papers; the last twelve pages are made up of the testimony and judgments made during the trial itself.

TESTIMONY OF HEINZ ZEUNER

I know Mr. Plagge since the year 1940 and have always been together with him until the end of the war. I couldn't think of any superior that was more concerned about the well-being of his subordinates than him. I was the sub-superior of food administration in the motor vehicle reparation park that he commanded when we came first to Russia. He was very worried about the food rations and whether all his people were really satisfied and so I met with him almost daily. He was especially concerned about the civilian workers in the park and I had to get extra rations for them (potatoes, flour, vegetables . . .). For example, he ordered weekly observations about his workers' weight to convince himself that they got enough food. I had the job to observe that the German officers never received better rations than the workers. That's what he always wanted me to check. He himself lived without out special luxury or any comfort. I observed especially his great sense of justice, he always required that there would not be any injustice in his park, particularly when it was against Jews. Jewish men, women and children hid in his park for weeks with his knowledge, until the SD (German secret service) brought all the Jews to Wilna. For example he gave an ID card of motor vehicle workers to a Jewish Doctor and his seventy-five-year-old father so they didn't get arrested. He also freed his Polish engineer from the prison when he was sent there without due process. When the German authorities started to displace Polish workers to Germany he gave many of them the needed ID cards even though they were not qualified for the job.

Today I'm wondering why he never got in trouble for all these activities.

There was always the danger that the SD and the German civil administration would have discovered his activities in the park.

He was mostly worried about how to get us safely into English or American captivity, and on May 2nd 1945 he achieved that goal. We all liked and respected him very much.

This explanation is the whole truth. I know that lying leads to hard punishments.

I was never a member of the "party" myself.

ADAM STAHL

DECLARATION IN LIEU OF AN OATH

Mr. Dipl. Ing. (qualified engineer) Plagge worked from 1932 to 1937 as an engineer and from 1937 until the war started as technical counselor of the management in the same business as me.

He was a very nice and helpful superior and against all kinds of injustice.

He never discriminated against any employees that not only ignored the NSDAP and its organizations, but criticized them openly.

I can confirm that Mr. Plagge was always nice and respectful towards me and the whole business would like seeing him working here again.

Copy (stamp July 30, 1947)

Medical Doctor H. Greve, Specialist in Orthopaedics

(16) Benheim-Auerbach May 27th, 47

Report

Mr Karl Plagge, Neukirchen, because of Infantile Paralysis of both legs has a decrease of working capacity of 50%.

Patient has great difficulty in walking and standing.

Dr Greve   e.h.

14440

Dr. Greve

(16) Benheim—Auerbach

COPY

Dr. Braunwarth

Specialist in Internal Medicine

MEDICAL REPORT

On his own request, I give Mr Karl Plagge, age 48 at this time, residing in Benheim, Darmstaedter Street 13, the following medical report:

Previous Infantile Paralysis—fall of 45 in the prisoner of war imprisoning—worsening of the old paresis.

Finding: Atrophy of the right and left muscle quadriceps. Thigh circumference (12 cm up from the patella, left 38 cm, right 36.5. Clear atrophy of the peroneasmusculature right. circumference left 36 cm, right 35cm. Patellar reflex left just barely visible, right weak positive. Achilles reflex right weaker than left.

Kneebending flexion strong, extension weak especially left. Plantarflexion bilaterally strong, dorsalflexion left weakened, right just barely seen. Paralytic dropped right foot.

Mr Plagge is only of limited work capacity.

Dr Braunwarth

Specialist in Internal Medicine

Dr Braunworth   e.h.

LAWYER ALFRED STUMPFF

DECLARATION IN LIEU OF AN OATH

As purpose of the investigation of the "Spruchkammer" (German court of the denazification trials) I state the following in presence of an oath:

Mr. Dipl. Ing. (qualified engineer) Karl Plagge, whom I knew only as an older student in the high school of Darmstadt, was my direct superior in the motor vehicle repair park in Wilna from June 16th 1942 until October 2nd 1942, where I served as a high lieutenant.

During that time I found that Major Plagge had an honorable and human mentality and strongly rejected the German policy of full extermination of the whole Jewish population in the occupied "Ostgebiete" (eastern territories, Poland, the Baltics, Russia . . .). He openly explained that to me in our discussions. Major Plagge demonstrated his opinions by really helping the endangered people, this not only took great courage but was also very dangerous for his position and himself. I will describe this with the following examples:

1. The large Jewish population of Wilna was herded into a ghetto. There the German administration distinguished between the "usable Jews" (with their wives and children) who could work for the Deutsche Wehrmacht or

the war economy, who lived in a special part (after my memory it was called Ghetto A). The rest of the "unusable Jews" became victims of extermination *aktions* and lived for a while in another part (Ghetto B). The employment in a factory of the Wehrmacht meant longer survival for the Jews during that time. Mr. Plagge employed in his factory Jewish workers in great numbers; when I served in Wilna they numbered about 250. There were a great number of Jews that weren't really useful or necessary for the work that had to be done.

The park employed, for example, Jews as haircutters, shoemakers, tailors, and cooks. Jewish women and girls worked as cleaning workers and garden workers. Additionally, there was a Jewish doctor for the observation of the civil workers' health. Naturally, the park wasn't allowed to employ such people and Mr. Plagge could have gotten in serious trouble by doing so. These people were camouflaged to the outside as professional workers of the motor vehicle repair park. I knew from personal discussions with Mr. Plagge that he employed the majority of these Jews only to save them from the extermination and murder of the SD and other "party" offices.

2. Mr. Plagge himself always treated the Jews in a very proper and human way and wanted his subordinates to do so as well. A good example for that is the following incident that represented the only violation of Plagge's rules towards a Jewish worker.

One day I accidentally saw how a sergeant that came from Wiesbaden (today's capital of Hesse, before the capital of Nassau) and who was very proud to be a member of the civil SS, threatened a Jewish worker and trampled on his leg. When I confronted the sergeant with the incorrectness of his behavior he excused himself by saying the Jew lied to him. He then used the common national-socialistic phrases that the Jews are our enemies and aren't worthy of protection from a German. I told him that it is disgraceful for a soldier to threaten and to kick a defenseless person and that if he really wanted to fight Germany's enemies he should serve on the front. He declared that he was a member of the SS and made veiled threats to tell the local administration about this incident.

I reported instantly to Major Plagge about this case. He then reprimanded the sergeant strongly and transferred him inside the park so that he couldn't come in contact with the Jewish workers anymore. He also ordered him to report to the front administration which, as far as I know, the sergeant did.

This is a case where Mr. Plagge acted to defend his Jewish workers from the *aktions* and the behavior of this dangerous person.

3. The Jews got their food rations in the ghetto and didn't have any right to get it from our park administration. Even so, they got an extra lunch during the time I served there just like the Polish workers; it was mostly a warm soup or another warm meal. Because the park didn't have any right to obtain extra food, the whole administration and particularly Major Plagge was always worried about how to get food like potatoes, vegetables, and horsemeat. That was the reason why the park was so popular as a working place.

4. I don't know the following case from my own experience, but know of it because Mr. Plagge told me himself. The wife and children of one of our Jewish workers visited relatives in the so-called Ghetto B ("unusable Jews"), where they were arrested during a military police raid and brought to an extermination camp. In his despair the Jewish worker beseeched Major Plagge to save his family. He immediately went to the camp and after a long discussion with the commandment freed the worker's wife and children.

5. Mr. Plagge energetically supported the amelioration of our Polish workers' living standard. Because the German administration placed Wilna under Lithuanian sovereignty the Polish population was discriminated against by the Lithuanians in order to get enough food rations and other life amenities. So, Mr. Plagge organized a special food supply for the Polish civil workers and their families. This turned out to be very difficult and he had to put a great effort into overcoming the resistance of the Territorial Commissioner (who can be compared in his duties to a district administrator) at the beginning. That's how it was guaranteed that the employed Poles really got their whole food rations. As an extra, the park provided them also with a warm meal every day.

These written incidents are only some examples out of many regarding Mr. Plagge's activities to help the victims of the National Socialism in a manner that I never saw anywhere else during the war. Mr. Plagge not only disliked the National Socialist methods emotionally and within himself, but he also tried to actively do everything he could against them, helping many people at great risk to himself. I also want people to know I told Mr. Plagge in one of our discussions that if the war would end unfavorably for Germany and if he was in danger, he always could go back to Wilna because the Jewish community located there would surely help him.

At last I have to say that after my discharge from the park I didn't see him again, and that I didn't correspond with him from about January 1945 until the spring of 1947. I knew that he was a member of the NSDAP and that's why I think that my statement is so important for his process. I am going to get personally in touch with him and I will be his witness in the process to relieve him from all accusations.

CHRISTIAN BARTHOLOMAE
DECLARATION IN LIEU OF AN OATH

As leader of the motor vehicle reparation park, Mr. Plagge was my superior from April 6th 1941 until the end of the war. I knew him as a fair and benevolent man who always tried to prevent injustice and unfairness. He was not only a very good superior, but he also tried to help the population (in the park and in Wilna) regardless of nationality, religion and race. During my time serving in Wilna in September 1941 he gave me the order to liberate the Jews Zablocki and Trananricz from the Lukiezki prison. A few days later I got the order to free the parents of two Jewish haircutters from the SD prison.

During the same time he accommodated thousands of Jews with wives and children in the park territory. He fed them and protected them from death and persecution. After that he gave them "passage tickets" in order to have the liberty to go to the city without fearing persecution. The Jewish doctor Wolfson and his father were employed as workmen in order to save them from execution. Doctor Wolfson was thus able to continue his work as a physician. In 1943 the German administration arrested the whole Lithuanian "intelligence" (lawyers, politicians, teachers, etc. . . .). A part of those hostages were to be shot as act of retribution. Mr. Plagge courageously liberated one of those hostages, the physician Doctor Baluk.

He prevented a part of the "Sauckel Program," which was created by the military administration to expel all of the Polish population from Wilna (Lithuania). He did so by employing large numbers of Polish people from Wilna in the park and by giving them the necessary workers' IDs. Through his action many Poles could stay and were freed from persecution.

At the request of a father, Mr. Plagge gave me the order to free this man's son from the prison, if necessary by using force of arms. I found out that Mr. Plagge was a member of the NSDAP only after the surrender. I never thought that he could be a member after his actions against the Nazis.

I wrote this paper in lieu of an oath. I never was a member of the NSDAP nor any Nazi organization.

KARL PLAGGE

POLITICAL CV (CURRICULUM VITAE) (RESUME, LIFE STORY)

I was born the 10th of July 1897 in Darmstadt/Hesse. My father was a practicing physician and died when I was six years old. I came to the army in 1916 directly from high school and fought on the Western Front in the battles of the Somme, of Verdun and of Flanders. In 1917 I became an English prisoner of war and was freed in 1920. I had to give up my dream of becoming a doctor because I didn't have enough money. So I studied mechanical engineering and chemistry at the University of Darmstadt. When the situation on the job market became worse in 1930 I became specialized in medical chemistry at the chemical-physiological and hygienical Institute of the University of Frankfurt-am-Main. In 1932 I opened a pharmaceutical investigation laboratory in my mother's house to earn a living for myself.

Under the impression of the growing unemployment and the expanding misery throughout the population in 1931 I joined the NSDAP (National-Sozialistische Deutsche Arbeiter Partei, National Socialist German Workers Party) in about January 1932. I was attracted by their promises (removal of unemployment, governmental employment projects, limitations of the highest wages) which gave me hope that it could get better. For myself I didn't expect any special amenities besides sharing in an economical revival throughout the country. I never wanted to work in a special paid office job, even though I had the opportunity, because I never wanted any financial advantages from the party. I really believed during that time in Hitler's social promises and declarations of peace. I thought to fight for a good thing, because I believed that you are always free to join and leave a party.

But very soon after Hitler came to power (spring of 1933), I realized that I couldn't always agree with some of the party's measures. I couldn't understand their personal policies against their defeated political opponents because I was a man that believed in compromises between political interests and not in the inconsiderate removal of all opponents. Also the loud-mouthed habits and the general show-off behavior of many of the party administrators and members wasn't very appealing to me. I also disliked the unscientific doctrines about the racial question. But I believed during that time that those unlikable aspects were only transitional and were going to disappear, leaving a fair and humane political administration.

That was the reason why I saw it as my duty to intervene and mediate and so, on my Ortsgruppenleiter's (town group leader) insistence, I became Blockleiter (house block leader). After a few weeks I gave up this job because I disliked it. As compensation for this job I began to make some speeches for my town group about my scientific areas of knowledge (technics and science), and after sometime I attained the rank of a Zellenleiter (tenants leader) but I never acted as Zellenleiter. I always refused to participate in the required ideological teachings, and so I was forbidden any ideology in my speeches. That was always my wish because I never liked the strange ideological goals of the party. I also never bought a Nazi uniform (required dress) even though it was a duty.

Because of my scientific interests I was requested to lead the Educational Institute of the DAF the "NS Kraft durch Freude" (National-Socialistic Force through Joy). I hesitated for quite a long time, but after I was sure that it was ideology-free (courses about science, foreign-languages, etc. . . . without party influence), I took the job. I was strongly motivated to lead this institute in a very apolitical manner of scientific and linguistic education.

But when the party continued to send me people that poisoned my institute with their ideology, it caused a break between me and the party. It followed a serious discussion with the Kreisschulungsleiter (district education leader, superintendent) who accused me of diluting the "idea." He also made the accusation that I was friendly with Jews and freemasons and that I helped Jews in my laboratory. He degraded me from my post and told me he could bring me before the party court. His comments about the Jews and freemasons were an allusion to my friendship with Mr. Dipl. Ing. Kurt Hesse, whose wife was of non-Aryan origin, and with Doctor Bruno Guenther, who was a freemason. I never told Mr. Hesse nor Mr. Guenther about this discussion, because I didn't want to risk our friendship because they were in a very threatened and dangerous situation. Witnesses to our friendly relations are Mr. Hesse and Mr. Guenther, who can swear that I always had Jewish patients in my institute. A witness of my discontent with the party's policies is Mr. Blome from the Hessenwerke (factory) who knew my opinions about the Nazi propaganda.

As consequence of that "crash" I didn't participate in any more party activities but began to act against the Nazis. My relationship with my nonideological and non-Aryan friends stayed very good. A witness for my basic attitude as man is the business counselor of the Hessenwerke where I worked in 1934, first as technical counselor and then as project and development engineer, before my laboratory earned its own profits. Other witnesses are Mr. Adam Stahl and Mr. Michel, Hessenwerke.

When the Nazis worsened the brutally anti-Jewish orientation of their policies, I tried to help my suffering friend Kurt Hesse even more and became the godfather of his son. This was shortly after the burning of the synagogues. His wife Erika had to endure a lot of moral and mental tortures due to her non-Aryan heritage. I had an inner need to stay very friendly with my two anti-fascist friend families (Hesse and Guenther) who had to endure some bad tortures and hardships. In the spring of 1939 I was as representative of the Hessenwerke at a specialist conference and was deeply shocked when I heard the speech of Doctor Ley. Here I clearly recognized that this man was rushing in a criminal manner toward war. I also told Mr. and Mrs. Hesse about this shock and they can testify to this.

At the beginning of the war the Wehrmacht drafted me very quickly. I had been a lieutenant during World War One and became now, in the course of six years, first an engineer officer then later a major. I have to say that I never enlisted voluntarily because I still suffered from the consequences of my polio, an illness acquired during my British captivity after World War I. Being a soldier was physically very difficult for me. I took the opportunity to leave the NSDAP in the same manner that all soldiers had the ability to take and didn't pay any member's payments after September 1939. This was because I was in strong opposition to the regime.

When I became head of the Kraftfahrpark (motor vehicle repair park) in Poland and Russia, I saw the civil population there in a very poor condition, without any rights or legal protection. There existed "soldier's letters" that informed the members of the German army that the Polish people were inferior and that the German soldier had to act as a "Herrenmensch" (master man), a superior human being. I never understood this kind of behavior and never acted in the manner as specified in our orders. I took the decision always to act against the Nazi rules and to also give my subordinates the order to act in very humane manner towards the civilian population.

During my service I had the chance to help many of the opponents of the national-socialist regime in foreign countries, to free them from prisons and even to save their lives. I took upon myself a great deal of risk because I hindered the SD and the party in their actions. There were some serious clashes between the SD leadership and me. Also my superior office reproached me for being too emotional and sentimental in my behavior towards the civil population. Because of my social actions, toward the end, they forbade all new measures I wanted to take. But I was not going to let them hinder me in doing all kinds of things in my power to alleviate the condition of my workers and the civilian population. I did not volunteer for this war and did not want to prolong the conflict by spurring on my labor to produce the needed resources with even greater efficiency. Due to the collapse of the middle of the front, the military administration dissolved the park and I was transferred to a military workshop which I took as a personal slight. I think the reason for the closing of the motor vehicle repair park had to do with the fact that my regiment commander accused me of being too soft in the treatment of my workers.

The following paragraphs describe my actions, showing how I tried to help the victims and opponents of the National Socialism in the occupied territories:

1. Prevention of the carrying out of orders during the "Sauckel *Aktion*" (deportation of foreign workers to German armament factories) by giving labor IDs of the park and the motor vehicle workshop school to frequently unnecessary and unqualified people. Witnesses are: Georg Raab, Friedrich Asmus, Heinz Zeuner, Hermann Schulz, and Christian Bartholomae.

2. Prevention of the deportation of citizens of Lithuania to the slate mines of Estonia by the forces of the SD. Through my appeal against this *aktion* at the SD administration office, I was able to accomplish that a large number of men, women and children could stay in their homeland. Witnesses: the same as 1.

3. Liberation of individuals from the prisons of the SD, who I knew were arrested innocently. Witnesses: the same as 1. and Doctor of the law Alfred Stumpff.

I don't know if I was under surveillance by the SD because of my hostile mentality toward the NS system, but I became aware of the disapproval of high SD officers because I caused so many problems for them.

I predicted the development of this irresponsibly started and careless war. A witness is my chauffeur over many years, Schulz, who always knew about my opinion and also Doctor Bruno Guenther.

The war and the sad development of the national-socialist system destroyed an ideal in myself and even before the end of this terrible war I was deeply embittered towards all the people who deceived and tricked me, those who were responsible for the whole misery and hardship of the war. That was the reason why, in 1945, I tried to prevent all bloodshed and destruction and led my whole division into American captivity. Witnesses: Raab, Asmus, Zeuner, Bartholomae.

At last I want to mention that I still suffer from the aftereffects of a skull injury that I got during the war through two car accidents. As consequence I have more problems with my legs as an after effect of the polio that I contracted during my English captivity after World War One. (See also Medical Bulletin.)

As consequence of my physical handicap and my remote housing situation in Neunkirchen, Odenwald (little town in a huge forest on the Hessian-Wuerttembergian border) I couldn't participate in compensation actions of physical work. But I am doing everything in my power to support the reconstruction within my capabilities and within the existing organizations in an attempt to ameliorate the current situation of misery. Witnesses are the mayor of the community of Luetzelbach-Neunkirchen, Mr. Brunner; the leader of the labor welfare of Luetzelbach-Neunkirchen and Brandau, Doctor Abel; and the member of the town council of Neunkirchen Mr. Kaffenberger.

Karl Plagge
[BRK]

EXPLANATION OF GEORGE RAAB

During my service at the motor vehicle repair park I was in the rank of a staff sergeant and my duty was to work on personal affairs. I frequently talked with Major Plagge about the discriminating treatment the civilians had to endure by the German civil offices, the SD and the military police. I always knew that he hated the NS methods of handling civilian affairs and he did everything in his power to help, defend and protect these miserable people.

The following paragraphs describe cases I exactly remember:

1. Case of the engineer Schulz

That Pole was under arrest for about three months in the Lukischki prison in Wilna. He was a teacher at the National College of Technology in Wilna. Mr. Plagge heard about his predicament through the director (principal) of that institute. Plagge then went to the SD office and demanded an investigation of his papers. He was able to liberate the engineer himself immediately from the prison.

2. Case of doctor of medicine Baluk

This physician was arrested during a police raid that was the consequence of the shooting of a Lithuanian police officer. The plan was to shoot him with the other hostages, but Mr. Plagge was able to prevent his death at the last moment.

3. Case of the accountant Urniascz

This Pole was also arrested in the same police raid and was deported to the punishment camp Parvinischki (Lithuania) "auf Kriegsdauer" (until the end of the war). Mr. Plagge was also able to liberate him through his intervention at the SD office. Mr. Urniascz was freed after an arrest of six weeks and was able to return to his family.

4. Case of the medical doctor Wolfsohn

This Jewish doctor and his old father were to be deported during a big *aktion* of the military administration in the Jewish ghetto of Wilna. He asked for help from Mr. Plagge, who gave him and his father the needed IDs of park workers. He didn't have the qualification to work in the park.

5. Case of the deportation of Jews

The military administration planned to deport about 100 people (men, women and children) to the slate mines in Estonia. They were already in a transport train when a friend of theirs informed Mr. Plagge. He went immediately to the train station and ordered them to leave the train, even giving them military protection. The highest SD officer of Wilna then arrived after Plagge left and ordered the military escort to bring them back in the train. They left for Estonia. Subsequently, there was a serious clash between Plagge and the SD officer. Plagge was very furious and desperate.

6. Case of the prevention of the Saukel *Aktion*

Many parents of young people that had to go to Germany to work in armament factories asked Mr. Plagge for help during that time. Plagge ordered to give many of them ID cards for the park, so they could stay, despite the fact that they had never worked in the park. He also founded a motor vehicle workshop school for the education of young Polish workers. About 300 Poles worked officially there. Plagge had arranged guarantees for them to go to the school, so they could stay in their homeland. This happened after long discussions with the military administration.

7. Case of the persecution of Jews

Mr. Plagge freed a large number of Jews (about 70) from the Lukischki prison. These Jews were to be deported to extermination camps, but were saved because of his protest at the SD office. He knew those workers personally and told the SD officials that they were indispensable for his park, but in reality they weren't and he knew that. He was allowed to enter the prison and he not only freed the workers but also their family members. All those people really loved him from then on for that action.

8. I also knew that he allowed during the persecutions a number of Jews to hide with his knowledge on park territory until the end of the SD aktions.

9. Social institutions for the labor force

Major Plagge also created a lot of social institutions for the well-being of his civil workers.

a) A park kitchen that served a wholesome lunch for the park workers but also to the workers who worked in faraway workshops belonging to the park

b) Creation of park-owned stores that supplied the workers and their families with food and meat

c) Creation of a park-owned hospital for the workers and their families (about 40 beds) supplied by army owned medications

d) Creation of a "Unterstuetzungskasse" (cash) that supported civil workers that were in debt

e) Workers' supply of shoes, underwear, and working clothing, accomplished through a lot of negotiation with the Lithuanian offices

f) Workers' supply of winter potatoes and wood, accomplished through a lot of negotiations with offices and distribution centers, but also through his own wood cutting program.

Mr. Plagge never profited from any of his actions, neither did the park.

On the contrary, his actions in favor of Jews and foreign workers (Poles, Lithuanians) carried a high risk for him, because he often had serious conflicts with the dangerous SD. There was also the risk that different people were aware that he was helping and supporting enemies of the state.

This explanation is the truth and nothing but the truth and I know that a crime against the laws of the Military Government could result in severe punishment.

KARL PLAGGE

TESTIMONY

At the beginning of 1944, one of my officers reported to me as the disciplinary superior officer that the captain Plisch had said during the previous evening the following words: "One should shoot Adolf Hitler, the earlier the better." Witnessing for this statement was a certain paymaster Mueller who was also a member of my unit. So I found myself in a very difficult situation. On the one hand I liked Captain Plisch because he was an honest and decent character, but on the other hand the accusation was quite serious. I feared that some officers would report it to a higher and more influential officer if I were to acquit him of that "crime."

All soldiers of the German army knew what kinds of inhuman decisions and judgements were given to those who committed similar "crimes" from the military court.

Despite the danger I decided to defend the captain and to protect him from his unhappy destiny, which would result in the death penalty because he openly expressed an opinion that many of us had thought about. At first I ordered paymaster Mueller to my office. I had a little discussion with him about what the consequences for Captain Plisch would be—that he would have to go to the military court because his *action* promoted the "disintegration of the Wehrmacht." I discovered that paymaster Mueller was a like-minded man, which allowed me to put down the incident. But because the officer who reported the case wanted a better examination of the incident, we decided together what words to use as we drew up the protocol papers.

The result of our discussion was a written interrogation in lieu of witnesses that contained only diverse unimportant expressions but not the incriminating ones as reported. I showed this protocol to the informing officer and told him that the incident was cleared up. But I also said him that I was wondering how he could denounce a comrade who was careless. He hesitated and was angry, but in the end agreed with the document and declined further examination of the case. The incident was so filed away and nobody of the three knowing people spoke ever about it again.

For me as the superior officer, the decision was very risky because the denouncing officer could always accuse me of high treason and tampering with witnesses. It had happened on occasion in similar incidents which became known to other people due to accident and that the next higher office sent all involved people to the military court, where they faced often severe sentences. Also, there was a high risk because the character of the denouncing officer was unfathomable. He himself was a heavy drinker who often said irresponsible words under the influence of alcohol and whose action then could never be predicted.

But I took that risk because a breach of duty (after the legitimacy of that time) seemed to me quite less serious than to send a man to the military court where he would have to face the final decision.

Herbert Mueller, former paymaster (in handwriting):

I confirm in lieu of an oath that the incident described by the witness (Mr. Plagge) is true and that all the details happened the described way. It was very risky for the former Major Plagge and me to handle the case the way we did.

KARL PLAGGE
To the "Spruchkammer" Darmstadt County
file number DL/St/St
my Spruchkammer file

I am going to send all needed papers for the above-mentioned (file number) affair. I exuse myself for the delay but it took me time to get all the exonerating materials with the certified signatures.
With best wishes
Karl Plagge

FRIEDRICH ASMUS
TESTIMONY IN LIEU OF AN OATH
The former major of the Wehrmacht Plagge was my direct superior during the war for about three and a half years. During this time he never emerged politically to my knowledge and he never made any kind of provocative speech. It was known in our unit that comrades that were opponents of National-Socialism were never disadvantaged but found a like-minded man in Major Plagge. "Big Nazis, Jew-eaters and harassing people" were neutralized, displaced or removed from the unit. I know about people, of higher rank than me who acted in a too National-Socialistic way who were forced to leave the unit. Slave driving methods were not tolerated. When, on September 1st, in the early morning, the deportation of Jews to the unknown

was ordered, Plagge immediately contacted the ordering SD offices to prevent the worst. He didn't care if the Jews worked in our factory or anywhere else. He crossed out and sabotaged the orders of the SD and the risk for himself was very high. During the next day he was successful and liberated a large number of heads of families with their wives and children from the clutches of the SD. He also always fought against the misery in the camps of the Polish civil workers who worked mainly in the repair workshops. He got them clothing, firewood, necessary food, and cigarettes. I had the impression that Plagge was constantly thinking about how he could help the population in a situation that became steadily worse. An example of Major Plagge's concerns toward the population is this sentence a Polish motor vehicle repair worker expressed the day we left Wilna: "As long as you were here, all days were Sundays for us."

These are only some small recollections. By the way Plagge was very respected and beloved by all people that knew him.

I would say the same things as witness on the court.

HESSIAN STATE DEPARTMENT
THE SECRETARY FOR POLITICAL LIBERATION
STATEMENT OF CLAIM
I file a suit against Dipl. Ing. Karl Plagge
born July 7th 1897 in Darmstadt
living in Neunkirchen in the Odenwald
Because of the law for liberation of the national-socialism and militarism of March, 5th 1946, I demand an oral trial and put Mr. Dipl. Ing. Karl Plagge in Group 2 of the Activists
explanation:
The person in question has the profession of qualified engineer
His yearly income in the year of 1943 is RM (Reichsmark) 9,000
in 1945 RM 3,000
his money value in the bank is RM 4,402
his things of value are RM 300
The accused is married and without religion
The person in question was a member of the NSDAP from 12.01.31 until 1939
he was towngroup education leader and appartment leader
he was also a member of
DAF 1934 to 1939 and was KDF job leader,

NSV 1934 to 1944,

RLB 1939 to 1944, he was air defense officer starting from 1939,

Verein Deutscher Ingenieure (Confederation of German Engineers) 1926 to 1944 and NS-Kriegerbund (Nazi Warrior Confederation)

The person in question counts also to the in the law mentioned people under D/2/1, D/2/4, F/2/1c and C/2/1 of part A and part B.

Until the person in question can prove his innocence after article 10 of the law we have to believe that he fills at least one field of article 7.

The official documents tell that he just moved to his new community and so no information is available. The official documents from his former community confirm the data on his registration paper. In one of his papers, the person in question tells the Spruchkammer that he joined the NSDAP in 1932 in good belief and that he was given the post of a houseblock leader in 1935, but held it for only a few weeks.

In 1936, he took the post of a towngroup education leader of the DAF. He thought it would be only scientific but when people were sent to make political speeches he had a serious fight with the county education leader and in 1938 he quit all his political posts.

When the war started in 1939 he was drafted to the Wehrmacht and came to Poland where he served as the leader of a motor vehicle repair park. During his serving time there according to numerous witnesses he protected Poles and Jews from the persecution of the SD, liberated them from prisons and defended them. If this information can be proven by the Spruchkammer, article 13 of the law would be satisfied.

THE SPRUCHKAMMER DARMSTADT-COUNTY

INVITATION TO THE TRIAL

Mr. Karl Plagge of Neunkirchen,

on account of the bill of indictment from the public plaintiff that you received with this paper you are ordered to come to the trial on Monday February 9th 1948 at 1 pm to the Spruchkammer Darmstadt-County. You have to be on time at the court.

You will be informed about:

1. The pieces of evidence are on the backside of the bill of indictment.

2. In the case of your unexcused absence the court has the right to hold proceedings without you or can force you to attend the trial by police order and public punishment.

3. You have the right to bring your own witnesses and pieces of evidence to the court or to apply for it.

PUBLIC SESSION OF THE SPRUCHKAMMER DARMSTADT-
COUNTY MINUTES OF THE PUBLIC SESSION ON FEBRUARY
9TH 1948
members present:
Gustav Kraemer as chairman,
Jean Kraemer,
Heinrich Lotz,
both assessors,
Hans Feigk as public plaintiff,
Emmy J. Hebberling as minute-taker,
in the oral hearing of the trial against
Karl Plagge, born 07/10/1897 of Neunkirchen
and his lawyer Reinher Klingelhoeffer,
and the witnesses
Dr. Stumpff, Christian Bartholomae,
Kurt Hesse, Maria Eichamueller
The invited witnesses know about the subject
of the trial and have the duty to tell only the truth.

[Note: In the Spruchkammer trial transcript, the prosecutors' questions are not included; only a solidus (/) marks the place where a question is asked. The witnesses' answers are recorded in full.]

The witnesses and the accused are under oath and have to tell the truth and only the truth. A violation leads to severe punishment according to public law. Asked about his personal situation the person in question responded:

I am 50 years old, institution teacher, married, no children, without religion, I left my church in 1934, no PG deployment, I am physically handicapped because of my legs and couldn't serve at the front. I had polio that became worse during the war.

Drafted 08/28/39 in the Wehrmacht. During WWI and at the beginning of WWII, I was a lieutenant. In Hammelburg I had a military practice. That was 1937 or 1938. It was one month long. I quit the Wehrmacht as a major. I was in English captivity until 08/04/1945.

The bill of indictment of 01/06/1948 was read, the indictment was pronounced orally by the public plaintiff.

The person in question was been asked if he wanted to respond to the indictment.

He said:

"I joined the party 1931 in good faith. I wasn't tricked and I didn't join because I was under any influence, I don't want anyone to believe that I was a victim. I joined free because I thought during that time I would serve something good. I later took a post because I had still the faith in serving a good organization. I am not one of those people that likes something but lets others work for it. I thought I really had to serve the organization. I also wanted the post. I attained the rank of a block leader despite my handicap. I was ordered to make speeches. My speeches were always only technical, never ideological. I am not a great speaker. I never had problems talking about something that I was interested in. There existed many interesting things in the technique back then, for example the electrification and the economical problems such as rubber production. I never ever thought about preparing for a war. I thought I would serve something peaceful. That was my strong conviction. The witnesses can prove that. I also later made speeches on the Volksbildungsstaette (people's educational institute). Most of the people there were really interested. As a human who was thinking I came increasingly in conflict with the measures of the regime. I spoke about it to my friends, in particular to my friend Kurt Hesse.

"I had a conflict with the district education leader. My speeches were always purely scientific. That fact met resistance. They wanted me to work ideologically. They accused me of diluting the ideas and that I stood in contact with freemasons and Jews. My consequence was that I quit my job at the Volksbildungsstaette (people's education institute). That was in 1937/1938. I was really worried when I was in Stuttgart (today's capital of Baden-Wuerttemberg) and heard the speech of Dr Ley that stirred up the people to war. That was during the spring of 1939. I told Hesse back then that Germany was heading into a fatal time. Germany was heading into a war. Many people didn't believe it."

(/) "Meeting Iron and metals. It must have been in April of 1939. The war was coming. First I was here but then I was ordered to a motor vehicle repair park and came to Russia or Poland (depending on the borders before WW2, during WW2 and after WW2), to Wilna because I was an engineer."

(/) "It happened like that: I was in the military camp Hammelberg. I couldn't ride horses because of my leg. So they didn't let me serve. When there was the mobilization I reported to the military leader's office. So I served as air defense officer. I had to go to the camps to check the air defense systems there and how well they worked. I did that half a year and then I came to Poland. There I decided to work against the Nazis. I saw unbelievable things that I couldn't support anymore." (/) "When the war against Russia started." (/) "During the war in Poland I was in Darmstadt. I was the responsible leader for the mobilization of motor vehicles here in Darmstadt. That was in July 1941. It was planned that we had to serve in Serbia but the administration changed it and we came to Russia. The important question for me was what could I do against those unbelievable things. First of all was the thing with Warsaw. I never hesitated to help those poor people that were persecuted, tortured and displaced. They were either Jews or Poles." (/) "I heard that. It was daily gossip in Wilna." (/) "They were liquidated in Lithuania, displaced and never came back." (/) "I never heard about this but I won't doubt it." (/) "I never saw photographs about it. It was enough for me what I saw and heard. I helped all the people that asked me for help."

(/) "I believe that." (/) "I tried to protect those people from death. I was successful in many cases. I want you to hear the witnesses speak about that. I myself was not in contact with the SD but had many difficulties with it. I wasn't very liked there. But they didn't persecute me. When I spoke with some of them personally then they admitted the cruel things they were doing." (/) "But all of them said they had orders to follow and they wouldn't act against orders.

"A man named Hensel I believe.

"I wanted to do something against it. I hid many Jews in the park. I also liberated Poles. I gave them jobs in my motor vehicle repair park. Through the park I helped many people." (/) "There were over 1000 people who worked at the park (altogether with my soldiers). There were 250 German soldiers in the park. The rest were civilians. It sometimes depended. I cared about the civil population. I created many stores in the city where the Jews in particular could shop for their goods. I created also some hospitals and visited sick Poles who lived in misery." (/) "I did that because I thought it was my duty. There needed to be people who were doing something good for the German reputation in foreign countries. I was ashamed.

"Then we had to leave. The Russians came and the front was displaced

westward, we came into captivity." (/) "Why did I do that ? I had a humanistic, anti-national-socialist opinion. I always believed in compromise. There
was a strong conflict between the party and me."

(/) "I brought my unit without casualties into American captivity." (/) Yes,
there was a serious breakdown." (/) "My wife entered the party in 1936. But
she tried also earlier to enter. She also became alienated by the ideas. I would
want you to ask the witness Hesse about it. He is my best friend." (/) "I was
never at a party convention." (/) "I always hoped that all the bad things were
only temporary. That was the theme of my talks with my friend Hesse. He
thought it was a revival of inferior instincts." (/) "I entered the NSBDT
through the VDA. Hegemann gave me the post.

"That was in 1938. I was listed as subject leader. I never heard about it. I
didn't have an official function.

"I had this job in the Volksbildungsstaette. I never knew what rank I had."

(/) "Some time after I took the job in the Volksbildungsstaette. I was
forbidden to make ideological speeches because I never visited ideological
conventions.

"That must have been in 1936." (/) "The clash with the Volksbildungsstaette was 1937."

(/) "I did that one year.

"I only spoke about technical questions. I didn't want to speak about
ideology. I was never sure about it. That was the Gervinus school." (/) "Town
group leader Diehl; it is possible that he moved.

"1934 as block leader.

"Collect money." (/) "I couldn't do it." (/) "I couldn't walk up steps. As
consequence the town group leader ordered me to make speeches. I had to
do something.

"I became job leader.

"Education leader from 1935 to 1936. Can I ask: What do you understand
under the term job leader ??? The block leader gave me the post of an apartment leader." (/) "I left the church because of the following reasons: We
always had a group of young people interested in those questions. Religious
things are very important to me. We had a lot of priest in our family. I didn't
like what I saw. One day I had a talk with my father who was a priest. He
wanted me to believe in the articles of the confession of Augsburg.

"It was a little creed for a Christian. I can only believe in something that
I can seriously take for true. That's why I thought it would be honest to leave

the church. I found my opinion in heavy fights with myself. I am not against religion. But I performed a separation, because I couldn't believe in that what we had to believe. There was no compromise solution for me like for so many German Christians. I still think that I am kind of religious anyway. My behavior is following an obvious direction and I know for myself what is right and what is wrong. I never had the feeling that I was wrong in my actions. If not, I wouldn't have done it. My witnesses can support that." (/) "I naturally agree to bear the consequences for all things I've done when proven that they were wrong.

"I wouldn't have become the godfather of my friend Kurt Hesse's son in this case." (/) "I gave a lot of people worker's ID cards without considering their qualification. There was, for example, a Jewish doctor that asked me for a job. At first I was shocked because what could I do with a doctor in the park. But I couldn't send him back and so he officially worked as a grinder in the park. He never did anything technical in his whole life. He also worked as a doctor for the civilians of the park. I also gave his seventy-five-year-old father a job." (/) "We lied a lot to help our workers. I was often in great danger without even knowing about it. I recognized that only afterwards." (/) "I gave out these kinds of cards since the Sauckel aktion. I told the SD that women and children are not able to work in working camps. So many women and children weren't displaced.

"I read the book Mein Kampf. 1929."

Examination of witnesses

Witness Alfred Stumpff,
Not related, 47 years, lawyer, Pg since 05-01-1937, group leader in the NSKK, no function, no trial yet
"I went to the Humanistisches Gymnasium (high school). I know Mr. Plagge personally since February of 1941 when I came to the park. I was there for three months. We talked more during the last days of his service there. That was June of 1942 when I came back to Wilna. I was first lieutenant. I stayed there until 10-01-1942. During this time I got most of information I am talking about now." (/) "Our park was an institute to repair motor vehicles. There was a large number of employees working at the park, about 700 to 800 Poles and about 250 Jews. We also got later 15 or 20 Russian POWs. Probably that's important. Jewish workers were employed, but also many Jews that were never craftsmen in their lives were employed. They

worked mostly in the garden and the kitchen. There was also a Jewish doctor who studied in Germany. They were employed also as tailors and shoemakers. There were some difficulties to explain to the administration the employment of those people. The Territory Commissar was the superior who was responsible. All the reports went through the Military Administration. We often talked about that. The Jews would die in the concentration camps, that was what we knew when we wouldn't protect them anymore. The ghetto was separated between the Jews that were useful for the military and those that couldn't work. The 'useful' Jews weren't persecuted. Also their wives and children were safe. Plagge tried to camouflage some Jews as 'useful' workers. He saved so about 250 people." (/) "There are always people that are never satisfied. Plagge had to worry about those who tried to investigate some cases. I especially remember one case. It was the wife and the children of a Jewish worker of the park who got displaced. We knew that it was a 'cleaning aktion.' The husband asked Plagge for help. Plagge not only did what some ordinary man would have done, but he went personally to the administration and didn't shut up until they freed the wife and her children. I know this case only from word of mouth. Plagge also tried his best to ameliorate the food and nutritional situation in the park. The Jews were persecuted in the ghetto. He was successful in supplying them with more food. He also gave them some warm soup at lunch time. The Polish workers also got a meal for lunch. We ourselves were poor. It was very difficult. The administration provided the Poles with some food but not the Jews. We also had some Russian POWs. Plagge always fought for these people. He bought them music instruments for their free time. An important thing was that we had many Polish workers. The Poles had a hard time. Wilna became separated from Poland during the war. There was a Polish and a Lithuanian population. The Poles complained about the nutrition situation.

"They got nutrition tickets but no food. The Greeks and the Lithuanians got their food but not the Poles. Plagge thought that we had to do something ourselves. He wanted to help them but he didn't go the bureaucratic way. He created the civil food supply. We rented stores and gave the population the needed food, so we could guarantee that the workers got their part. The Poles were very happy about it. This system worked until the end, I heard from other witnesses who stayed longer than I did. I was so impressed that I told Plagge that if the war would end in a bad way for Germany he could go to Wilna and the Jewish community would surely help him out." (/) "We didn't have any differences or problems." (/) "It was an often dangerous project. We had a meeting with the Territorial Commissar about the food situation of the Polish workers. We hoped back then that we wouldn't get into any trouble. We feared that people in the administration would work against us.

"I believe they were about 250 people. Among them were also Nazis. There was one sergeant whom I caught on a Sunday morning hitting and kicking a Jewish worker. He kicked him in his butt. Then I intervened and I was very outraged. I had a strong discussion with that sergeant. He told me the Jew was lying to him. I rejected that argument even when he told me that he was a member of the SS. 'The Jew is our enemy,' etc. . . . He told me. I replied by suggesting that he could report to the battle front if he really wanted to fight. I reported the incident to Plagge and he had an even more serious discussion with the sergeant and ordered him to report to the front. Normally Plagge didn't have the right to do that, but afterward the sergeant himself filed an application for going to the front and so he disappeared from the park very quickly after the incident."

WITNESS CHRISTIAN BARTHOLOMAE,
NOT RELATED, NOT ACCUSED BY THE LAW
"It was the 6th of April 1941 in Darmstadt when I received the command to report to a military working group whose officer in command was Plagge. We went eastwards, until the captivity on the 2nd of May 1945." (/) "He was my superior. I was sergeant." (/) "I left the Wehrmacht as sergeant." (/) "We installed there a workshop for motor vehicle installation for the front. The officer in command was the troop leader who was himself a subordinate of Major Plagge. I didn't have much personal contact to him." (/) "In the case of personal problems I knew that I could go to him." (/) "We had also roll calls and he always asked who was who when one went passed by him." (/) "I can't tell this exactly because I spent my whole day in the workshop." (/) "We had to go daily to an officers meeting and the boss was always present." (/) "I could tell him all what I wanted to. He was always worried about us and tried to free us from all difficulties.

"I was a soldier from 10-22-1940 until 09-09-1945." (/) "That was normal because I come from a soldier's family.

"I didn't know that he was a Pg [Party member]. I wasn't told this until I was in the American POW camp by Hermann Schulz. That was in 1945." (/)

"I know it because it was in my workshop. I had back then about 20 Jews working as helpers. One morning one Jew had a stupid look. I asked him what was going on, and he told me that another Jew had disappeared. I immediately contacted Plagge and he liberated the Jew very quickly from the prison. Two days later another Jew had disappeared and Plagge again freed him." (/) "It was not as easy. The Warrant Officer Wolf, from the SD caused me many problems. The Jew was freed. He worked as glazier in the park." (/) "Because the Jews were ordered to us." (/) "They were arrested accidentally. If we hadn't freed them then they would have disappeared forever." (/) "Dr. Wolfsohn and his father were saved from execution. Dr. Wolfsohn himself told me that Plagge saved his life and that he has to thank him forever." (/) "He worked as doctor in our park." (/) "I knew that from Wolfsohn personally." (/) "That was the huge aktion against the Lithuanian intelligence. The order was to arrest the intelligence. He liberated at his own risk Dr. Balleuk and two Poles." (/) "I don't remember how it ended but it was very dangerous to do anything." (/) "One had to take some risk." (/) "I know about the incident from Dr Balleuk and the two Poles." (/) "The man who asked for help was Polish, the rest I forgot. He came and wanted to see the Major. His son worked for us. Plagge immediately sent someone there. He ordered us to use our arms if there would be any resistance. The boy was liberated." (/) "It was a very unusual situation there. One couldn't only give in, one had to defend oneself against the SD."

WITNESS MARIA EICHAMUELLER,

OF DARMSTADT, HOUSEWIFE, NOT RELATED

"I saw Mr. Plagge today morning the first time in my life. I don't know him. I have to say the following words: The last Christmas I was in Ludwigsburg near Stuttgart. My girlfriend whom I visited knows the Jewish lawyer Dr Paula Zanka who is in charge of the Jews in the camp. Through the help of my girlfriend she asked me to look for a Mr. Plagge here in Darmstadt with the reason that there are different Jews in her camp that want to thank Mr. Plagge. They told her that Plagge had always cared about them and that he helped them in a difficult time. They want to support him with their food and money if he lived in misery. There is also a Jewish father in Stuttgart who says that Plagge saved his son's life. I immediately went to the police in Darmstadt to find Mr. Plagge when I came home. I found different Plagges but not the one I looked for. On Saturday I accidentally read in the newspaper that there is a trial with a Mr. Plagge going on. I immediately came here but couldn't find the responsible superior on Saturday. So I came here today to hear if it is really the right Plagge from Wilna. (/) The Jewish camp is in Ludwigsburg."

WITNESS KURT HESSE,

NOT RELATED, NOT ACCUSED BY THE LAW

"I've know him since 1932. Back then he applied for a job in my business. I couldn't give him a full job as engineer. He stood in a free working relation to me. We often had discussions together. We also talked about politics.

"I only learned later that he was a Pg. I didn't care about it when he applied for a job. That was in 1935. I am Aryan but my wife is Jewish. I stood under increasing pressure due to this. Plagge was always good to me and gave me advice. He supported me mentally and was honest to my family. He never tried to excuse the crimes committed by the Nazis. He believed those were only a phenomenon at the beginning that would disappear after a while. In 1938 I needed to hire a full time engineer. I needed someone in a high position who was a member of the party or an adjacent organization. But I didn't want someone who would make propaganda to come into my business. I knew that he wouldn't make propaganda and that I could trust him. He was liked throughout the business. He always cared about all employees." (/) "That was since the spring of 1938. Normally I would have needed an electronic engineer but I decided to hire him anyway. A reason was also to have someone for 'outside,' someone who could help make it seem as if the business was national-socialistic. I never regretted having hired him. In 1938 when the synagogues burned throughout Germany he told me how despicable and abhorrent he thought it was. He was in a time of inner mental conflict. In 1938 also he was very worried about the future shortly after the attack on the Czech part of Czechoslovakia [in German: Bohemia and Moravia].He sometimes thought he talked to me in too open a manner. The third event in 1938 that shocked him fundamentally was the meeting of German engineers in Stuttgart. He went there as a representative of my business because many technical and scientific speeches were being made. I also went there. We spoke a short time after the convention. He was totally shocked, I had problems recognizing him. He couldn't get over the fact that Dr. Ley said in the most uninhibited manner that in three years the German flag would wave over Warsaw. By then he had mentally left his former party. And his anti-Nazi opinion was still growing. At the beginning of the war he got drafted. We wrote each other letters. I saw that he had completely changed. He didn't have any of his former convictions." (/) "During the war I saw him when he returned from Poland for vacation. He visited me first in 1941 or 1942. After that I saw him two or three times. He was the opposite of a Nazi." (/) "He never was an official, he was idealistic. People always liked him. He was never mean to anyone. He acted as an human." (/) "He was in contact with the NSDAK because he made technical speeches at the DAF. I heard later that he wanted to quit. I always knew him as an honest person. He is my boy's godfather even though he knew that my son is 'mixed.' I knew that I could always trust him."

After the examination of each witness and the reading of each piece of evidence the person in question was asked if he has to say anything.
The public plaintiff, the person in question and the lawyers had the right to address their opinion to the court.
The public plaintiff gives the right to decide about the case to the court.
The person in question and his lawyer moved for classification as group 4 of the hangers-on of the national-socialistic regime.
The person in question had the right to address his speech at last.
"I agree with the words of my lawyer."

The leader of the court declared on February 9th 1948 after secret consultation of the Spruchkammer through the reading of the Spruch formula, the announcement of the reasons and under the truth of the law the following decision:
The person in question, Karl Plagge, born 07-10-1897, living in Neunkirchen/Odenwald is classified after paragraph 12/I as *hanger-on (fellow traveler)*.
After paragraph 18/I he has to pay an unique extra payment of RM (Reichsmark, currency) 100.-
Explanation:
The superior judge
Kraemer
The asssessors
Albrecht
Jean Kraemer
for the correctness
Hebberling

The person in question was a member of the NSDAP since 12-01-1931, block leader from 1934 to 1935, town group education leader (apartment leader) from 1935 to 1936. He was in the rank of a KDF job leader in the DAF whose member he was since 1934. He left the church in 1934. Because of his rank of lieutenant during WWi (1914–1918), he was drafted into the Wehrmacht in 1939 and served most of the war time as leader of a motor vehicle repair park, at last he had the rank of a major. The official offices can't tell anything about his political opinion. In his own testimony the person in question explained that he joined the NSDAP in 1931 in good faith and after a long period of unemployment. He took the posts that were proposed because he was convinced to serve a good organization. He had to quit his function as block leader because of his handicap, so he became town group education leader. He was forbidden to make ideological speeches because he refused to visit the obligatory ideological education courses of the party.

The cost of the trial has to be paid by the person in question. The cost is RM 9000.

His speeches were always of an only technical nature (electrification). Also in his job as office leader of the KDF he was concerned only with educative questions never with ideological themes. He decided himself to quit his post as town group education leader when he was ordered to prepare ideological projects and speeches. In 1937 he became so antagonistic to the national-socialistic government, because of the ideological goals expressed by Dr. Ley during the convention of German engineers in Stuttgart, that he returned to his position as office leader of the KDF. When the war broke out he was immediately drafted and first he served as air defense officer in Darmstadt. Later he had to serve in the motor vehicle department before he was ordered to the East front shortly after the German attack on Russia. There he was the leader of the motor vehicle repair park in Wilna. There were about 250 German soldiers who served in the park and about 700 to 800 civilian workers, only Poles and Lithuanian Jews. As long as those people were working in the park, they were protected from the raids of the SD and the Gestapo. Through his personal effort, he freed numerous people who were arrested by the SD and gave them jobs in the park. He saved the life of a Jewish doctor who was a hostage. Another doctor got the needed papers that proved the employment in the park for himself and his old father. He also protected several hundreds of ethnic Poles who should be displaced as factory workers to Germany (Sauckel *Aktion*) by giving them jobs in the park. Those Poles could so stay together with their families in Wilna. Because of the irregular supply of food of the Jews and the Poles, he organized the creation of their own jobs in the city to assure their daily supply with nutrition. The terrible incidents that he saw opened his eyes and he then understood the violent ways of the Nazi regime. The witness Stumpff, who worked for a longer while in the park, told the Spruchkammer that the person in question employed, against the law of the Nazi government, Jews as qualified workers, even when they were not qualified to do their work. He also told the Kammer the case of the Jewish wife who was arrested with their children and later liberated by the person in question who spoke personally with the responsible SD officers. The witness also explained that the Jews in question would relieve the person in question from his burden when they could appear at the court. Sergeant Batholomae, who also served in the park confirmed the witness Stumpff's explanation about the Jews and Poles. The surprise witness, Maria Eichamueller explained that she heard from her girl-friend of Stuttgart that the Jewish lawyer Mrs. Paula Zanker from Wilna, who is occupied in a Jewish deportation camp in Ludwigsburg, wants to find the person in question in Darmstadt because many Jews from Wilna in this camp want to support the person in question if he lives in misery. There are many Jews in this camp who want to meet personally the person in question to thank him for his engagement in saving their lives.

The son of one camp member is still alive because of the person in question's effort. The witness Hesse who is married to the non-Aryan women has known the person in question since 1932. He explained that the person in question was never a fanatic member of the nazi movement but always tolerant and helpful to all people regardless of race and faith. He also told the Kammer that the person in question was very good for his business because, on one hand, he was politically correct to the exterior but didn't act as a Nazi in the business itself. The witness also could ascertain that the person in question was already in 1938 totally antagonistic to the regime and his old values. He was very liked by all members of the business.

As consequence of his formal incrimination the person in question is placed in class 2 of the addendum of the law. To prove if the state of affairs of paragraphs 5, 7, 8 and 9 are fulfilled, it is needed to examine the time before and during the war separately. The person in question joined without doubts the Nazi movement because of idealism. He left the church in 1934 and became block leader, town group education leader, and KDF office leader the same year. The examinations demanded by the plaintiff didn't show any activist membership. The explanations of the witness Hesse prove that despite his membership of the NSDAP, he never left his way of humanity and tolerance. The explanations of former Wehrmacht soldiers prove that he never fulfilled, as an officer, the conditions of paragraph 8.

During his military time there were many actions that could relieve the person in question from his burden. The incidents described by himself weren't only confirmed by the former members of the Wehrmacht but also by the appearance of the witness Maria Eichamueller. His actions in favor of Poles and Jews show resistance described in paragraph 13 if it could have proven that it was of anti-national-socialist nature. The help offered by the deported Jews in Ludwigsburg shows that the person in question participated in an uncommon manner in the saving of lives of persecuted people. As resume the Kammer observed that the person in question was not a persecutor nor a militarist nor a beneficiary of the Nazi regime in the sense of the law. He proved that despite his early participation in the nazi movement that he rejected later its methods and ideals and that he also fought against them. In the end, the Kammer had to answer the question if the person in question would best fit in group 5 after paragraph 13 or in group 4 after paragraph 12/I. Resulting from the belief that the anti-national-socialistic motive of his actions is not proven, that probably his human attitude was more important, the Kammer finishes the trial with the categorization of the person in question into group 4 of the fellow travelers or hangers-on. The reason is that he has to be seen through his attitude as a nominal member of the NS movement.

The superior judge
Kraemer
For the correctness
Hebberling
(minute taker)
Spruchkammer Darmstadt-County
State of Hesse

APPENDIX B

Letter of Karl Plagge to Strauss

This letter, written by Karl Plagge in 1956, was given to Marianne Viefhaus by Dr. Hans Madsen, who found them among the papers of Anke Madsen-Plagge after her death. The translation seen below is based on efforts by Mimi Sherwin, Joerg Fiebelkorn, and Pearl Good.

Dipl.-Ing. Karl Plagge   Darmstadt, April 26, 1956
                                                       Otto-Hesse.Str. 4
                                                       Telefon 5532

Respected Attorney:

How deeply I have regretted that, while on the same train from Stuttgart to Mühlacker, we could not ride together and talk about the various shattering experiences of that time. You asked me why I never wanted to write down all these experiences. I answered that up until now I did not have the necessary time as you will understand when you know that as the technical manager and procurement officer of a large electro technical factory I have been overwhelmed with work.

However, the reason I gave was superficial. It is my desire to also give you the inner reason for my silence. I do not know if you are aquainted with the book by Albert Camus, *The Plague*. This book describes the story of a physician, Dr. Rieux, who lived in a city where suddenly there was an outbreak of the bubonic plague. In case you may have read this book, I would like to say that it was, and is, my endeavor to perhaps emulate Dr. Rieux.

When I read the book for the first time after the war, it was as if I was reading my own thoughts that, during the war, kept going through my head again and again. The fate of the hapless Jews and the pain that these people had to endure never appeared to me to be other than what it in reality was, namely a disgraceful outrage.

However, as perceived by a political person, this outrage is not directed in the same measure against the people who made themselves instruments for turning into murderers. I wasn't able to recognize the boundaries where the limit of guilt began or ended and, in a broader sense, as a German, I myself bear this guilt. From this plague there was no refuge. One had to be a witness of this outrage, in the course of which the only choice that remained, was to hate or love the God who permitted all these things. This was the cause for me to revise my religious views, and I resisted loving a creation that martyred people and would even gas children and would let people be guilty as happened here. If the order of the world was determined through death, then it was perhaps better for God not to believe in Him and, instead, to struggle against death with all one's strength, without lifting one's eyes to heaven, where God was silent. If on earth there should only be "Scourges and Victims," then it is an obligation to stand, not on the side of the castigator, but to espouse the cause of the victim. I have spoken with many of these "Scourges" who were responsible for the horror and have long reflected upon their words. I have perceived these men as blind tools of a hallucination, and I must tell you that these people have also moved me to pity, because I saw what a dreadful schism dwelt in their souls. They weren't in a position to resist against the outbreak of that stupidity, inertia, and bestiality that is imparted to people on the way as the unfortunate heirs of their heritage.

In my canteen, in which long-distance lorry drivers from all over the East came together when their vehicles were refueled or repaired by us, I once met a drunk SD man, who was breaking down crying because his terrible conscience oppressed him to his very foundation. He belonged to an execution squad which for months had committed horrible abuses. He sought to drown his despair in alcohol. I sat next to him and tried to look into his soul. What I found was a man with deadly psychic wounds, a human wreck, who was held together only through the power of military discipline. He was not, or only quite dimly, aware of what he had perpetrated and his attempts at justification resulted in a terrifying ignorance.

The realization came to me that the evil in the world almost always originates from unawareness, ignorance and weakness. People are more good than bad, but they are more or less ignorant and one calls that virtue and vice. The most hopeless vice is ignorance, which believes that it knows everything and for this reason presumes the right to kill. The soul of the murderer is blind. To true goodness and love belongs also the greatest possible clarity of vision.

As to how I achieved keeping so many Jews that were entrusted to me alive, sadly far too few, at least until the breakup of my park, there presented a simple formula. I always tried to help my conversation partner to see the situation clearly. To that end I used a certain tactic which consisted of not provoking my conversation partner nor enraging him. Because we lived in a time where a person who dared to assert that $2 \times 2 = 4$, could be punished with death. However, it was granted to me, by the civil administration and the SD to come into contact with people with whom I could bring about a certain clarity at least in the moment of decision. It usually turned out that in the end my opponent said: "You are correct, handle it as you think it is right."

Perhaps other places lacked only a little determination to similarly act to prevent and reduce the horror. I have never felt that this took special courage. It required only a certain strength that anyone can derive from the depths of moral feelings which exist in all human beings. Beyond that perhaps, in addition, a little good will, an occasional good idea and devotion to the task at hand is necessary. I didn't have the feeling that I was exposing myself to special danger because my arguments were always reasonable, honorable and indisputable on the humane as well as the technical level.

Only in one single case, a sergeant, who was transferred to me from a penal squadron, tried to blackmail me with the charge of aiding Jews and to report me for court-martial. This cost me, certainly, many sleepless nights— because I am basically no "hero" but actually quite a nervous person—but I succeeded in defending myself against this man and sending him away.

I asked the following question to the district commissioner of the city of Wilno: can an officer with a sense of honor idly watch the murder of defenseless people? The question was no more than right and reasonable. The district commissioner sat silent for a long time in front of me thinking this over. Then he said, "I would never give my daughter to a man who has dirtied his hands here with the blood of the defenseless." It was not really an answer to my question but, on the strength of that, I could tell the commissioner: "Then these murders will stop in my sphere of influence!" He thereupon gave me his hand. Nevertheless, what scenes came later is well known. When I succeeded on a dark, ghastly September night to penetrate the doomed ghetto which was surrounded by Ukrainian SS, with two machine guns and took hundreds of Jews on rapidly commandeered trucks to the hastily contrived camp on Subocz Street, the only consequence was that the SD leader let me know that he thought me a fool. He had a bad conscience because he had broken his word to me that he would protect my people.

When they wanted to carry away the Jewish women as being useless mouths to feed, there suddenly appeared 100 Dutch sewing machines for repairing armed forces materials. It was a trick I prepared as I foresaw this development. Henceforth, no one dared to interfere with such an organized war economy.

However, I was unable to prevent the murder of the children. I was on leave during these days. Whether it would have been dared in my presence and succeeded I do not know. Those children who remained hid in prepared known hiding places and they survived until the final evacuation of the park.

When I returned from the war, there were also difficult times for me as I had lost everything and I had to build my existence again anew. Nevertheless, how much more fortunate I was than the Jewish families that I visited at that time in Stuttgart. Mr. Leo Greisdorf told me then, "You have lost everything, as have we, but you can walk through the streets that you walked as a child. We, however, have become homeless and will always be full of longing, thinking back on the streets of our hometowns." I then became very quiet, thinking about what I expected from the world and its people. What one experiences becomes engraved into ones consciousness but remains in a different form from the way that is seen in today's politics, literature, and contemporary history.

In Camus's book the evil of the world is represented in general by the plague, which tramples through the unlucky city and spreads its microbes. So we also are always again exposed to danger in a moment of absent-mindedness, being infected or infecting others. What is given by nature is the microbes. Everything else, health, integrity, purity, is the consequence of the will, which can never be allowed to weaken. So I stand at a distance, an observer of the apocalypse of our time. There, where I stand, I try to do as much as my strength will allow.

I venture to conclude with the words of Albert Camus, who at the end of his book describes how Dr. Rieux observed the celebration of joy that was organized by the people after the end of the plague epidemic.

"While Rieux listened to the cries of joy, that rose out of the city, he was reminded that this joyfulness was constantly threatened, because he knew, what was unknown to this happy crowd and can be read in books: that the plague bacillus never dies out or disappears, but is able to slumber for decades in the furniture and in the laundry. It patiently waits in the rooms, the cellars, the luggage, the handkerchiefs and the bundles of old papers and that perhaps the day will come, when the plague, to the misfortune and instruction of the people, will awaken its rats and send them out, so that they die in a happy city."

Can you now understand why yet today I keep silent?

In my description of the events, the murderers do not creep around as sullen villains but as pitiable schizophrenic natures whose acuity of consciousness was unimaginably reduced. Some soldiers were not heroic resistance fighters, but simple people with perhaps a little dram more insight and a breath more heart than the masses around them. So you see, my dear Attorney, that this would be a less attractive story for today's public which demands sensations, heroes, and criminals. The depiction of the *Plague* brings no headlines, but requires reflection and meditation. I submit myself to this in free quiet hours. What remained and remains to us as long as we live is: a little friendship, a little love and, lastly, solitude filled with good thoughts. All those who make a greater demand on mankind or have turned away to something beyond mankind that they can never conceive, would be disappointed and receive no answer.

Forgive me, that as a stranger I disclose my inner thoughts to you. After our conversation which brought back so many memories of difficult times, it mattered to me to make a rough draft in writing what goes through my head in the nights.

I enclose a writing of Mr. Leo Greisdorf, which he wrote out for me in a kind way as a precaution in order to do me a service of friendship. So far as I can remember, Mr. Greisdorf was a teacher in Vilna and later also worked in the Park. To begin with, I personally did not know him, thus I was even more touched at that time by his gratitude and helpfulness. Who knows how he is doing now in Canada where he decided to emigrate. Perhaps he is in need? Would it be possible for you to find his address? Should he be in need, I would gladly help as far as I can.

If you should be in touch with Dr. Moses Feigenberg, I ask you to send him my regards, as well as to all those who know me—in case the latter, after all the injustice they suffered, place value on remembering the time and the people they came into contact with in those days. Perhaps send Dr. Feigenberg my letter. Since I am in the middle of preparations for the Hanover fair, I dictated this letter in a hurry. Some turns of phrases originate from the above-mentioned book of the French existentialist.

With friendly greetings,
Signed Plagge

Good Family Tree

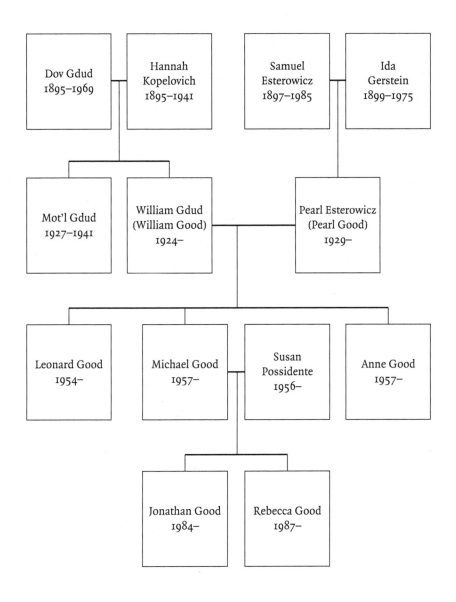

Index